DOCTOR ON THE MOVE

by

Ray Cope   R.D. M.B. F.R.C.P.Ed D.M.R.D. D.T.M.& H.

(Emeritus Professor of Radiology and Orthopaedic Surgery,
University of Missouri, USA).

i

Printed by Directory Services llc,
Lincoln, Nebraska, USA.

Published by Dr Ray Cope
908 Martin Drive, Columbia MO 65203, USA.

Website address for the book (wth order form)
www.doctoronthemove.com

ISBN 0-615-12891-2

Key to flags on front cover of book,
from above down and left to right.

Liverpool FC, British Merchant Navy, Brazil, Ecuador,

Australia, United States, title and author, Mexico, Scotland,

Malta, Royal Navy, Sri Lanka, Waterloo RFC.

For Helen and Frances

CONTENTS

Abbreviations

ATC	Air Training Corps
BBC	British Broadcasting Corporation
BMH	British Military Hospital
CBs	Christian Brothers
CP	Canadian Pacific
CPO	Chief Petty Officer
DMRD	Diploma of Medical Radio Diagnosis
DTM&H	Diploma of Tropical Medicine & Hygiene
FC	Football Club
FOAC	Flag Officer Aircraft Carriers
FRCR	Fellow of the Royal Collage of Radiologists
Gib	Gibraltar
GP	General Practitioner
Hibs	Hibernian FC
IRA	Irish Republican Army
ISS	International Skeletal Society
MFV	Motorised Fishing Vessel
MRCP	Member of the Royal College of Physicians
MTS	Merchant Taylors School, Crosby
MU	University of Missouri
Mizzou	University of Missouri
NBC	National Broadcasting Corporation
NHS	National Health Service
NMOH	Naval Medical Officer of Health
P&O	Peninsular and Oriental Shipping Line
PMO	Principal Medical Officer
PO	Petty Officer
PWD	Public Works Department
RAF	Royal Air Force
RFC	Rugby Football Club
RL	Rugby League
RMR	Royal Marine Reserves
RN	Royal Navy
RNAS	Royal Naval Air Station
RNH	Royal Naval Hospital
RNR	Royal Naval Reserve
RNVR	Royal Naval Volunteer Reserve
RSNA	Radiologic Society of North America
RU	Rugby Union
RWF	Royal Welsh Fusiliers
SBNO	Senior British Naval Officer
TA	Territorial Army
UAU	Universities Athletic Union
VAD	Volunteer Aid Detachment
WRNS	Womens Royal Naval Service

ACKNOWLEDGEMENTS

I am grateful to many for contributions and assistance with this book. They include Professor Anthony Hudson of Blundellsands, Merseyside: George DeRitter of the Old Birkonian Archives Team, Merseyside: Jim Jenkinson of the Merseyside Former Boxers Association: Many readers of the *Liverpool Echo* and patrons of *The Crack* public house, Liverpool: David Ashby of the Naval Historical Branch, Ministry of Defense, London: Commander David Hobbs RN, Curator, Fleet Air Arm Museum, Yeovilton, Somerset: Graham Pepper of the Shaw Savill Society, UK: Mrs Natalie Cutler of Kensington, London: Sir Michael Quinlan of Banbury, Oxfordshire: Commander John Exworthy RN (ret'd) of Chandler's Ford, Hampshire: Dr Vernon Pugh of Wareham, Dorset: Jerome Farrell of Fleet, Hampshire: Alistair Syme, editor the *Denbigh Free Press* and a multitude of its readers: Duncan Smith, Librarian, *Aberdeen Journals Ltd*: Dr John Taaffe of Tullamore, Dr Niall Tierney of Dublin and Alan Reardon, secretary of the Lahinch Golf Club, Co Clare, all of Ireland: Dr B. Cissa, Chief of Communications, Health Service of the French Army, Toulon, France: Brothers Julian McDonald and Bob Wallace of Waverley College, Sydney, Pam Betts of the Edmund Rice Directorate, Brisbane and Neville Lockett of North Turramurra, NSW, all of Australia: Judith Nefsky and Stephen Lyon of Canadian Pacific Railway Archives, Montreal, Canada: Emeritus Professor Haskell Hinnant of the Department of English and Dr Anthony Lupo of the Department of Atmospheric Sciences, University of Missouri, Neil Carr of the Lincoln Financial Group, Mrs Bettina Havig of the Boonslick Quilters, Mrs Winifred Krause and Dick Mull, all of Columbia, Missouri, USA.

I am indebted to Ray O'Brien for his foreword, to former Liverpudlians Dr Laurie Bergman of Glenview, Illinois, USA and Pedr Davis of Kyle Bay, NSW, Australia, for reading my manuscript and to all three for valuable suggestions. My daughter Helen provided much computer assistance and my wife Frances provided all manner of help, especially computer searches and the design of the book front cover, without which the book could never have been completed.

PREFACE

Some years ago, I wrote a book that achieved some small success. *From Mersey to Missouri: A New and Different World* was originally envisaged as an autobiography but the final text was more a comparison between the United States and Britain and contained a great deal of data about the former. Several friends wrote to me, saying that they had enjoyed the book but were somewhat disappointed that I had not included more personal material.

The question may arise as to why I should think that a second book would be of interest. *Doctor On The Move* is an attempt to rectify the sentiments above and I believe that I have now composed a true autobiography, very different to its predecessor and covering my whole life, which I trust will satisfy friends as well as a broader readership. I have visited a whole host of interesting and sometimes exotic places, such as Sri Lanka, Australia, Ecuador, Brazil, Canada and, of course, the United States, with most of these visits unreported in the first book. I have also met all manner of interesting personalities, some of them famous, such as Dr Hillary, the future President of Ireland, Lady Edwina Mountbatten, the President of Ireland, Lord Longford, Lord Vivian, Noel Coward, Danny Kaye and sporting greats including Sir Leary Constantine, Matt Busby and Bill Shankly. The word "serendipity", used and explained in the book, comes to mind in this context and perhaps explains my travels and acquaintances, as well as accounting for the title of the book.

This second effort of mine does contain some repetition, because of considerations of continuity, but this is minimal. The overwhelming majority of the text is new, with many previously unreported anecdotes and details of places, persons and events that might be of general interest, and all the illustrations are also new. I hope that these reminiscences will entertain the reader and give some small fraction of the enjoyment that I have experienced in remembering what has formed the text and setting it all down on paper.

Ray Cope
Columbia, April 2005

FOREWORD

Gracious me! Push! Old Push, the music master. He taught me much of what know about music. He taught my father before me. And in between, though far closer to my time at school, he taught Ray Cope. The difference is that Ray recalls it all so much more clearly and vividly than I.

That is the beauty of this book, a worthy successor to Ray's earlier work *From Mersey to Missouri* and a piece of social history not to be missed by those who claim to take an interest in people - who does what, why and when. Ray's memory is so much more fertile and vibrant than is Joe Average's and he turns his exceptional gift into an absorbing and utterly enjoyable piece of autobiography. So much of his life and work strikes chords in my own inner self. He went to St Mary's College, Crosby: so did I. He went to University: me too. He served in the Royal Navy: I also. He participated in rugby football and in other sports: snap! But then our paths diverged - his into a career given over to Medicine, Academia and Travel, mine to a more humdrum existence in Politics (more honestly, Bureaucracy), the Water Industry and Urban Regeneration. Between us, we could earn a crust in several corners of the globe.

Ray's style is never boring nor didactic. He is ever the story teller, the raconteur. His stories have a purpose. They help him to paint meaningful canvasses of which the infill is the detail of which I have spoken. Something between Michael Palin and Bill Bryson, perhaps, with a touch of Daniel Defoe thrown in for good measure.

I dare say that not many of his readers will have known *Old Push* or, for that matter, the several hundred characters who strut on to these pages for their brief moment of fame or infamy, whichever; but I do not doubt that this will dilute the reader's pleasure in the slightest. The book will, I guess, delight all who recall their own schooldays with affection or with some other emotion. It will appeal to all who have served their country: and appeal also to academics, medical practitioners, out and out travel devotees and to normal, decent family members.

A short story of my own to finish. When Ray suggested that I might write this foreword, it broke a silence between us (in no way hostile, simply the vicissitudes of life!) lasting over 30 years.

Together with the material he sent me was enclosed a photograph of myself and 20 plus other sufferers in the school's annual cross-country race. I recognized neither myself nor anyone else on the photo. Ray, who is perhaps five years my senior, pointed out myself, by position in the race (second) and the date when the photo had been taken!

Do be assured, prospective reader. Ray Cope has many other rabbits to pull out of his capacious hat. They are worth examining. I commend this book to your attention. I believe that you will find it an excellent read.

Ray O'Brien   C.B.E. M.A. (Oxon) I.P.F.A.
Sometime Chief Executive, Merseyside County Council

I shall be telling this with a sigh
Somewhere ages and ages hence:
Two roads diverged in a wood and I -
I took the one less traveled by
And that has made all the difference.

Robert Frost, *The Road Not Taken*

ONE

Early Days

Born in 1930, the same year as Amy Johnson flew solo from Croydon to Darwin, I was christened John Raymond, these words, of course, being on my birth certificate. However, I was always known as Raymond to family and Ray to friends, this creating some problems in later life. My early years were spent in the borough of Crosby, once in Lancashire but in Merseyside from 1974 following the regional changes of the Heath government. John Gladstone, whose son William Ewart Gladstone was the British Prime Minister on no less than four occasions, was living at 62 Rodney Street, Liverpool in the early 19th century when the city had a population of less than 100,000. Gladstone senior built a large house and two churches in open country north of Liverpool at Seaforth, later to become part of Crosby. The borough continues further northwards to Waterloo, where my family lived, to Crosby itself and finally to Blundellsands, the more upmarket end. The latter was memorably described as being "the debtor's retreat" by Wilfred Pickles in one of his *Down Your Way* BBC radio programs. Waterloo was built to accommodate the increasing population of the great port city of Liverpool in the late nineteenth century. With the famous victory of the same name still fresh in British memories, the new suburb bore such street names as Murat, Blucher, Wellington and Hougemont. Crosby and Blundellsands were developed later.

When I was a boy, the Blundells were an old recusant family, still living in an extant hall and walled estate at Little Crosby, which was amid countryside a little further north. In much earlier times, and especially prior to the Reformation, their estates had been much larger and extended to the coast, hence "Blundell Sands". The family name was popularly supposed to derive from Blondell, a squire who, after King Richard the Lionheart had been imprisoned on his way home from the Third Crusade, searched central Europe for his monarch. Blondell was alleged to sing a few bars of a popular song of the period, a favourite of the king's, around a large succession of castles, eventually hearing a reply from within one of them. This indicated the presence of his monarch, or so it was said, who was eventually released. The loyal squire was then knighted, and the lands around Crosby settled on him.

My early childhood was largely uneventful. I attended a parochial school, from which, on my second day, I ran home in mid-morning. This greatly embarrassed my mother, an ex-schoolteacher who knew the Headmistress personally. I was dragged back to the school for the afternoon session, after being suitably admonished and threatened with enormous penalties should I ever repeat such a performance. One of my classmates was Sheena, a young lady who lived near me and whose seventh birthday party I attended. I later discovered that her father was Matt Busby, then captain of Liverpool Football Club (FC) and a Scottish international player. He was later to be Sir Matt Busby of Manchester United FC fame.

Some in the class came from backgrounds that were poor and deprived. One of the teachers had an obsession with cleanliness of the upper parts and the young pupils had their necks intensely scrutinised by her at frequent intervals. Should they fail this examination, a basin on a raised stand was brought into the classroom and the unfortunate child would have to wash the offending neck in full view of the entire class, after which it was once more inspected for cleanliness. Recalling this practice now, I wonder at the uproar that would erupt should it ever be repeated in the politically correct world of the twenty-first century, especially that of the USA.

The British Empire, invariably coloured red, occupied a great deal of the globe in these days and the monarchy appeared to be permanent and above any criticism. Empire Day was celebrated with great gusto each year, in my case with a party at school and an early dismissal in late morning after the lusty singing of the Empire Day anthem. The first few lines of this were

What is the meaning of Empire Day, why do the cannons roar,
Why does the cry "God save the King", echo from shore to shore.

King George V and Queen Mary opened the Mersey Tunnel in 1934 and I was later informed that I had been present at this event with father but had little memory of it. The monarchs celebrated the silver anniversary of their coronation the following year. The coronation of Edward VIII, swiftly followed by his abdication, resulted in King George VI and Queen Elizabeth being crowned on May 12th, 1937. Each student was presented with a souvenir mug on these royal occasions and I still retain my three. In a few brief years, World War Two was upon us and at its conclusion the Empire began to disintegrate, beginning with the Indian sub-continent. In retrospect, it all appeared to occur so quickly!

Family holidays were spent mainly in North Wales, in farms, boarding houses and hotels on the periphery of Snowdonia and Conway Bay, at such polysyllabic places as Llanddeinolen, Llanberis, Deganwy and Llanfairfechan. Many years later, I was to enjoy the generous hospitality of my brother-in-law Captain Tom Donovan at his home on the Isle of Anglesey at Llanfairpwllgwyngyllgogerychwyrndrobwllllantysiliogogogoch, situated near Menai Bridge. Unsurprisingly, it is the town with the longest name in the UK and is commonly referred to simply as Llanfair PG. Memories of these boyhood holidays include freezing seawater, incessant rain and lounges devoid of any interest. I always dreaded Sundays, when I was not allowed to "play out" and all the men seemed to be ill-tempered. Father, who was virtually teetotal, told me that this was because they couldn't get a drink but there were usually different kinds of squash and lemonade available and I couldn't fathom his explanation. Many years later, I was to enjoy singing, usually in rugby clubs after a game, a humorous ditty, the first verse of which was

If you ever go to Wales, where they have those splendid ales
And you want a drink on Sunday, you will have to wait 'til Monday

Following a vote in 1968, East Wales became "wet" on Sundays although most of the West remained "dry". In 1996, Wales became almost universally "wet" on the Sabbath.

Several uncles would transport us by car to and from our vacation site. A café called The *Singing Kettle*, just off the A55 trunk road at Lloc, near Holywell, was invariably visited both going to and returning from our vacations. It had a large copper kettle at its entrance and served teas and light refreshments. It was a pleasant enough pit stop but calls there came to have an almost religious importance to my mother, aunts and other older relatives who might be with us; it could never be passed without a visit. Indeed, I became convinced that visiting this establishment constituted the highpoint of the vacation for mother and I wondered, after a particularly wet and boring holiday, why we simply didn't just go there, take our tea and then go home! The café changed ownership a number of times, with the Greenall Whitley brewery becoming owners in 1971. The premises were closed in 1990, this being rather surprising as there was now more local housing and the A55 had become a dual carriageway with increased traffic. The final indignity occurred when a McDonalds fast food outlet opened on the site in 2001!

In 1938, father took us on holiday up to Edinburgh, where we stayed at Joppa. A daytrip to the British Empire Exhibition at Bellahouston Park, Glasgow, proved to be most enjoyable, with each dominion having its own pavilion. In retrospect, it beat London's infamous Millennium Dome hands down, both for value and entertainment. A visit to a Deutsche Kriegsmarine three-masted sailing ship, used for training purposes and berthed in Leith Docks, was also most enjoyable. The German naval crew was extremely affable and helpful, being given high marks by the visiting Scots; and this barely 12 months before the outbreak of the war.

My family seemed to visit Liverpool or Southport at least once monthly, always on Saturday afternoon. On one occasion, I had been inspected and pronounced "fit to travel" and told to stay clean and await my parents outside. The road had recently been tarred, with pebbles then thrown on it. I thought it imperative to investigate this and soon had my newly acquired shorts, blazer and shirt covered in the black, sticky stuff. Father went ballistic when he saw me! I received a painful kick in the pants, was sent for an immediate bath and banished to my bedroom for several hours. The afternoon's expedition was, of course, cancelled.

On another occasion, my family visited a news theatre in Liverpool after shopping had been completed and prior to afternoon tea. Mother became concerned about a man who was, she claimed, constantly changing his seat and moving about the cinema in a furtive fashion. No one else was aware of this and we rudely told her to forget it and watch the screen. Some minutes later, there was a large bang immediately in front of us, followed by exclamations of anguish from adjacent moviegoers. We became aware of a nasty, stinging sensation in our eyes and noses and, with the lights now on, we were hurriedly ushered out by father. Apparently, a member of the Irish Republican Army (IRA) had set off a tear gas bomb, which fortunately did little harm although several people had to visit the Casualty department of the Liverpool Royal Infirmary. My mother's fears had proved to be correct, a point that she made with both perseverance and force. This episode was part of a rash of similar acts, including the bombing of post boxes, carried out by the IRA at this period.

My mother's youngest sister, Clare, lived across the road from us with my grandmother. A spinster, she taught at my elementary school and took the "scholarship class", this being, of course, the infamous Eleven Plus Examination. A teacher of the old school, she achieved results with scholarly material that was not always outstanding. Former pupils remembered her with love and affection and I was often asked in later life if I was a relative of hers. A strict disciplinarian, she achieved results without any recourse to punishment. A frequent ruse of hers, when she had to leave the classroom for some reason, was to say to her pupils "Remember, you are now on your honour. No talking or skylarking". Amazingly, this never failed to work, even with the most rebellious child. I doubt if such methods would be successful in present times.

In the late 30s, the Territorial Army (TA) began recruiting and spending weekends and holidays under canvas in parks and countryside. The "Terriers", as they were called, were admired by some, especially the more senior citizens, but others treated them with more irreverence. A common joke was the suggestion that many had joined the TA simply to obtain extra time off work or to escape from their wives! As relations with Nazi Germany cooled and war became more likely, the Terriers were given increasing respect.

A branch of my mother's family was Irish, with the male members being almost entirely officers of the British Army or Merchant Navy. One maternal cousin was a Lieutenant Colonel and his son approached him in 1938, saying that he wished to join the Army. His father was suitably pleased, especially when his son declined the offer of any "string pulling" on his behalf. The young man went off and nothing was heard of him for some time until his family received a postcard. He was well and enjoying life in Ireland, having enlisted in the Army of the Irish Republic on the Curragh! Most of my family thought that this was hilariously funny, except mother who was considerably saddened.

Father took me aside after this news and, conspiratorially, told me that it this sort of amusing situation was typically Irish. It reminded him, he claimed, of an incident that had involved him during the Great War, in which he had been a volunteer in the King's Regiment, one of Lord Derby's "Liverpool Pals" battalions and part of the hastily raised, and often inadequately trained, divisions forming the "New Army" of Lord Kitchener. After being wounded in France, he was recovering in Blighty in 1916 when the Easter Rising took place in Dublin. At the time, England was denuded of fighting men, save for cooks, bottle washers, new entry recruits in the very earliest stages of training and convalescent soldiers who had been wounded in action.

Father was sent to Dublin shortly after the rising had been suppressed and had to escort a political prisoner by rail to Cork City. The gentleman concerned was bound for Spike Island, a notorious prison in Cork harbour. Dressed in uniform and carrying a cumbersome rifle, father had been given a small sum of money to tide him over until his return to barracks in Dublin. After several hours, the prisoner sitting in the train beside my father started to stir and wriggle and was told to stop doing this. In fact, he was merely retrieving his packed lunch from the deep recesses of his coat, after which he kindly offered one of his appetizing chicken sandwiches to father, who abruptly refused it. Approaching Cork City, the prisoner asked dad where he would stay the night, it being too late to make the return journey. Father snapped that he needn't worry about that but the man persisted, saying that father would be unlikely to get into any British Army accommodation in Cork City. He then handed over a piece of paper, on which was scribbled an address, and told Dad to use this if all else failed.

After the prisoner had been released to two military policemen, father trudged around Cork City trying to get a bed for the night in a military establishment but, as his prisoner had rightly forecast, to no avail. He could not afford a hotel and wondered if he should investigate the address that he had been given. He was concerned, of course, that this might constitute a trap, a ruse to put him into rebel hands. Eventually, he was so hungry, tired and generally fed-up that he decided to try it. At the given address, the lady opening the door frowned severely when she saw the army uniform and asked how Dad had her address. He answered, quite honestly, that Sean Doyle had given it to him. Asked how he knew Sean, he replied that they had both traveled down together on the Dublin train and that Mr Doyle had told him to call. He was made very welcome, given a hot meal, a good bed and, after a hearty breakfast, returned to Dublin after all payment for his lodging had been refused. Father did not think that this was Mr Doyle's home but that it belonged to either relatives or close friends. Soon after this short Irish interlude, father returned to the carnage of Flanders.

On Sunday, September 3rd 1939, I was at my grandmother's house, sprawled on the floor, sketching and doodling. The radio was turned on just before 11.00 am. After the chimes of Big Ben, the Prime Minister, Neville Chamberlain, announced that Britain and France, having had no reply from Germany concerning their ultimatum concerning the invasion of Poland, had therefore declared war. I was not entirely aware that World War Two had begun and asked my Aunt Clare what she was doing. She was, in fact, tying a luggage label, with my name and address written on it in large capitals, on to my braces. Further enquiries elicited the information that this was in case I was injured during a bombing raid, and if disfigured, rescuers would know who I was!

Father received some very bad news now and had to endure hard times subsequently. The building company run by him and his brother had constructed some bungalows in nearby Formby. These were completed in mid-1939 and I would occasionally visit them with him at weekends when the houses were on show. With the outbreak of the war, these buildings were immediately confiscated by the Army for the housing of military personnel, although why these particular dwellings should be so coveted was a mystery to us all. To the best of my knowledge, he received little if any payment from any official source at the time. The bungalows were returned to him several months after the end of the war, in very poor condition. It is probable that he received some monies at this time but, even if this was the case, he was very considerably out of pocket over the whole affair.

Very little in the way of building supplies were available once war had been declared, unless work was being done for the Armed

Services or for civilian defence, and a policy of labour direction was in force. Now 50 years old, Dad might have been able to challenge this, especially as he had been a First World War One volunteer and had been injured in that war; but he did not choose to do so. He was directed to the Liverpool docks, where he worked as a stevedore. This was not the most pleasant or socially superior kind of work but was, of course, of vital national importance at the time. One day, working at unloading a ship, three large and very healthy-looking dockers approached him and asked what he thought he was doing. Father was puzzled by the question and asked for clarification. He was told that he was working far too hard and was "showing up" the rest of that particular gang, who might possibly have to play "catch-up" if he didn't slow down. No threats were actually made but my father was aware that something unpleasant would occur unless he fell into line. The average docker working with dad was at least 15 years younger and this was at a desperate stage of the war!

Luftwaffe air raids did not involve the north-west of England immediately after the declaration of war but many gardens were now filled with Anderson shelters, essentially comprising sandbags placed over a metallic frame. Brick shelters were also built in many roads, reducing them to only a narrow single lane. Neither of these constructions would, of course, protect against a direct hit by a bomb, or even a near miss; but it was claimed they would give protection against flying glass and rubble. Many schools had sand-bagged bomb shelters, usually built partly below ground level and often very damp, and I remember going into these several times a week for practice drills. Inside, everyone would have to don their gasmask, which was constantly carried on the person. Mine always had an unpleasant smell of rubber and the eyepiece soon misted up. Applications of soap were said to prevent this but never did so in my case. Wearing the gasmask was a somewhat claustrophobic experience and I doubt if I could have endured it for very long.

Next to our house lived a German spinster of late middle age. I never thought to enquire how it was that she came to be in England. She had a cat for company, few if any friends and took in a succession of lodgers, mainly male schoolmasters. At this time, although long registered as an alien, she came to experience considerable problems. She had to report to the local police station at frequent intervals and some of the less charitable and more vindictive neighbours began to talk acrimoniously about her. She was clearly in a very invidious position, especially when the bombing of Merseyside began or when local householders lost relatives and friends in the war. She was a quiet, kindly soul and my family and I felt very sorry for her. We made a point of being especially friendly towards her and of assisting her with shopping, small jobs about her house, etc. She asked father to write a letter on her behalf, which he did. I am uncertain as to where this letter was directed and what effect, if any, it had. She died suddenly, this being quite unrelated to any air raid, after which the very people who had spoken against her strenuously protested as to their great friendship and regard.

In the Spring of 1940, I began to feel extremely tired and soon came to realise, in spite of my tender years, that something was seriously amiss. I became febrile, with painful and swollen joints, accompanied by profuse sweating. I had rheumatic fever, the disease that is said to lick the joints but bite the heart. There was no room for a small boy with a non-surgical condition in British hospitals of the time. Wholesale discharges of patients were taking place, to accommodate the ever-increasing number of war injuries from France and the increasing civilian casualties on the home front from Luftwaffe bombing. So I was nursed at home by my devoted mother. Cortisone was not yet available and I was treated with large doses of aspirin, which I found to be most unpleasant. As well as giving rise to considerable nausea, tinnitus was another disagreeable complication of this therapy. My condition gradually improved although the general practitioner (GP) in charge of my care was very concerned, so I learned later, about my cardiac status. Each day, my Aunt Clare left me homework so that I would not lag too far behind my classmates and I found tackling this very helpful in passing the long hours.

The "phony war" continued and nothing much happened in the north-west of England for some time. In late May 1940, the British Expeditionary Force (BEF) in France began falling back on the channel ports after the surrender of the Belgium Army. With French military resistance all but ineffective and the German army pouring through its lines, France now sued for peace and the BEF began its famous withdrawal from France. This "miracle of Dunkirk" involved more than 330,000 British and French troops being lifted from the port and open beaches to the north, principally by an arma-

9

da of small craft crewed, in the main, by British civilians. Even a ten-year-old sick boy could realise that things were very grave. My ubiquitous Aunt Clare, visiting me one day, brightly observed: "It's all over now. The Germans will be here at any moment". She was not being particularly defeatist, merely expressing the probability that many shared with her at this terrible time for Britain.

After graduated ambulation, I resumed attendance at school again after having missed about 15 weeks of lessons. Restrictions were placed on my physical activities. I found these irksome in the extreme and soon disregarded them whenever it was possible to do so without parental awareness. Largely because of the dedication of my aunt with respect to her coaching of me at my home, the school work that I had missed did not appear to be significant. In fact, I had no trouble with the Eleven Plus Exam and was awarded a "County" scholarship, which would have enabled me to attend the excellent Merchant Taylors school (MTS). This had many famous former pupils including Lord Runcie, the Archbishop of Canterbury during the 1980s. At this time, the lesser "Free Place" scholarship gave entry to either St Mary's College or to Waterloo Grammar school. In fact, I entered St Mary's for religious reasons. This school had been established in 1919 by the Irish Christian Brothers (CBs), this religious order having been started in Waterford, Ireland, in 1802 by Ignatius Rice, a local merchant, to combat the very considerable educational deficiencies in Ireland following more than two centuries of penal enactments. Within a short time, the CBs had schools all over that country and later many famous former pupils. These included many of those who became prominent in public life, such as Liam Cosgrave, Charlie Haughey and Bertie Ahern, all holding the office of Taoiseach, and others such as Eamon Andrews. There were many CBs establishments in England and also in Australia, New Zealand, South Africa, Canada and Gibraltar. Primary schools, industrial schools, schools for the deaf and orphanages were in place in many countries but only secondary schools were present in in England. If perhaps somewhat lacking the prestige of some long established schools run by other religious orders, these CBs schools have made huge contributions to the education of countless boys, especially those from less privileged backgrounds, while charging only modest fees.

Claremont House formed the initial nucleus of the school. It has eagles on its main gates, these indicating that it was the former United States (US) consulate for Liverpool. Famous Old Boys of the school include Lord Birt, Director General of the BBC and advisor to Prime Minister Tony Blair: Sir Ivor Roberts, British Ambassador to Ireland and Italy: Roger McGough, founder member of *The Scaffold*, playright, broadcaster, children's author and poet: Professor Laurie Taylor, well-known sociologist and TV personality: Ray O'Brien, holder of many important positions including Chief Executive of the Severn/Trent Water Authority and of the Nottinghamshire and Merseyside County Councils: William Hanrahan, BBC and Sky producer and presenter and Managing Director and owner of the TV company *Hanrahan Media*: John Sullivan, speech writer for Margaret Thatcher: Kevin McNamara, Labour MP for Hull North and Shadow Secretary for Northern Island for many years: Sean Curran, a BBC correspondent: Colonel Kevin Hughes of the Royal Artillery, later an administrator for Post-Graduate Affairs and Research at Macquarie University, Sydney, when he had become an international expert on roses: and John Cain, a jovial and popular captain of Waterloo RFC who played for Lancashire on many occasions and who, after being passed over for several years, finally won a rugby cap for England.

John Birt's autobiography *The Harder Path* was published by Time Warner Books towards the end of 2002. A review by Michael Vestey, whose writings I had enjoyed previously, in *The Spectator* of November 16th 2002 claimed that the clue to Birt's advancement and success lay in the "brutal Irish Christian Brothers school he attended, where beatings with the strap were carried out sadistically every day". It was also alleged that the school tended to produce authoritarian figures who knew how to be submissive towards the masters to avoid punishments; in other words, "creeps". On reading this, I thought "what a load of rubbish" and fired off an immediate e-mail to the *The Speccie* which, to my considerable annoyance, was not published.

Discussions with friends about Vestey's article led me to do some research into the CBs schools and, following more conversations, to discovering and listing some of their more celebrated Old Boys. I could find no comprehensive list of the latter but was informed of the following associations in England.

St Ambrose's, Altrincham. Skiffle player and singer Lonnie

Donnegan: Actor Brendan Charleston: John Bason, Financial Director of Associated British Foods: and rugby players Michael Worsley (England) and Dylan O'Grady (Ireland).

St Anselm's, Birkenhead. Judge Denis Clark: Peter Stanford, writer and BBC presenter: Michael McParland, Sky TV broadcaster and barrister: James Walton, Daily Telegraph TV critic: Football Association Chief Executive Mark Palios: and rugby players Austin Healey and Ben Johnston (England) and Simon Mason and Alastair Saverimutto (Ireland).

St Boniface's, Plymouth. Sir John Gingell, Black Rod from 1936 to 1941: and rugby players Colin Pinnegar (England) and Liam Mooney (Ireland).

St Brendan's, Bristol. Field Marshall Sir William Slim, Commander of the 14th Army in Burma and Governor General of Australia: and England rugby players Mike Rafter and Mark Reagan.

St Edward's, Liverpool. Labour MP and Minister for State Affairs Peter Kilfoyle: Judges Michael Byrne and John Morgan: Sir Eugene Goosens, conductor and his brother Leon Goosens, oboist: violinist David Nolan: Michael Williams, actor and husband of Dame Judi Dench: Sir Brian Pearse, Chief Executive Midland Bank: Sir Terry Leahy, Chief Executive of Tesco: and England rugby players Mike Slemen and Kyran Bracken.

St Joseph's, Blackpool. Lord Tom McNally, Judge and political advisor to James Callaghan: George Carman, famous barrister, respected and feared in equal measures in court: and Professor Anthony Hudson, Emeritus Professor of Common Law and Dean of the Faculty of Law, University of Liverpool. This is the only former CBs school in England that no longer exists.

St Joseph's, Stoke on Trent (a second CBs school of this name). Dominic Cork, the Derbyshire, Lancashire and England cricketer.

Prior Park, Bath. Cardinal Cormac Murphy O'Connor of Westminster: Sir Cameron Mackintosh, theatrical impressario and producer: Kenneth Macdonald QC, Director of Public Prosecutions: Peter Levi, poet and Emeritus Professor of Literature, Oxford University: John Beamish, Ambassador to Peru and Mexico: Hugh Scully, BBC presenter: and rugby internationals John Palmer (England), Damian Cronin (Scotland) and Jim Murphy O'Connor (Ireland). This was the only CBs college in England that was ranked as a public school during my time as a schoolboy.

I now tried to recall a few of the many well known CBs Old Boys that I had heard of in Australia and enlised some informed help in this quest. Among many famous former pupils are acclaimed writers Thomas Keneally and Morris West, both of whom have written a multitude of novels and acquired many awards. Keneally wrote *Schilder's Ark*, on which Spielberg based his movie *Schindler's List*. West was himself a member of the CBs order for 12 years, with *The Shoes of the Fisherman* being his best known work. General Peter Cosgrove, Chief of the Australian Armed Forces in the early part of the third millenium, is another distinguished CBs former pupil as are a whole host of Australian rugby union (RU) international players including Michael Lynagh and George Gregan, both of whom were Wallaby captains. Bob Dwyer was coach of the victorious Wallabies in the RU World Cup of 1991 and Brad Fittler was captain of the Rugby League (RL) Kangaroos. Among many famous cricketers were Bill O'Reilly, known as "Tiger", the legendary Aussie bowler of the 1930s, and Keith Stackpole, the opening bat for his country in the late 1960s and the early 70s, who scored a double century against England at Brisbane and was *Wisden* cricketer of the year in 1973. Neale Fraser, who won 20 major tennis titles, was ranked number one in world tennis in 1959 and 1960 and was captain and later manager of Australia in Davis Cup competition and Herb Elliot, the Olympic 1500 metre winner at the 1960 Rome Olympics and regarded by many as being one of the most outstanding middle-distance runners of all time, are other products of the CBs.

These afore mentioned names represent a mere fraction of the many celebrated alumni of the CBs in England and Australia. None of these, and few if any of my school acquaintances, fit the description of a "creep".

The CBs as a religious order has spectacularly declined over last 30 years, largely due to a lack of vocations. In general, however, the vast majority of the CBs schools in England continue today with lay staff and this is also the case with their 38 schools in Australia. St Mary's College, Crosby, was the first former CBs institution in England to become an independent school and it is now also co-educational. This school, and several others that were formerly run by the CBs, now have principals who attend the Headmaster's Conference, this being the traditional definition of a "public school".

TWO

ST MARY'S COLLEGE

Punishments at my old school were given on the hand with a leather strap, which was thought to have a piece of whalebone inside. I doubt if this was significantly more painful than a cane and the frequency of administration was probably no more than in most public and grammar schools of the day. No doubt there were some with sadistic tendencies among the staff, and I can remember one definitely eccentric figure, but such characters would be met in any large school. I particularly remember receiving the strap on two occasions. The first was when, at the age of about 12, I wrote a long essay without any paragraphs. As punishment, I was given the choice of a very lengthy writing assignment or the strap. After some hesitation, I chose the latter and the Brother involved, with a twinkle in his eye, laid the strap very gently across my palm a few times; clearly, I had made the correct decision in his opinion.

The other occasion was definitely more painful. In the Sixth form, when 16 years of age, I was found guilty of throwing snowballs at the boys emerging from the school into the playground at mid-morning break, most of them en route to the tuck shop. The mass of boys formed a hard-to-miss target and the actions of myself and a few accomplices created confusion and havoc. I was given "six of the best" on both hands, which were still cold and numb from the snow. The pain was agonising and I was fearful that I might not be able to control the tears in my eyes. I was unable to hold a pen for more than an hour afterwards. However, there was no doubt that I had earned such a punishment and my only regret was that those involved with me had escaped scot-free.

The single incident that I can recall in which a Brother acted less than kindly occurred immediately after I had joined the school in the Third form. Another new boy stood out, wearing what was obviously a brand-new suit, dress that was very unusual for the majority of the boys who wore grey shorts and a school blazer. He was furnished with a very large geometry set, containing compasses, protractors, etc as well as a huge selection of pens, coloured pencils and other learning accessories. He had the best in sports kit and his parents had clearly spared no expense in fitting him out. Unfortunately, he was far from being good at his lessons and his deficiencies were cruelly exposed, in more ways than one, on a daily basis. We all felt that he could have been treated with less roughness, which resulted in no appreciable improvement in his learning; perhaps a removal to a lower form was indicated. Inevitably, he left the school after a few weeks of this treatment and I never heard of him again.

On the whole, despite this example, the Brothers were dedicated and enthusiastic teachers. They were a celibate religious community, living a fairly relaxed life under simple vows that could be readily dispensed. They were virtually all university graduates and many could be considered as being "muscular Christians", being none the worse for this. Outside school hours, they were agreeable, friendly and even gregarious and I often played soccer with them at weekends. In addition, a group of them would visit my home for tea and sandwiches in the late afternoon on a fairly regular basis.

There were many lay masters in addition to the Brothers, of course. Mr Fred Boraston, who taught Music, was quite memorable. An older man, he had a superb knowledge of music but was very conservative in his tastes, loathing Jazz and Swing. He dressed in a black jacket and waistcoat, black striped trousers, with a winged collar and black tie but this very professional appearance was somewhat diminished by the large, black boots that he invariably sported. He was very keen on his students breathing by using the diaphragm, not the mouth, and would often prod incorrect breathers in the upper abdomen; this gave rise to his nickname of "Push". Two part-time females were added to the staff and taught Elocution and Ballroom Dancing. The latter exercise was enthusiastically received by most pupils and, with hindsight, this represented a quite enlightened attitude on the part of the Headmaster. Although Latin and French were new to me, I was happy in my new school and made decent educational progress. The teaching was, on the whole, very good although one or two of the staff had amusing idiosyncrasies. Thus our History teacher showed the not uncommon Irish difficulty in pronouncing the "th" sound correctly and his frequent rendering of "George the Turd" drove us regularly into gales of laughter, to his constant bemusement.

At the school, there was a system in place whereby second-hand books could be purchased officially. I did not avail myself of this very much, acquiring most of my books from my cousin John Farrell, who was a few years senior to me. John was a truly outstanding student, who was awarded the prestgious and very difficult-to-obtain State Scholarship at just 15 years, an amazingly early age to achieve this, followed by an exhibition to Downing College, Cambridge. He was also a finalist in the BBC sound radio *Brain of Britain* competition, during which, in a round on abbreviations, he had to admit that he did not know what "lbw" signified! John was no athlete and was, as a boy, rather corpulent; he had not played much cricket and had therefore not been given out "leg before wicket". On receiving his old text books, I was amused to find his name on the flyleaf changed, in many places, to "John Barrell", no doubt by some prankster in his class. After national service in the RAF, John graduated from Cambridge and became a university librarian. He worked at Hull University initially, where he was a colleague of the poet Phillip Larkin, and then happily spent the rest of his working life in the Bristol University library.

In the Spring of my first year, the school's annual cross-country race was held. It was suitably divided into various age groups, with different courses being run, most in relation to the Little Crosby estate and village. Participation in this race was compulsory and exemptions difficult to obtain. I was told that, because of my rheumatic history, I would be excused but I insisted on running. Many boys, who were reluctant athletes and dreaded this event, thought that I was mad to pass up this chance of escaping the race. My stance resulted in the expected brouhaha with mother but, because of father's indecision on the issue, I prevailed with some difficulty. At the time, I was quite small and very light. Two boys who had been at the school longer than myself already had run well the previous year and were strongly fancied in our 10-12 year-old age group. They both set off like greyhounds but I had reeled them in by the halfway mark and won easily, with no great difficulty. Father was suitably proud of me, mother simply relieved that I had not died during the competition, which I went on to win on three further occasions.

The war ground on, with air raids providing an excellent excuse for not doing one's homework; but the May Blitz of 1941 was something else. It extended over eight consecutive nights with nearly 1500 Liverpudlians being killed. Terrible though these figures were, they were soon equalled and then exceeded nightly by Royal Air Force (RAF) Bomber Command raids on German cities. For a couple of years, boys living in Bootle and Aintree brought to school almost daily reports of damage due to bombing. Crosby, areas "up the line" to Southport and those towards Ormskirk escaped most of the damage, all being further from Liverpool.There was sporadic news from one's classmates of the involvement in battle of a father, brother or other relative and occasionally this news would be grim. A large proportion of Merseyside families had maritime connections, with family members or relatives being especially in the Merchant Navy, and these contributed to the frequent unhappy tidings.

A succession of Old Boys revisited the school and some, presented at assembly to the entire student body, would give modest accounts of their wartime experiences. In addition to his often physically challenging work, father was out until after midnight several nights per week, and much later than this when there was an air raid, patrolling our locality as an Air Raid Warden. One house in our road was hit by an incendiary bomb, the resulting fire being easily controlled by the wardens. Also, he spent a couple of nights a week at the Crosby Conservative Club doing something here called "fire watching". In December 1941 came the news of the Japanese attack on Pearl Harbor followed two days later by the sinking of the *Repulse* and *Prince of Wales* by Japanese aircraft off the coast of Malaya. Two months later, in February 1942, came the fall of Singapore. A few weeks after this, we learned that my mother's cousin, Captain Frank Conway, had been among the prisoners. A career soldier in the Loyal North Lancashire regiment, he then spent more than three dreadful years as a prisoner of war in Changi gaol, his wife and children escaping on what was literally the last ship to leave Singapore.

Rationing was now in place in Britain and the "ration book" was needed for the acquisition of many food substances. There were no cakes on sale in shops and bananas and oranges seemed to have disappeared from the face of the earth. Sweets and chocolates, known as candy in the USA, were also rationed, and could only be bought using "coupons". The country was encouraged to "Dig for Victory" and some areas of many parks were converted into allotments. The park at the end of our road was put to this use and Aunt Clare, with my occasional assistance, worked hard on her patch of ground, growing many delicious vegetables. There was also a system of coupons for the purchase of clothes and this caused occasional problems with the purchase of caps, blazers, rugby jerseys, etc. However, in general, surprisingly little disruption in school life seemed to occur. We had several patriotic endeavors, including collecting for various financial drives, such as "Spitfire week", and were encouraged to collect aluminum, mainly in the form of saucepans. Most houses lost the iron railings around their gardens. We learned the national anthems of our many European allies, but Belgium, to our surprise, was never included. For many years, perhaps even now, I could remember the English words and tune of the French, Polish, Czech, Dutch and Norwegian anthems.

The blackout was in existence all this time and the precautions that it entailed had become a way of life. Windows and doors were carefully screened and many households, including my family's, had light wooden frames enclosing dark material which could be snugly fitted into windows. Bicycles and cars had the upper half of their lights either painted over or blanked off with a visor; the feeble light from these caused some difficulties in driving. Some cars were modified to get around the petrol rationing and had bags containing town gas on their roofs that provided enough power for driving the vehicle at a slowish speed.

One night, having been around at a classmate's house collaborating on our homework, I set off for home in pitch darkness. I was well acquainted with the area and was running. Approaching a steep kerb that I knew to be there, I jumped in the air and collided violently with a lamp post that I had overlooked. My forehead took the full force of the collision and it was no exaggeration to say that, literally, I saw stars. I was very dazed but had the sense to return to my friend's house, by which time I was sporting a swelling the size of a very large egg. He and his mother slowly walked me home. I had one day off school and then returned to full activities. This rapid recovery led to countless jokes at my expense about the thickness of my cranium.

At about the age of 12 years, I joined a Sea Scout troop that was well run and very active. Many friends were members and we used the stables, outhouses and lawn of a large house in

Blundellsands as our headquarters. There were three scoutmasters, the senior being an ex-master mariner who had served in sail. We became expert at boxing the compass, tying all sorts of knots and, much more difficult, splicing rope. The heavy navy blue jerseys, with "Sea Scouts" emblazoned in white on their front, were very comfortable in the winter but much less so in summery conditions. One of the great perks of our troop was our good luck in being able to spend days on the tugboats of the Rea Towing Company. Because of the war, the port of Liverpool was extremely busy, with crowded docks and many ships in the river waiting for berths. We came to know all the docks on both sides of the river and many scouts, myself included, obtained the "ship's pilot" proficiency badge after a series of splendid lectures from the ex-sea captain. Not uncommonly, scouts would go out to the Mersey Bar on tugs and some lucky boys got a trip to Avonmouth and back. In retrospect, my sea scouting days formed a rich and varied episode in my life.

However, little boys grow up and I soon joined the school's Air Training Corps (ATC) squadron. I kept on with the scouts for some time but, with increasing academic workloads, I was eventually forced to leave them. The school squadron held drills and lectures after school twice weekly and this sometimes interfered with games practices. Occasionally, flying experience was gained by visits to the Royal Air Force (RAF) station at Woodvale, near Southport, where a Polish squadron guarded Merseyside during most of the war years, and at the Royal Naval Air Station (RNAS) at Burscough, near Ormskirk. I enjoyed my days in the school squadron and soon was promoted to corporal. An annual camp was held at such RAF stations as Lindholme, near Rotherham, Tern Hill in Salop and St Athan, near Cardiff. The latter camp was most enjoyable. Bleddyn Williams, the famous Cardiff and Wales rugby centre, was an officer on the staff there and gave the young visitors several lectures on rugby, before refereeing a game dressed in uniform. The conditions were very warm and we played in gym shoes. During a particularly ragged passing movement involving the backs of one team, Bleddyn threw his whistle away, intercepted the ball, turned back upfield and ran through most of both teams before touching down. He came back, looking very sheepish, and explained that he simply couldn't resist what he had done!

Pedr Davis was a school friend who lived nearby. His father

was a Liverpool journalist who accepted a position on the *London Evening News* about this time. I was sorry to see Pedr go but promises of vacations at his new home in Wimbledon eased the pain. After a relatively short time in his new location, he returned to us, staying with previous neighbours. This was because of the V1 and V2 rocket raids on London and the South East, his parents thinking, quite rightly, that the buzz-bombs constituted a real threat. So he returned to his old school and I enjoyed his company for another year.

Bishop Halsall now arrived as the chaplain at Park House, an up-market, popular and very respected nursing home in Waterloo. It was owned and run by Augustinian nuns who specialised in Midwifery but also offered excellent general surgical and medical care. The bishop was technically the Bishop of Zabi, a defunct christian see in North Africa, and was the auxiliary Bishop of Liverpool; this appointment left him largely free for diocesan affairs. He asked my school for some altar servers and I was one of those persuaded to volunteer. He was an interesting and amiable man who gave his altar boys generous gifts at Christmas and at other times. He would take his altar boys to the Lake District on occasions, where we would all enjoy walking on the fells. One of my memories of the latter location is of the Bishop perspiring over an old stove in a mountain chalet while cooking lunch for a gaggle of boys, who were playing cards for money. For relaxation, he could often be seen helping his brother, a farmer, load hay or muck at the latter's farm, situated close to the village bearing their family surname.

During my association with Bishop Halsall, a story circulated about him and Fr John Heenan. Both had done their seminary training at the English College in Rome, traditionally the place where "high fliers" in the English church were sent. Joe Halsall, a hard-headed Lancashire man from a farming background, was said to be more down-to-earth than his more enthusiastic London friend. When the latter would discourse, often at breakfast, on schemes that he had envisioned, the former would listen and then invariably say "We are not impressed, Jackie". In the fullness of time, Fr Halsall was consecrated bishop and one of the first telegrams he received was said to be from Fr Heenan and read "We are not impressed. Jackie". A few years later, Fr Heenan was consecrated Bishop of Leeds. He was alleged to have received a telegram reading "We are still not impressed. Joe". This story was widely believed to be true and I am inclined to think that it was. Bishop Heenan went on to become Archbishop of Liverpool and finally Cardinal Archbishop of Westminster.

One of Bishop Halsall's great interests was the noble art of boxing. He was a very regular visitor at the Liverpool stadium and would occasionally take me along. We sat in the best seats, only five or six rows back from the ring and surrounded by aficionados, hangers-on and bookmakers. Other than a scarf across his neck, he made no attempt to disguise himself. At this time in the late 1940s, boxing, especially the professional variety, had not yet attracted the general opprobrium that it later gained; however, it was already frowned upon by many and generally thought of as being distinctly "non - U".

Nel Tarleton, the famous and very popular Liverpool boxer, had retired in 1945 but many other local fighters were prominent in the sport. In the mid-1940s, these included Ernie Roderick, brother-in-law of Tarleton and managed by him for a time. Also frequently seen at the stadium were Stan Rowan, Peter Fallon, Gus Foran, Bernie Pugh, Billy Ellaway, Wally Thom and Jimmy and Tommy Malloy, all from Merseyside or St Helens. A three-round exhibition bout in 1947 involved the "Brown Bomber", the great Joe Louis, boxing three rounds with his chief sparring partner. Louis, who had won the World Heavyweight Championship in 1937, was a member of a touring US Army boxing team, was 32 years old at the time and nearing the end of his wonderful career, yet his skills and athleticism were outstanding. Sugar Ray Robinson, Lee Savold and Randolph Turpin, all famous names in the sport, also boxed exhibitions there. The Liverpool stadium was the only purpose-built boxing facility in the country and contained no pillars, excellent views of the ring being available from all seats. Requiring only a new roof, it was inexplicably demolished in 1985.

The war against Germany finished on May 7th 1945 and the treaty was ratified on the following day. Wild celebrations followed Victory in Europe, or VE Day as it was called, and these included street parties, with tables and chairs being placed in many roads for al fresco eating and drinking. The Japanese formally surrendered aboard the *USS Missouri* on September 2nd and "Victory over Japan", or VJ day, gave rise to further rejoicing. The Booth family

Fig 1. VE Day Party, Waterloo. Tony Booth, later to be the father of Cherie Blair, is seated nearest to the camera, next to a boy wearing a paper hat.

lived directly across the road from us and I clearly remember Tony, their eldest child, being prominent in these celebrations and in other activities (Fig 1). This was the actor remembered by many as the "scouse git" and son-in-law of Alf Garnet in the TV series *Till Death Us Do Part*. Tony's father sailed in the Elder Demster ships, on the *Appapa, Accra and Auriol* out of Liverpool, for West Africa. In common with many seafarers, he would immediately enter a pub with friends on arriving back in Liverpool. Telephones were in short supply in our locality in the mid-1940s and Mr Booth, having no phone in his own house, would frequently phone my family and ask if we would cross the road and tell his wife that he would be home at a certain hour. I greatly resented this liberty on his part but mother, a great peacemaker, always insisted that we oblige.

Cherie, one of Tony Booth's seven daughters from four mothers, moved in with her grandparents in October 1954 across the road from my old house and lived there until 1972. By this time, I was away from my family home a great deal and neither met nor was aware of her. She attended Seafield convent school in Crosby, situated close to St Mary's College, and went on to become a highly successful QC as well as being the wife of Tony Blair, the British Prime Minister. Years later, following an interview related to a Liverpool visit when she was Chancellor of the John Moores

University, Liverpool, Cherie described many of her childhood memories in some detail for the Liverpool Echo. She reminisced about how she would pass a pawnbroker's shop and the level crossing at the Liverpool to Southport railway line, on her way to St Edmund's infant school, the same one that I had attended. This brought back vivid memories of these scenes to me.

In 1946, my relative Captain Conway arrived home after more three years in the Changi Prisoner-of-War camp, Singapore, where he and many others had received terrible treatment. He could not be repatriated from Malaya for several weeks because of his poor physical condition and was promptly admitted to the clinical unit of the Liverpool School of Tropical Medicine for treatment of multiple parasitic and deficiency diseases. He spent nearly three months there, visiting us as his condition improved. His wife had left him during his imprisonment and, all in all, he had endured a dreadful time. On these visits, which soon became regular and weekly, he and I would often play chess. He was very good at this game and taught me much. Apparently, chess had been a great consolation to him and others during his incarceration. They had played with handmade wooden pieces, usually on a mud floor ruled in squares.

I had grown a good deal by the time I sat my School Certificate examination and entered the sixth form. I enjoyed rugby and was making decent progress in the game but did not enjoy the confidence of the Brother in charge of rugby, never even getting the slightest consideration for the first XV. Accordingly, I turned increasingly to running and, with the backing of the headmaster of the time, formed a school cross-country team. I organised the fixtures but never scheduled any that clashed with first team rugby games. However, I still had difficulty in getting boys released from rugby practices for competition although, to some degree, this was overcome by the intervention of the Headmaster. Despite these problems, we did quite well during our first year of competition. We had several notable successes, including a win over a strong Liverpool University second-string team and a third place in the Sangster Cup for Merseyside and District schools. This trophy had been presented for competition by Vernon Sangster, the founder of Vernon Pools.

The annual school sports day illustrated the woeful ignorance about athletic matters that prevailed in the school at that time. All events were completed in one day, with little consideration being given to athletes competing in several events. A Victor Ludorum was declared each year, winning of which grossly favoured, of course, the sprinters and field events competitors. After considerable persistence, I managed to get the annual cross-country race counted as one win for Victor Ludorum, but the scales remained very heavily weighed against the middle-distance runner. In my last year at school, for instance, I won my first event, the 440 yards, in an excellent time. I triumphed over Peter Kelly, considered by most to be much faster than I, by running almost flat out virtually from the gun. Then I had to run the 880 yards only 20 minutes later, being beaten by a friend over whom I could usually triumph. Finally, after a long rest but still feeling totally exhausted, I ran the mile, which I managed to win in a very slow time. However, this was not enough and I finished runner-up in the Victor Ludorum stakes. Nevertheless, many congratulated me on my efforts and I was told a distinguished-looking older man wished to speak with me. I thought that I was in for more compliments but he simply asked "Are you related to Miss Halpin?"

I was a member of Waterloo Harriers, not one of the leading clubs of Merseyside, and trained with them at Barn Hey, a small and subsidiary ground of MTS. There were no showers available but at least it was possible to run on a track. Tom Pratt was the secretary and general factotum, working very hard at what was a basically thankless job; he was also a very good masseur. An ex-serviceman, a student at St Andrews University, did some enthusiastic coaching during his summer vacation but I did not avail myself of his expertise. However, Charlie Kelly was a second claim member of Waterloo, Liverpool Pembroke being his first claim club, and regularly trained with us for convenience. He was the elder brother of Peter, whom I had beaten in the school sports 440 yards race, and was a very good miler. In fact, he was an Irish international athlete, the best in the region with the possible exception of John Joe Barry of Wirral Harriers, who was also an Irish international and had represented Eire in the 1500 metres in the London Olympics. Charlie and I would often talk together about training and tactics and his advice was invaluable.

In these days, most of the athletic competition in the north of England seemed to involve handicapping although, of course, county and other major championships would clearly not take this form.

My first non-school competitive race was at the Earlestown Viaduct Sports where I competed in the junior half mile. On arriving at the track, I was horrified to see in the program that I was the back-marker, off just 28 yards, whereas some youths were way ahead of me, off distances up to 95 yards. After the gun, I set off as briskly as possible, finding it necessary to run very wide nearly all the way because of the great mass of competitors ahead. However, I came in third and won a distinctly tinny toast rack. This was the only race I ran as a junior and it cost me dear. On moving up to open competition, I was severely handicapped because of my third place finish in the junior ranks and never got among the prizes again.

At this time, I was using spiked running shoes made by Laws of Wimbledon for track competition. I had some slight problems with them and a local cobbler put a sponge heel on the outside of each shoe, which made a major improvement. Most local runners used the Foster shoe, which had been developed by Joe Foster of Bolton and was one of the first spiked running shoes in general use. Years after the war, this relatively small business was transformed into the Reebok company, named after a small African gazelle, which became a world giant in running shoes. Reebok sponsored a new soccer stadium for Bolton Wanderers, replacing the old Burnden Park and called, appropriately enough, the Reebok Stadium.

I now, like many of my friends, worked during the long summer vacation. Picking peas and potatoes for Crosby corporation was about the only employment available. I found it back-breaking and extremely tiring and was paid just sixpence an hour. Even allowing for the worth of the currency at this time and subsequent inflation, it was a truly beggarly rate of remuneration. The following year, I graduated to working on the harvest for a Little Crosby farmer. Although this was also tiring, it was much more enjoyable than my earlier forms of work and I now was paid at the munificent rate of one whole shilling an hour.

This heavy physical and unaccustomed work had another effect. I had entered the Lancashire County 440 yards Junior Championship race, which was to be held in conjunction with an athletic meeting at Croston, between Rufford and Preston. This was not really my event but I had run several very good one lap times in training and, like many middle-distance runners, I entertained delusional notions about my ability in running the quarter mile. There were three heats for this competition, with the first two in each heat and the fastest loser going on to the final. I was amazed to see several bookmakers present, busily accepting bets on the various races. I had never witnessed this before at any athletic meet and was further surprised to find that I was the strong favourite in my event.

I felt very tired and "heavy legged" during my warm-up and bitterly regretted not taking at least the previous day off from harvesting. My worse fears were confirmed after the gun went off. I had neither speed nor stamina, came third in my heat and was not even the fastest loser; but my troubles were not yet over. On slowly walking back to the changing tent, a red-faced and clearly drunken man in a loud check suit accosted me and began shouting loudly and gesticulating wildly. I was quite alarmed and couldn't understand for some time what, in a very broad Lancashire accent, he was saying. Eventually, I realised that he was accusing me of "throwing the race" and deliberately losing, presumably to assist someone's betting strategy. I was very relieved when a policeman arrived on the scene and sent the man on his way.

In the summer of 1945, I went down to Wimbledon and spent several most enjoyable weeks with Pedr Davis and his family. Rambles on Wimbledon Common and visits to Surbiton lagoon figured prominently in the holiday. Pedr lived close to the All England Tennis Club, which had been bombed in the London blitz and was now occupied by the US Army. It was still not completely repaired and one day Pedr, his brother, some others and myself managed, quite illegally, to gain entry to the famous club ground and knock a ball about on the damaged centre court for a few minutes, so that we could later boast of "playing on the Centre Court". A couple of American soldiers saw us skylarking, escorted us to their canteen for a dressing down and gave us each a coke to drink before shooing us off the premises. This was the first experience of coca-cola for us all.

Following another vacation at Pedr's home, he and I took off with Michael Quinlan, a friend of Pedr's, on a cycle tour, staying each night at youth hostels. The first day we had to cross London from the south-west to the north-east but this proved to be less daunting than I had feared. We stayed near Castle Hedingham on this night, headed on to Norwich and the Norfolk Broads and then covered a big circular route through the Midlands and finally back to London. The trip took about 12 days and was most enjoyable, apart from Michael's bicycle being wrecked by an overtaking lorry near Bletchley. He was fortunate to escape unscathed and had to take the train home. After national service in the RAF, Michael entered Oxford University. After securing a Double First, he joined the Civil Service where he had a most distinguished career, being Permanent Secretary at both the Employment and Defence Departments before being knighted.

The early months of 1947 saw the whole country blanketed by snow for weeks on end. This period was said to be the snowiest of the twentieth century and most areas were intensely cold. Snow fell somewhere in the UK on every day between January 22nd and March 17th, with many villages completely cut off for days. On Merseyside, road crews kept the main roads clear for the most part but many side roads were impassable for long periods. I remember father piling coal and ashen residues in the late evening on the kitchen fire to keep it alight during the long night. I usually walked to school, rather than cycling, and boys from more distant homes were frequently very late in arriving. All sporting fixtures were cancelled and the railways suffered major disruptions.

At school, the Arts Sixth form had good teaching and was well advised on career options. In the Science Sixth, we had excellent Chemistry tuition from the Brother in charge of rugby and good Maths and Applied Maths instruction. After some initial attraction to Engineering, I had by now decided on a career in Medicine, although there was no family tradition of any sort for this choice. Physics and Biology were required subjects but, because of the war, male teachers were in short supply and the teaching of the former was poor and was non-existent in the latter. Norman de Vere, an Irishman, had arrived to teach Physics. He was a former medical student at Trinity College, Dublin, whose undergraduate career had run into major difficulties. His family owned and ran the *Western People*, a newspaper widely read in the West of Ireland, and he stoutly claimed that, but for the war, he would have competed for Ireland as a middle distance athlete in the Tokyo Olympics of 1940. Although genial, sociable, and very interested in athletics, his grasp of Physics was considerably less than overwhelming. I remember him telling us that it was probable that we would find "something about the atomic bomb" on our exam papers and he was often seen copying on to the blackboard from magazines such as *Scientific American*. He eventually went back to his medical studies, qualified at University College, Galway, and after working in Africa, finally became a GP in Dublin. I was highly annoyed about this situation and was forced to forget about Biology, which Mr de Vere subsequently taught but at a time that was far too late for me, and I obtained an outside tutor to help me with Physics.

In the end, I obtained examination results that were excellent in Chemistry, good in Pure Maths and Applied Maths and reasonably good in Physics; these won me a Lancashire County Major scholarship. I had applied to the Faculty of Medicine of the University of Liverpool for admission. There was considerable initial confusion because I had applied in the name "Raymond John" and my birth and other certificates were all in the name "John Raymond". With some difficulty, I managed to get this sorted out, convinced that it must have made a very bad impression. However, I was accepted for the following year, which meant that I had virtually to waste another year in the Sixth form. A large number of ex-servicemen were still applying for university places and were being given priority over school leavers. Another student had been far more perspicacious than I. A year behind me at St Mary's, he left for the Southport Technical College and after a couple of years there, having studied both Physics and Biology, he began medical school at Liverpool with me but in the second year; so he had effectively gained two years on me. At the time, the Liverpool medical school was well thought of, with many of the faculty and honorary consultants being internationally known. However, it was not good tactics to apply to only one University and I had done this only because of the lack of any guidance in the matter.

During my final year at school, I was promoted to the dizzy heights of Flight Sergeant in the school ATC squadron. I competed in the ATC northern athletic championships at RAF Cosford, near Wolverhampton, where a large hangar was the only indoor arena for athletic competition in Britain until a much better facility opened in Glasgow. At Cosford, I won the 800 metres and so qualified for a place in the national competition, held that year at RAF Halton, near Wendover, in Buckinghamshire. The standard was, in my opinion, very high with one of the Liverpool competitors being Ken Box. A student at the Holt High School in Childwall, Liverpool, he went on to become a well-known international sprinter and represented Britain in the 1956 Melbourne Olympics. I came third in the 880 yards race at Halton on Friday afternoon and was told that I would be a reserve for the annual meeting against the Sea and Army cadets. I was also informed it was imperative that I remain until the conclusion of the meeting on Saturday.

This seemed a waste of time to me, especially as I had now completely finished with all activities connected with my school and I had a much better idea. I hitch-hiked to Wembley, hoping to acquire a ticket for admission on the Sunday, the last day of the 1948 Olympics. This would have included the finish of the marathon, the relays and the closing ceremonies but was unsuccessful in this. From London, I hitch-hiked home and did quite a lot of this successfully before getting my own transport, after which I would often pick up others looking for lifts. Both as a hitch-hiker and as a motorist, I never encountered any problems but, because of the growth of motorways and the increasing risk of violence, hitch-hiking all but disappeared from the British scene long before the turn of the century.

THREE

The University of Liverpool

I entered the Faculty of Medicine at Liverpool University in September 1948, the same year as the National Health Service (NHS) was inaugurated in the United Kingdom (UK). Some 90 plus students made up my year, the majority being ex-service men. Four other former pupils of St Mary's joined with me but only three of us would finally qualify in Medicine. There was an Anglican parson in his 40s and ten females among the first year entrants. The number of females would be vastly larger these days and would even constitute more than 50% of the student intake in some US medical schools. 77 students finally graduated in 1954, several being initially from the year ahead.

As expected, my first year was very easy and most pleasant. I was excused Physics and Chemistry because of my school results and just had to take Botany and Zoology in the MB Part 1 exam, with which I had no difficulty. In the final term of that year, I took the course in Organic Chemistry, which was normally done in the second year. I had a good deal of spare time, much of which I invested in learning bridge in the Student's Union. Early in my student career, I formed the opinion that the that the Engineers had the best esprit de corps, that the Architects were the best dressed, tending to favour Clydella and Viyella type shirts, self coloured woollen ties and corduroy jackets, and that the Vets were the most pleasant group.

There were debates in the Student's Union and many interesting talks, some of which I attended in my early student years. I remember, quite vividly, an evening debate on the motion that "This house believes that the comedian does more for the community than the politician", or words to that effect. The motion was proposed by Gilly Potter, a well known humorist of the period, and opposed by the Reverend Longbottom, with both having a student seconder. Longbottom was a minister of religion, active and not unsuccessful in local politics, where he stood as a "Protestant", this being somewhat similar to the future tradition of the Rev Ian Paisley of Ulster. Although Mr Potter did not bother, for most part, to speak specifically to the motion, the house voted overwhelmingly in its favour. On another occasion, a talk was given by Lord Longford. I spoke with him later and was asked if I would escort him to the station, the noble Lord apparently declining a taxi. The tall, rather untidy, Minister for the British Zone of Germany, looked as if he had dressed in a great rush and had the air of an absent-minded professor. We walked down Brownlow Hill together to Lime Street station where I saw him onto the London train. I found him very informed about all manner of subjects, as well as being most generous in spirit.

One day, I encountered George Wilmot at the mail slots. He was an ex-Bevin Boy, one of those who had become coal miners instead of doing national service in the Armed Forces. He was also President of the Guild of Undergraduates that year and I had previously met him when he competed for the University against my school in a cross-country race. He was an old boy of Birkenhead School, a Merseyside institution that included in its distinguished list of former pupils the famous barrister FE Smith who became the first Earl of Birkenhead, as well Secretary for India and Lord Chancellor. A friend of Wilmot's then chanced to pass by. This was Graham Routledge, also an Old Birkonian and a freshman in the Law school. Wilmot introduced us and asked if either of us would take the place on the Guild council that was reserved for a fresher's representative. We both declined, much to George's annoyance, but Graham and I became firm friends, seeing a good deal of each other especially in *Mrs Mac's*, the university pub of the time, now long since disappeared and whose proper name I never did discover, and in other popular taverns.

These included a hostelry in Rice St adjacent to the Liverpool Art School, which was said to be over 150 years old. It was originally called *The Ruthin Castle* and then *Ye Cracke* but was generally known simply as *The Crack*. It contained a snug called *The War Office* where, it was claimed, armchair military enthusiasts had closely analysed and criticised the tactics employed in the Boer War. It was later frequented by Roger McGough and Mike McCartney of the *Scaffold* group, John Lennon in his days as an art student and by Franz Stamfl, a musical polymath, broadcaster, writer, and humourist. *The Philharmonic* was another popular tavern, a picturesque Victorian pile near the Philharmonic Hall. The latter was where the Royal Liverpool Philharmonic Orchestra played, with Franz

Stamfl principal flautist, and where I would receive my degrees. This pub had two rooms opening off the main lounge called *Brahms* and *Liszt* and superb mosaics and ceramics in the men's toilet which were, not infrequently, photographed by tourists, not least by American females!

Graham and I seemed to visit the same watering holes, with he bursting not uncommonly into *Lloyd George knows my father, father knows Lloyd George*, these nine words being constantly repeated to the tune of *Onward Christian Soldiers*. Graham was always splendid company and graduated with flying colours in his Law finals. He later abandoned Law for the Church, being ordained in the Anglican ministry and eventually appointed Canon Resident of St Paul's Cathedral, before his untimely death in 1989. His sister Patricia was also a student with us but I never met her. After beginning in repertory at the Liverpool Playhouse, Pat went on to enjoy a highly successful career. She won Tony, Olivier and many other awards, including Top TV Comedy Actresss and Personality of the Year, and was made a CBE. As well as many movie and stage appearances, her roles as Hetty Wainthropp in the BBC TV series of the same name and more especially as Hyacinth Bucket, pronounced "Bouquet", in the TV series *Keeping Up Appearances* were particularly popular and well known.

One Saturday afternoon in the summer, I went to St George's Hall, Liverpool, to hear the great Paul Robeson sing. The son of a minister of religion, Robeson had attended Rutgers University in New Jersey. He had been an outstanding college football payer and was one of the first African-Americans to play as a professional. After graduating in Law, he joined a prestigious New York City law firm. He had a wonderfully deep, strong voice and was famous for songs such as *Old Man River*. The occasion had been promoted by the local communist party and, to my frustration, I had to listen to a great deal of left wing cant before the great man was presented and began to entertain. Robeson was, of course, used by the Soviet Union and communist parties throughout the world for their own ends, while playing on his understandable hatred of racism. Father was most annoyed when he learned how I had spent my afternoon.

Early in my first university term, the Fresher's cross-country race was held. The university course had virtually no "country" in its length but did include several steep hills. Alan Parker, the university team captain, acted as our hare or guide and some 20 competitors started, several being ex-servicemen of formidable shape and appearance. In fact, I managed to win relatively easily but was discouraged, despite my victory, by the nonchalant ease with which Parker, just ahead of me to show the freshmen the way, strolled around the course, following which he indulged in some further, and probably more intensive, training. I was then included in the first team fixture, away to Durham University a few days later. We travelled there by train on Friday afternoon and, on the morning of the competition, our hosts showed us around the University, then the castle and finally the cathedral. At the end of this tour, I noticed there were only a couple of my teammates with me. The more experienced runners had been here before and were wise to the Durham ploy, aimed at wearing out the opposition before the competition. I wondered why these veterans had not shared this knowledge with the rest of the team. I did quite well in the this race but found the rest of the season heavy going and did not distinguish myself. There were five runners on our team who had represented the Universities Athletic Union (UAU), effectively English Universities minus Oxbridge. The team always performed well but I found things to be getting progressively tougher. When George Wilmot passed me one day on a hill, as I was puffing and struggling, I realised that I was not performing up to my expectations, remembering that I had beaten him easily when competing against him for my school. After the end of this season, I did not run cross-country for the University again.

I continued to compete for the university track team for several years, with considerable personal satisfaction and pleasure but with only modest success. Occasionally, I wondered if I would have done better had I not had my brush with rheumatic fever but decided that there was no point in dwelling on this. After the track team had competed east of the Pennines, our coach would invariably pull into a pub en route home. A favourite of ours was *Help the Poor Struggler* near Oldham, with the sign outside depicting a man kicking his heels with a noose around his neck. This was run by Albert Pierrepoint, at the time also the Hangman of England, but is now long destroyed. On one occasion, a late season track meeting was run in Yorkshire immediately before the degree ceremonies. Several important dignitaries were going to be awarded honorary degrees, including the French Ambassador to Britain. The rather tatty quadrangle amid the main university buildings had been tarted up with flowerbeds and a central fountain. On the morning of the big day, a large notice bearing the words "Please do not urinate in the reservoir" was seen adjacent to the fountain and had to be rapidly removed. I recalled it being wrestled from its supports on the way home from our track meet but had no idea how it had been transported to the quad.

Fig 2. Alan Parker and the author, before a cross-country race at Durham University, 1948.

Alan Parker was outstanding on both the track and cross-country teams. A tall, well-built man (Fig 2) from Barrow, he used to run to and from his digs to the University. After graduating with a BSc Honours degree, he tried to qualify for the British team in the 1500 metres for the 1952 Helsinki Olympics, where Bannister secured a fourth place in the final. He was unsuccessful in this but, with great resolve, won a place for the 5000 metres. He was second in the fastest of the three heats in 14 min 18.2 secs, easing up close behind Schade of Germany, who set a new Olympic record in this heat. Parker's time was less than one second slower than Gaston Rieff's 5,000 metre previous Olympic record set in the London Olympics of 1948 and faster than any Briton had run previously. He was eight and nine seconds respectively faster than Pirie and Chataway were in their heats and a whopping 38 seconds quicker than the great John Landy, who failed to qualify in another heat for the final. Alan paid a heavy price for this fast time, however, and ran nearly 20 seconds slower in the final, won by the great Zatopek, although still finishing in the first dozen.

George Park was the best sprinter on the university team for many years. He was a medical student, two years ahead of myself, and a true amateur. He would warm-up in an old pair of trousers, with a cricket sweater over a rugby shirt. If it was raining, he would add a flat cap and carry an umbrella. He made a strange sight, plodding around the track under his brolly as he warmed up and this frequently gave rise to amusement and even derision; but George invariably had the last laugh. He was an excellent sprinter and rarely lost. I remember one season when, at the Leeds University track, he ran a remarkably fast 220 yards; in fact, he headed the UK times that season for this distance until well into July.

At the end of one track season in the early 1950s, a late additional fixture was added against the Army's Officer Cadet Training Unit at Eaton Hall, the Duke of Westminster's lovely estate near Chester. Because of prior commitments, many of the regular team were unavailable and our team numbers were correspondingly small, with several athletes having to take on multiple events. The military treated the occasion very seriously. There were flags everywhere, with Generals and other VIPs shaded by an awning in a stand near the finishing line, and dozens of marquees. The cadet's team numbers appeared to be massive. However, we won fairly convincingly and were right royally entertained at the conclusion of the events. The question of a rugby fixture for the cadets, who apparently had two blank midweek slots, now arose. The track team usually contained several university rugby players but they were absent on this occasion. With the start of the rugby season only a couple of months away, I was prevailed upon to bring a team over mid-week in late September.

I managed to get together a reasonably decent XV, drawing

on members of the St Mary's Old Boys, Liverpool University and Waterloo clubs. We were all apprehensive about the presence of John Hyde in the opposing ranks. He was a cadet at Eaton Hall and had played for the Northampton club, for East Midlands and for an England Under-19 Group team as a schoolboy and was to shortly get a full cap with the England team against France; however, he did not appear against us. Early in the first half, our hooker, John O'Shea, injured his leg in what was clearly a serious manner. The cadets gave us a replacement player but he was not a specialised hooker. This seriously handicapped us but our scratch team played well and we lost only narrowly. In fact, John had fractured his lower leg and I visited him that evening in a Liverpool hospital. He had been just behind me at St Mary's and was a year below me at medical school. His injury required extensive treatment and caused him to miss much class work and an important examination. He sat this at a slightly later date, passed with flying colours and his graduation as a physician was not delayed. He went on to become a consultant pathologist at Clatterbridge hospital.

On the way to and from the athletic grounds, which were situated at some distance from the University on the south side of Liverpool, I would pass an undistinguished street close to dilapidated tram sheds. This was Penny Lane, later elevated to fame by *The Beatles*. John Lennon had lived at 251 Menlove Avenue, quite close to Wyncote, the university sports ground. Yoko Ono bought this house many years later and presented it to the nation. In 2002, she unveiled a seven-foot high statue of Lennon at Liverpool Airport, which was subsequently called the John Lennon Airport.

At the end of my first university year, I worked as a lift attendant at the Adelphi hotel. At this time, it was run by British Railways, had a good reputation and was immeasurably superior to the shabby hotel that it became many years later. I wore a winged collar, black bow tie and a navy blue suit with "Britsh Railways" embroidered in yellow on the jacket's maroon collar. Many years later, at the announcement of the wedding between Prince Charles and Mrs Parker Bowles in early 2005, I saw the Prince on TV wearing a garish dinner jacket, with a red collar and cuffs. Although not nearly as smart, it immediately reminded me of my old hotel uniform. A Sandhurst Army cadet, recovering from some illness, was my colleague. The hotel contained many American and Canadian guests, usually staying there overnight before joining their ship for a trans-Atlantic crossing. The demise of the North Atlantic passenger ship was still more than 15 years ahead and four Cunarders and three Canadian Pacific (CP) ships regularly sailed from Liverpool to New York and Montreal respectively.

My work was generally boring and not a little tiring, but had its moments. Thus for a period of a couple of weeks, I would pick up Danny Kaye at a specific time at the mezzanine floor of the hotel in the late evening. He was appearing at the nearby Empire theatre and would enter the hotel via the garage at the rear before making his way to meet me on the mezzanine floor to take the lift, so avoiding the crowds of fans and autograph hunters awaiting him in the main foyer. I found Kaye to be charming and generous.

In later years, I worked on the Christmas rush for the Post Office for several years and in the summer had a variety of jobs, including working for the Inland Revenue, the Merseyside and North Wales Electricity Board and for the NAAFI store and canteen at RAF Jurby in the Isle of Man, during which time I acted as a Marshal for the motorcycling Manx Grand Prix. The beginning of my clinical training in various hospitals saw the end of all this casual work.

In my second year at University, I took up rugby in the winter months and, after one season playing with St Mary's Old Boys, joined Waterloo Rugby Football Club (RFC). They ran five teams at this time and I had many happy years playing for the junior teams. Nearly all players remained after the game for several hours for social drinking and the invariable communal singing of songs, bawdy but amusing and very traditional. These songs included such hoary favourites as *The good ship Venus, The one-eyed Riley, Little Angeline, The Ball of Kirriemuir, The Eagles they fly high in Mobile*, the derivation of which I was never able to discover but suspected that it had originated during World War Two, and many others. Following England's great win in the Rugby World Cup of 2003, correspondence in the *Sunday Telegraph* disclosed the fact that *Swing Low, Sweet Chariot*, the anthem of the England rugby supporters, had been a popular post-match song in rugby pavilions at an earlier time. Apparently, it had been accompanied by a set of stylised gestures appropriate to the words. This was news to me and it was certainly not sung in the clubhouses that I knew, where the players were entertained by considerably more colourful and risque numbers. Sometimes "beer races" would be held between the home and visiting teams. 15 or so pints of beer would be lined up on the bar in front of each team, who would then engage in an alcoholic relay race. Having drunk his pint, each contestant would have to place his pint glass upside down on his head to prove that he had drunk the entire contents, before racing back to touch his next team-mate. Memories of this kind of behaviour now make me feel more than a little nauseous! Because of the drink and driving laws, and for various other reasons such as the changing youth culture, both beer races and singing had disappeared from the rugby clubhouse long before the end of the millennium.

It was difficult for medical students to play for university teams because laboratory sessions and clinical work ruled out participation in midweek games. Nevertheless, I played in a few Wednesday matches for the university junior teams in my early years at medical school and took great interest in the university first XV. At that time in the late 1940s and early 1950s, this was a very strong team, with Dennis Greenwood, a Yorkshire county player and England trialist, playing at centre alongside Edgar Knight, another outstanding player. Alan Milligan was scrum half, university captain and also captain of Cumberland and his partner at stand-off was Billy Cartmell, a Lancashire county player. The team had an excellent hooker and Reg Bazely and Vic Tindall played on the wings, both winning many caps for England. Tindall later became a Liverpool and District referee and went on to be Professor of Obstetrics and Gynaecology at Manchester University.

I saw the home team lose narrowly to a powerful Queen's University, Belfast, side. Kyle and Strathdee were the visitor's halfbacks, both celebrated Irish internationals, as was Henderson at centre. There was a group of Ulster players backing up this trio but Liverpool ran them close in a wonderful game. Liverpool advanced to the final of the UAU knockout competition in this season, where they were defeated narrowly by Loughborough who were skippered by Ken Jones, the British athletic team captain and Welsh international rugby player.

Brian Nordgren was a New Zealander and a student in the renowned Faculty of Architecture at Liverpool University during these years. He was a superb rugby player but RL, not RU, was his game. He played for the all-conquering Wigan team of the time and frequently trained on his own at Wyncote. It is possible that he might have joined in with the university rugby club's training on occasions. The Lancashire RU became aware of this situation and threatened the university club with expulsion if they did not speedily put an end to it. The Guild of Undergraduates now came into the picture, stating that as Nordgren was a fully paid-up, bona fide student, he was perfectly entitled to use the facilities at Wyncote. An awkward situation was averted when Nordgren announced, most sportingly, that he would train elsewhere in future.

In the third millennium, RU clubs were endeavouring to sign top RL players, after years of snubbing them and refusing them entry into their pavilions. In many cases, salaries larger than they were already getting were on offer and some RU clubs,such as Leeds and Orrell, had close ties with their RL neighbours. Then in 2005, Andrew Farrell, the captain of the Wigan and Great Britain RL teams, was recruited for Saracens RFC and the England RU team and the latter's squad training camp was run in conjunction with Leeds Rhinos, the RL Super League champions.

One of my very few claims to any sort of minimalist rugby fame occurred in the North of England Senior Sevens competition at the Manchester RFC during the early 1950s. The Waterloo first team had been scheduled to play against the North of Ireland club earlier in the season. Severe gales had delayed their ship at the Mersey bar for many hours and they arrived in Belfast very late on Saturday afternoon and far too late to play. Over drinks at the North club, the fixture was then rearranged for the last week of the season, the very date of the Sevens. A Waterloo team did compete at Manchester comprising a collection of junior team players and one first team player, Mike Rowe; the latter insisted, most surprisingly, that I be captain. Assisted by an opening round bye and a lucky draw, we progressed to the semi-finals, where we were narrowly beaten 3-0 by Fylde, who went on to win the final. Another unusual but happy rugby memory came via Brian Goodman, a friend, former MTS student and Waterloo member who was to live permanently in the USA soon after graduation. He was captain of the Clare College, Cambridge University rugby team, which was undertaking a tour to the Channel Islands over the New Year. He asked me if I would join them to make up the college numbers. I was happy to oblige, with another Waterloo non-college member, for what was a most enjoyable trip. One of the more welcoming local clubs was always Old Birkonian, at their pleasant ground and pavilion on the Wirral. Here I frequently enjoyed their generous post-game hospitality, usually met my friend Graham and never had anything less than a most happy time. Unfortunately, because of falling player numbers and persistent vandalism, the Old Birkonian club was forced to close its doors at the end of the 1974-75 season, amalgamating with Birkenhead Park RFC.

Notwithstanding time spent playing bridge and rugby, I managed to pass my first big examination, known as Second MB and comprising Anatomy, Physiology and Biochemistry. The illustrations in my anatomy book consistently failed to match cadaveric appearances; hence I had spent all too little time in the dissecting room. Physiology and Biochemistry posed no problem but I was seriously concerned about the Anatomy exam, especially the oral, which was conducted over a cadaver. With a mixture of luck, bluster and a small amount of knowledge, I managed to fool the external examiner and scrape a pass.

With this exam out of the way, I began clinical studies in the wards and clinics of the four main teaching hospitals of the time. The Liverpool Royal Infirmary, immediately adjacent to the medical school, was the biggest of these and I did two clerkships there in Medicine. A surgical clerkship was completed at the at the less prestigious Stanley Hospital and another at the famous Royal Southern Hospital. The latter was situated on the south side of the city near the docks and in a very run-down area. It took a brisk 20 minutes walk to get there from the medical school, passing very close to Nelson Street, where Hugh Owen Thomas had lived, his house being destroyed in the Liverpool blitz. Thomas was a son of *The Bonesetter of Crosshall Street*, a most famous, although unqualified, early orthopaedist. I enjoyed all my clerkships, including my two in Surgery. Although having no tendency to feel queasy or faint, I did not enjoy watching operations and learned very little from my visits to the operating theatre. Having to stand behind the surgical team, as well as fellow students and nurses, I was rarely able to see the operating field and hence was unable to follow the surgeon's descriptions as to what he was exposing and doing. I'm sure that these experiences greatly influenced my impending choice of house jobs.

On Friday, many of my year would get together, whenever

possible, for lunch at one of the many excellent Chinese restaurants near Great George Square. *The Far East* was the best known of these and one of the largest. Dishes containing chicken and occasionlly pork were available here during most of the war years and a local joke was that this selection was accompanied by a marked paucity of cats in the neighbourhood! In fact, the food was always of a high calibre. Where it originated, I know not but I was certain that the joke bore no relationship to actuality. This area of Chinese gastronomy was close to the former home of the great Sir Robert Jones, nephew of the younger Thomas and dubbed *The Father of Orthopaedic Surgery*, who had spent most of his illustrious career at the Royal Southern Hospital.

The next exam, Final MB Part 1, in Pharmacology and Therapeutics, was a breeze. I found the subjects both interesting and unchallenging, was one of only two students to earn a distinction and was awarded the J Hill Abrahm prize. It carried with it 50 pounds, this being a huge sum at that time to add to my impoverished finances. It was promptly invested in a motorbike, a small BSA 125 cc competition model that was really quite unsuitable for my needs. I had some hair-raising experiences on this machine, often with Eric Wylie, a fellow student who lived close by, who usually travelled with me and who became a GP in Parbold. Driving into the University in the rain, on slick, cobbled streets and across tram tracks, was often quite alarming and led to not infrequent skids and even some falls.

Final MB Part 2 now followed, comprising Pathology and Bacteriology, a formidable test with a significant failure rate. Once passed this hurdle, it was generally accepted that one would qualify in Medicine at some time. I was not too concerned about the Bacteriology section, although it turned out that this would be the most critical for me. A question on the written paper asked about Gram negative bacilli causing meningitis. This referred to bacteria that did not take up the Gram stain. In the tense exam atmosphere, I immediately thought of the meningococcus, which is also Gram negative and is a frequent cause of meningitis, and wrote extensively about this organism. Now bacilli are shaped like rods while cocci are like small, circular islands and the question referred to a whole group of bacilli, such as Haemophilus Influenzae. So I mistakenly wrote about Gram negative cocci, not Gram negative bacilli. When discussing the examination immediately afterwards with other students, my mistake became sickeningly obvious. I thought my chances of passing were now minute.

However, I gave the matter considerable thought and came up with a stratagem for the viva voce. This exam proceeded quietly to begin with and I thought that I was doing well. Then came the inevitable. Professor Downie, the Professor of Bacteriology and a most kindly, helpful and respected man, asked me why I had written about a coccus in question three when the question clearly indicated that a bacillus was to be discussed. I crossed my fingers and answered that I thought that the question was ambiguous; that the word "bacillus" had a general meaning of "organism", as well as its more specific morphological sense. This, of course, was a load of rubbish but it seemed to amuse the external examiner, who chuckled to himself and smiled broadly. Professor Downie was clearly irritated, defended his choice of words and then abruptly asked me about the very issue that I had so stupidly mixed up. Of course, I was now very well prepared for this and gave a comprehensive account of the Gram negative bacilli concerned. I passed the exam! More than a dozen fellow students had made the same mistake as did I and few were rewarded with a pass. I got to know Professor Downie quite well in his retirement, when we lived near each other and occasionally met on the golf course. He told me that he remembered well both my mistake and my highly original defence at the oral examination.

By now, I was getting towards the end of my undergraduate medical student days, with life becoming more serious. The Final MB Part 3 exam was in Public Health and Forensic Medicine. I found the latter subject to be very interesting and I passed the exam with a distinction. I now "lived in" for 12 weeks at the Liverpool Maternity Hospital at Oxford Street, during which I performed a number of normal deliveries "on the district", most of these being in slum dwellings.

Medicine, Surgery and Obstetrics and Gynaecology, together with their associated sub-specialties, comprised the subjects of the final qualifying examination in Medicine, Final MB Part 4, leading to the award of the Batchelor of Medicine and Surgery, or the MB ChB, degrees. Professor Sir Henry Cohen, later Lord Cohen of Birkenhead, had a most popular teaching session in Medicine each Friday afternoon known as "the circus", which was held in a new portion of the medical school, a large lecture theatre with steeply banked seats. The lecturers in Medicine and the Professor's senior registrars would comb the wards looking for rare clinical cases; however, the Professor was rarely, if ever, defeated by his juniors. In the absence of Sir Henry, other consultant physicians would run this circus and one of these, Dr Baker Bates, had a favourite expression. If a student answered a question with some exceedingly uncommon condition, he would invariably respond with "pigs might fly but they're rare birds". One day, with the auditorium packed, a student deliberately provoked him and the expected reply came out. At this, some dozen students rose from the higher seats at the back and each launched a large pig with a pair of wings, made of balsa wood and brightly coloured tissue paper, to shouts of "Pigs DO fly and they're NOT so rare!" The pigs glided about the auditorium accompanied by wild cheering and general mayhem.

Having sold my motorbike to an architectural student, I had just about enough money to buy a second-hand sports car with a loan from father. It was a 1936 BSA Scout, allegedly from the same stable as Daimler and Lanchester although I found this hard to believe. It looked quite sporty and attractive from a distance but this appearance was very deceptive. It was nearly 20 years old and had clocked up a huge mileage. The crankshaft was oval and, as I could not afford to have it reground, the big-end bearings gave way at very regular intervals. When this occurred, I would take the sparking plug off the involved cylinder to get rid of the compression and then drive the car on three cylinders until such time as I could afford to have repairs made. In fact, I think I drove this car nearly as much on three cylinders as on four! Of course, this led to a marked decrease in the output of the already feeble engine and to such embarrassments as being overtaken by slow trucks on hills.

Midway through my sixth and final year, I went to London to sit the Conjoint examination run by the Royal Colleges of Medicine and Surgery. This was a safety first ploy not uncommonly employed, in case of problems with university final exams. Possession of the MRCS LRCP Conjoint qualification, would then avoid any delay in beginning house jobs and acquiring medical registration. Depending on when it was taken, possession of this alternate professional qualification could even result in the student beginning his house jobs, or internship, at an earlier date. Both the written papers and clinical examinations were held at Queen Square, London WC1, just off Southampton Road and close to Russell Square and the National Hospitals for Nervous Diseases and Sick Children.

I decided to take the exams in Pathology, Surgery and Medicine and drove down for an afternoon paper in the latter. Well aware of the limitations of my old car, I had considered going down on the day previous to the exam. However, this would involve the expense of an overnight hotel stay somewhere and I decided on an early start instead. I set off from home about 7.00 am and stopped briefly to eat a sandwich lunch that mother had provided. All was going well and I thought I would arrive in plenty of time when, near Towcester, a big end went! Although well used to this situation, the business of finding which cylinder was involved and removing the plug always took some time and was invariably a dirty business. Unfortunately, it was pouring with rain and this emergency procedure took much longer than usual. London traffic was very heavy and I arrived at the examination hall just after 3.00 pm.

I went immediately to the bathroom where I tried to clean myself up and get dry. I entered the examination room some 15 minutes later, having missed 50 per cent of the three hour exam beginning at 2.00 pm. I realised that my chances of success were minuscule but tried to do my best in the short time remaining. My arrival, dirty, dishevelled and rushed, attracted a good deal of attention from the other candidates. A big man on my left, in particular, seemed to find me an object of great interest but purely in a negative way. His face revealed his utter disdain for me, my appearance and my late entrance. I thought he looked familiar but put these thoughts aside as I began to scribble furiously. Some months after this unfortunate incident, I suddenly realised who my disapproving exam neighbour had been when, on May 6th 1954, he won a mile race on the Iffley Road track in Oxford in 3 minutes 59.4 seconds. It was, of course, none other than the world-famous athlete, Roger Bannister! I was correct in thinking that I would fail the exam in Medicine although I passed the other parts. Some months later, I passed all parts of the Liverpool final degree with no trouble and never bothered to complete my extra Conjoint qualification. I was only 23 years old when graduating in Medicine so I don't believe the delay in entering medical school, or the necessity of doing the first year course, was very significant; in fact, on mature reflection, it was probably a considerable blessing in disguise. In addition, my subsequent travels more than compensated for living at home for most of my time at medical school.

During most of my student years, culminating with graduation in 1954, some form of rationing was still in force and these post-war years were alleged to be drab and gloomy by many historians, often giving their opinion with the benefit of considerable hindsight. It was said that the ascent of Everest by Edmund Hillary and Sherpa Tenzing in May 1953, the Queen's coronation a few days later and Bannister's great run in 1954 had momentarily relieved this darkness. I was never aware of these feelings, nor were any of my friends. I attributed these allegations of darkness and depression to poetic license gone astray and to the need for journalistic and historical copy.

FOUR

Houseman and Naval Officer

1954 was the first year that British medical graduates were compelled to complete a year as a houseman or intern in a designated pre-registration post before becoming fully registered and free to practise Medicine in any location. I was determined to avoid the frantic lobbying and sucking-up in which many indulged to secure house appointments in teaching hospitals. There would have been a high probability of the latter necessitating working for six months as a house surgeon in General Surgery, where holding a retractor in the operating theatre for hours on end would form a major part of the experience. I had no intention of doing this and hence elected to take a post in Obstetrics and Gynaecology, beginning in September, 1954, at Ormskirk District Hospital, situated in a pleasant market town between Liverpool and Preston. The two gynaecologists there also had appointments in the Liverpool teaching hospitals and were well respected. This proved to be a happy choice although it involved much night work. I estimated that I rarely, if ever, worked less than 80 hours per week and frequently more than 100. For these labours, I was paid a paltry 425 pounds a year. Even excluding much additional "on call" time, this worked out at about one shilling an hour, or much the same rate as I had been paid for harvesting six years earlier. After board, keep and laundry had been deducted, I ended up with the magnificent sum of just 21 pounds each month!

By now, my car was proving to be a major headache and I determined to exchange it. Visits to local garages and car sales rooms elicited little or no interest and my busy schedule precluded any attempt to sell it privately. After discussion with a knowledgeable friend, I resolved to try and trade it in for another vehicle in London. Second-hand car sales dealerships on the North Circular Road, many operating from bombed sites, were my specific targets. I managed to get a couple of days off immediately before the New Year and drove to north London. The first two visits were not promising but I found what I was after at the third. The car in question was a 1935 Riley Nine, even older than my present car but in excellent condition, or so I thought. It had an aluminum body, knock-on wire wheels, twin carburetors, a sunroof, attractive red leather seats and a pre-selector gear box. The salesman and I argued about prices for some time and I managed to beat him down a few pounds. I then handed over my car and the 100 or so pounds of balance and took off up north. I felt very pleased with myself, quite sure that I had bested the salesman.

At a spot within a few miles of my big-end disaster en route to the Conjoint exam a few months earlier, the car broke down. I was devastated! I had no idea what was wrong but suspected that the gearbox was at fault. I arranged for a tow into a garage, where they advised me to consult a more specialised firm in Northampton. This I did by phone and, assured that the car would be picked up and examined, I got a ride back to the A5. Much to my surprise and delight, I was successful with one of the first cars at which I waved my thumb and secured a lift back home. I suspected that I was going to be in for a very large repair bill and couldn't help thinking of this as I let in the New Year, with friends, at the *Bowler Hat Club* at Oxton on the Wirral. During the course of the evening, I got into conversation with a very fit looking gentleman who appeared to be in his early thirties. He told me that I was wearing a very serious expression, asked about my worries and was very sympathetic when I gave him an abridged account of them. It appeared that he was a dentist and played for the local Neston Cricket Club. A friend took me aside and asked if I knew to whom I had been talking. When I admitted that I had no idea, he told me that it had been Ken Cranston, whose soaring cricketing fortunes I had followed for years. After leaving Liverpool and District cricket, he had taken over the captaincy of Lancashire at the start of the 1947 season. He had then been selected to lead England as captain after a mere 13 first-class games. As an all-rounder, his play was steady rather than spectacular, his test batting average being 15 and top score 45. His taking of the last four South African wickets in one over in the Headingley test was his finest performance for his country. He played eight tests in all and, after the 1948 county season, returned to club cricket. Thus he had a very short, very satisfactory and highly unusual international career, unbelievable in terms of the twenty-first century. I was correct in my guess as to the car's problem. I had to go down to Northampton a few weeks later to retrieve it, after handing over a very large cheque.

For my second pre-registration job, I was pleased to secure a house physician position at Sefton General Hospital, a large complex on the south side of Liverpool. Again, some of its consultants were on the staff of the teaching hospitals and it had a good reputation. I learned a lot of Medicine there and enjoyed this period. However, after the Casualty officers left at 5.00 pm, the house physicians had to cover this work until 8.00 am, this occurring for me about once every eight or nine days. This period invariably proved to be a very busy 15 hours. I had no problems with this but, in addition to seeing patients, we had to group and cross match any blood required. This should have been done by a laboratory technician and it was quite ridiculous, in that day and age, that this was not the case. The Pathology department gave us a very short course in this subject, using a "tile" method. This situation meant that I and others would frequently have to leave a crowded Casualty department for 20 minutes or more to arrange compatible blood for a patient, using a dated and crude technique. I would then worry all night if I had done this correctly in my haste and would hurry to the Pathology department next morning for reassurance on this score. Many thought that this department was seriously at fault and that the hospital "powers that be" should never have countenanced this situation, which appeared to be unique among area hospitals at this time. However, I must admit that I was unaware of any incompatible blood being administered in these circumstances.

A local GP earned the enmity of the housemen at regular intervals by his inconsiderate and often unprofessional actions, especially at night and at week-ends. On one occasion, a man with abdominal pain who rang him at 2.00 am was told to come to the GP's surgery and ring the bell. This he did, when the GP opened his bedroom window, threw a piece of paper out and yelled "Take that to Sefton". Surprised that he had not actually had a consultation with his doctor, or been examined by him, the patient proceed to the hospital and presented this dirty scrap to the houseman on duty, who read "? appdx". The patient was carefully examined, given some medicine and sent on his way.

The houseman then rang the GP about 3.00 am and informed him that the appendix was, in his judgement, present. Of course, the GP complained to the Medical Superintendent of the hospital, who read the riot act to the doctor concerned. At a subsequent meeting of the junior house staff, all agreed on the injustice of the situation and each houseman made a point of telling the Superintendent of their views and how, in the future, they would behave in exactly the same manner.

At the end of my 12 months as a houseman, I was given my certificate of Full Registration with the General Medical Council. I then was informed that I had to present myself for a medical examination for national service. This I did, meeting many of the students from my year there. A few were declared medically unfit for the Armed Services and, understandably, were disappointed. A small number, however, had been most anxious to avoid national service and had come up with all manner of excuses, such as flat feet, asthma, migraine, sick parents, etc. Some of these were successful and, in at least one case, the scrimshank concerned had the nerve to boast about it in later life. For my part, I was looking forward to such service immensely, after six long years in medical school and a hectic year as a houseman. In fact, I minimised my rheumatic history on the questionnaire filled in before the physical exam.

Eventually, I received a letter stating that I had been recommended by the War Office for a commission in the Royal Army Medical Corps. This did not please me at all as I wanted, very much, to join the Senior Service and had indicated this earlier. I suspected that doctors were apportioned in great chunks to each service, i.e. the first 60 to the Army, the next 40 to the RAF, then 30 to the Royal Navy (RN) etc. I really didn't know what, if anything, I could do about this situation. However, father, now back on his feet again in the building world, mentioned my predicament to a business acquaintance who knew Lord Fraser of North Cape. This man said that he was willing to mention my name to this great retired seadog who, as Admiral Sir Bruce Fraser, had been in command of the battleship *Duke of York* in the battle of North Cape in December 1943, way up on the north of Norway and well within the Arctic Circle. The German battle cruiser *Scharnhorst* had been seeking to attack the Murmansk convoy JW55B but had been sunk by the British ship and her attendant destroyers. I asked father's friend to contact him and, much to my delight, soon received a letter telling me that I was to be appointed as a Temporary Acting Surgeon Lieutenant in Her Majesty's Fleet.

I now had some six weeks before reporting at Portsmouth and had arranged to do a four week locum as a GP in North Wales. This would be "single handed" and I would be taking the place of the doctor who was going on vacation. An old lady would live in the doctor's house with me. I was a little uncertain about this but, in fact, it worked out well. She cooked my excellent meals and helped with the surgeries, whispering a few vital comments about many patients before they entered the consulting room. I was kept busy and really had little time off. There were two surgeries each day, with a third on market day; and I was "on call" every night and weekend. In fact, these "on call" duties proved to be very light with the country people being highly considerate. On one occasion, a young farmer called at my house and surgery at 2.00 am. The old lady living with me heard his knock and awoke me. It seemed that his wife was very ill and he had called to collect me, as I would never find his farm unaided. I said that I would follow him in my car but he insisted that I ride with him and, after my visit, he would then drive me back. His wife was, indeed, very ill but my treatment was efficacious and I was able to leave her after about an hour.

Then it was time to join up, going down to the RN barracks at Portsmouth, usually known as "Pompey" to its inhabitants and to the Navy. I was technically on the strength of *HMS Victory*, the former flagship of Admiral Horatio Nelson, while attending the Divisional Course; the RN barracks, Pompey, also came under the Victory name. Being only a national service recruit and Royal Naval Volunteer Reserve (RNVR) officer, my clothing allowance was substantially smaller than for those holding a permanent commission and uniforms were expensive. However, I managed to obtain an excellent used doeskin suit of "blues" and another only slightly inferior in serge, from a naval tailor on Portsmouth Hard. My cabin was small and had a washbasin but no running water. Admiralty stewards, nearly all retired ex-servicemen, would bring a cup of tea and hot water each morning. As well as parade ground skills, including saluting on the march with a cutlass, we were taught all manner of rules as detailed in the Queen's Regulations and Admiralty Instructions. These ranged from details of the pay of non-commissioned ranks, and how it could be deducted at source for families, to the running of a court-martial. We were also instructed in how to behave at a wardroom mess dinner. Personally, I found the latter to

Fig 3. The doctors and dentists of the September 1955 Divisional Course at the Royal Naval Barracks, Portsmouth. The author's medical school classmate, Surgeon Lieutenant Jack Laine, is standing, second from the left. The author is seated, second from the right. (Crown Copyright/MOD. Reproduced with the permission of the Controller of her Majesty's Stationery Office).

be rather insulting but the Navy took it very seriously and we even had a trial run-through before a compulsory real mess dinner.

The parade drills occupied most of each morning and I wondered at the emphasis given to them. Our group comprised four different sections. The largest were the new entry doctors and dentists and there were nine of us in this group (Fig 3). Dr Jack Laine, who had been in my year at medical school and later became a consultant surgeon in Wrexham, was one of these. The others included two Birmingham graduates, one of whom later became a consultant anaethetist and the other an academic anatomist, and a Guy's Hospital graduate who became a GP in Cornwall. Two medical graduates from Glasgow University and dentists from Manchester and Melbourne Universities completed the section but I never discovered what happened to them subsequently.

Then there were the officers, newly promoted from the non-commissioned ranks of the lower deck, and a few Commonwealth officers on long courses with the RN. Finally, there were Fleet Air Arm pilots, recently returned from prolonged training with the US Navy at Pensacola, Florida, on the new F4 or Phantom aircraft. Clearly, the first group was the most deficient in naval know-how and marching skills so the doctors and dentists felt most of the wrath of the Chief Petty Officer (CPO) gunner who drilled us mercilessly. He would bawl insults at anyone making a mistake, always finishing his tirade with "Sir". In fact, he had quite a sense of humour and a group of us took him out for drinks at the completion of the course. As we improved, we had to take part in morning Divisions under the eagle eye of the Commodore, a stocky, bearded man who carried a telescope under his arm and was accompanied by his bulldog, the latter wearing a navy blue jacket with *HMS Victory* emblazoned on it in white letters. This duo had a slightly improbable air and always suggested to me that they had escaped from an Ealing Studios comedy. The Royal Marine band was marvellous and made marching easy. The RN band, composed of ratings with varying instrumental abilities, was much less proficient and often seemed to magnify the faults of our awkward squad.

A squadron of Russian ships, consisting of two cruisers and four destroyers, arrived at Portsmouth in October 1955. The visit was part of a Russian/RN goodwill initiative with British ships simultaneously visiting Leningrad. One afternoon, the members of the Divisional Course went on board the cruiser *Sverdlov* with our CPO drill instructor. Two things impressed me about this ship. One was the absence of any hammocks, which were still quite extensively used in the RN; the Russian sailors, at least on this particular ship, slept in bunks. The other was the very inferior status of the Russian naval physicians, few of whom appeared to have officer status. It was widely rumoured, both in the RN and in the national press, that British frogmen had inspected the underwater aspects of some of the visiting Russian ships, as many of them were extremely manoeverable and that the Navy wished to learn the reason for this. In April 1956, another visit of Russian ships to Pompey, accompanied by Nikita Krushchev and Marshall Nikolai Bulganin, took place and resulted in a British frogman, Lionel "Buster" Crabb, going missing. His headless body, lacking both hands, turned up in Chichester harbour about a year later. It was popularly supposed that Crabb had been investigating the Russian hulls, some of which were thought now to have an extra propellor which could be lowered from their for'ard keel, when he had been apprehended by Russian security.

Square-bashing finished, we went to *HMS Dolphin*, the submarine headquarters, for a trip in a submarine and for instruction in such things as submarine escape. The 100 foot tower there, filled with water, was fascinating, with experienced divers positioned at various heights below the surface under cones containing oxygen, where they stayed for many hours. Trainees would emerge from an airlock at the base of the tower and rise to the surface far above. The principle of this "free ascent" was that, with pressure multiplied by volume being a constant, decreasing pressure during the ascent would cause remaining lung air to expand and so the volume would remain reasonably unchanged. The divers in the tower at different levels ensured that passing escapees did not breathe out too quickly, by placing a hand to their lips, or too slowly, with a push on their abdomen .

Time was then spent at *HMS Phoenix*, the Navy's atomic, bacteriological, chemical and defence centre; this was most interesting although somewhat depressing. The elements of atomic theory were mastered and drills following an atomic attack were discussed. We then went to nearby *HMS Hornet* for a ride in a very speedy patrol boat, powered by two Rolls-Royce Deltic engines. I remembered that the quite long train that had recently taken me from Liverpool to Euston had just one of these engines. The young midshipman in charge clearly enjoyed his assignment and we sped about the Solent at high speed. A few years later, I was sorry to learn that *Hornet* was to close and these potent speedsters taken out of service.

After the completion of the Divisional Course, the medical officers went across Portsmouth harbour to the Royal Naval Hospital (RNH) at Haslar. Here we learned about the specific duties of a naval medical officer. We had some brief instruction in Aviation Medicine, medical officers who had postings to air stations or carriers undergoing a longer course in this. We had instruction in Tropical Medicine also and learned about Emergency Dentistry, getting to know the dental surgical pack carried on all ships. One of my happier memories of these days was of the many hours I spent playing a very competitive and "cut throat" variety of croquet on the wardroom lawn at Haslar with my fellow physicians.

I enjoyed my time in Portsmouth and its environs. The Nuffield club near the barracks was a great haunt for junior officers. It had a lovely restaurant, a useful snack bar and lots of sporting activities. Both Hampshire and the Navy played cricket and rugby there and I turned out regularly for United Services Portsmouth second XV. The members of this club's sporting teams were overwhelmingly naval but the occasional soldier and airman did participate. The number of personnel in the Navy was always the smallest of the three services and the RN in those days still had quite a few seagoing ships and overseas establishments; so the naval pool of athletes in Britain was not large. In spite of this, many good athletes were present in Pompey, including my friend Dr John Wrighton. He had trained at Charing Cross Hospital and was a superb 440 yards runner. He was, in fact, the European champion, who later represented Great Britain in the 1960 Rome Olympics. Tremayne Rodd and Gordon Waddell, the half backs both for the Navy and Scotland, were often seen playing rugby. In later years, Rodd became a member of the House of Lords as Lord Rennell.

A considerable source of vexation for me was the Divisions, held on the parade ground of the barracks every Friday at 4.00 pm in the presence of the Commodore. These were taken very seriously, all officers wearing medals and carrying swords. These parades lasted at least an hour and seriously interfered with any plans of mine to sneak off a little early and drive home for a weekend. It was extremely difficult to get out of Divisions, with permission to be absent rarely given. So, frequently, I would head out at about 5.15 pm, thereby running into all dockyard and other traffic that was homeward bound. At this time, there were more than 20 naval establishments in the Portsmouth area and I seemed to encounter traffic from all of them as I fought my way north. John Callaghan, a great friend, was now teaching at Ratcliffe College, a public school near Leicester. Under these circumstances, I would often stay the night with him and carry on home on Saturday morning. John was heavily into tennis and was the Leicestershire County singles champion at this time; hence we would often spend time at the Leicestershire Club and County tennis club, having a few drinks afterwards. Sometimes we might use a little pub at Sileby, close to the school and near the home of Lady Elizabeth Barnett, and we once saw the star of *What's My Line* there. She was later convicted of shoplifting, the goods involved being worth the vast sum of 87 pence, and tragically committed suicide.

Through my visits to Ratciffe, I came to know one of the

pupils. John Willcox was an outstanding rugby player. He represented Fylde, Harlequins, Oxford University, the Army, Lancashire and England, the latter 16 times. On the British Lions tour of South Africa in 1962, he played in three of the four tests and was the leading scorer for the Lions. He was described by the press as "the man who knows no fear" and his composure while waiting under a high ball, with the opposing forwards bearing down on him, was remarkable. He became a master at Ampleforth College, in the East Riding. Meeting him there years later, when he was in his 30s and long past his prime, he told me that he still enjoyed playing for a local team, far removed in rugby excellence from his earlier clubs. One one occasion, he had been asked to play for their second team. In no way had he objected to this but admitted that he was surprised to be selected as a centre three-quarter, not a full-back!

One of the problems with these visits was the small matter of where I slept. I remember on one occasion being shown into the school's infirmary by John, a dormitory haven that we were forced to employ for my emergency sleeping quarters on this particular night. Much beer having been consumed earlier, I crept into a vacant bed, slept very well and awakened next morning to a chorus of juvenile voices. I half opened one eye and saw a lady in what appeared to be some kind of uniform talking to seven or eight young boys who were sitting up in bed. I was in time to hear the lady ask "But who is he?" to which the youngsters answered "We don't know, matron, but he arrived here in the middle of the night with Mr Callaghan and woke us all up". With burning ears, I feigned sleep until matron had left and then bolted for John's room, ignoring the stares and questions of my youthful audience.

Our postings now came through. To my chagrin, I found that I had been assigned to the Chatham Dockyard Surgery, a prospect that filled me with dismay. I spoke to several senior medical officers and was told that nothing could be done to change this; but I had other ideas. With some difficulty, I managed to schedule an interview in London with the Surgeon Captain in charge of all medical postings. His secretary was most suspicious of my request but, with obstinate persistence, I managed to wear her down. I now had to get time off to meet with him, also not an easy matter. Finally, however, I arrived at Waterloo Station on a Friday afternoon and took a taxi to Queen Anne's Mansions, a massive 14 storey building in Broadway

SW1, just off Victoria Street and near Caxton Hall. Completed towards the end of the nineteenth century, it lacked any external decoration and was now black with dirt. In his book *The Face of London*, Harold Clunn wrote of it during the early 1930s "it is, for real ugliness, unsurpassed by any other great building in all London". It was demolished in 1971, not before time in the opinion of many.

Here I met the Surgeon Captain. I had thought deeply about what I should say. Clearly, I must be polite but some respectful firmness was called for. I told him that I was most unhappy about my posting and that I had been hoping for either an overseas billet or a seagoing appointment. I now had to endure a long lecture about the Navy being a disciplined service and how all officers had to accept their assignments. I didn't like the sound of this at all and wondered how I could get him off this particular tack. To my surprise, he suddenly asked me if I would like a posting to Ceylon. I stammered an affirmative and that was that. Apparently the medical officer originally asigned there, who had a permanent commission, had successfully applied for training in Surgery and was going, very coincidentally, to Broadgreen Hospital, Liverpool, for two years. Mr John Shepherd was a consultant surgeon at Broadgreen and a Surgeon Captain RNVR, who frequently arranged training for many of the Navy's general surgeons.

I left the building in a hurry, was lucky to find an empty taxi and managed to catch a convenient train at Euston for a weekend at home. On Saturday over lunch, I casually mentioned to mother that I was off to Ceylon for 18 months, not to Chatham. She had been very happy with the first appointment and was now quite mortified with the change. I was in no way dishonest but mother somehow formed the impression that it was the Navy that had changed my posting and was now cruelly sending her darling son to such a faraway place. I had a few weeks to serve back at Pompey barracks, doing routine annual physical examinations etc, which I found very boring. I was given a couple of weeks embarkation leave and had to acquire tropical clothing. I was due to sail from Southampton on December 22nd and made all my goodbyes. A few days before leaving, I got a further communication stating that the troopship was delayed and would now sail on December 29th. I had mixed feelings about this although I would get another seven days of leave and be at home for Christmas. However, I was really rather

57

keen to get away and get on with things.

The Christmas period passed very quickly and I was soon boarding the *MS Dilwara* at Southampton. This was a British India line ship, far from new but very comfortable, with furnishings that were good and solid, although somewhat dated. The stewards and many of the cooks hailed from the Indian sub-continent and the food was superb. However, the ship was very slow, our cruising speed rarely exceeded 11 knots with the winning distance for the sweep-stake on the ship's daily run never exceeding 260 nautical miles. Dilwara was an official Army troopship and the majority of the pas-sengers were soldiers, most of whom were going to fight the com-munist insurrectionists in Malaya. A few RAF personnel were also with us. Somewhat to my alarm, I soon discovered that I was the only naval officer on board and was therefore the officer command-ing the small naval draft. There were about 25 naval non-commis-sioned ranks present, including a few CPOs and Petty Officers (POs). Most of them were going to Singapore but a couple were accompanying me to Trincomalee, my destination in Ceylon.

At this time, the sailor's daily rum allocation had not yet been discontinued and the members of the naval draft received their tot each day. This seemed to cause great resentment among the Army, who also tried to impose their own military way of doing things on the matelots. All this led to considerable ill-feeling and the sailors were soon regarded by the military as being nothing but trouble. After only a few days at sea, two senior CPOs came to me about this situation, claiming that they were being discriminated against. I was in a difficult position. Not only was I very much a new boy in service matters, having been in the service merely "half a dog watch", but, as a doctor, I was not an executive officer. While sympathetic to some of their complaints, I suspected that they were gilding the lily, at least to a degree. So nothing much changed. I attended each dis-tribution of the rum allowance, if only to convince myself that the cor-rect naval proprieties were being observed and that seamen drank their tots immediately. Only senior ratings were allowed to bottle it and drink at their pleasure.

Some troops were landed at Cyprus and then we arrived at Port Said. There was no shore leave here and we only stayed a short time. Items from fresh fruit to trinkets and cheap jewelry could be bought from the "bum boats" surrounding the ship, with the goods and monies being exchanged via baskets and a system of ropes. These vendors were not allowed on board, but the Gully-Gully man was. He and his kind were extremely skilled local magicians and conjurors, who delighted the passengers by producing a vast number of baby chickens from within individual's mouths, from inside the crowd's clothing, etc, as well as performing many other tricks and illusions.

We now entered the Suez Canal. The British were in the process of leaving this area and only a small number of troops remained. The Irish Guards were among them and provided much good-natured humour as we sailed by, yelling things like "throw us your women", the troops on board responding with taunts about the guards going home for weekends. However, everyone's level of humour and tolerance seemed to plummet when we reached the Red Sea, this being a well-known phenomenon; it was certainly very hot. Then we reached the red rocks of Aden. We all had a few hours ashore where all manner of bargains, especially in electrical goods and photographic equipment, could be obtained in the markets. On returning to the ship, I watched the approach of most of the naval draft in a tender.

To my horror, several of the returning sailors jumped, fully clothed, into the water and began swimming about. I imagined that this was some kind of gesture of defiance against the Army. After a few minutes, an Aden police launch went to their assistance but this was airily waved off. The Red Sea, including Aden harbour, had a bad name for shark attacks and I was extremely concerned. After fully 15 minutes, the swimmers condescended to climb back aboard their launch and eventually boarded the ship; they were promptly thrown into the brig. This incident further increased the poor standing of the Navy and I was told that I might be later involved in the court martial of the offenders. Fortunately, things quietened down and our passage across the Arabian Sea to Ceylon was uneventful. I delivered a written report of the incident at Aden to the resident naval officer at Colombo, who assured me that I would not be held accountable for the antics of the naval draft, which was a considerable relief.

I arrived in Ceylon in January 1956, about the same time as Sir Arthur Clarke, the famous British science fiction writer, chose to make this island nation his permanent home. The handful of sailors who landed, myself included, were checked into a hotel. Having been given a written introduction to a prominent Colombo orthopaedic surgeon who had trained in Liverpool, I phoned him and was picked up at the hotel. He showed me the sights of the city and took me to his home for drinks and a most enjoyable dinner. Next morning, we left Colombo in a coach and arrived in Trincomalee some nine hours later, after several stops. The heat of the day was incredible and I was amazed at the dense, lush jungle that crowded against the road. I checked into the wardroom of *HMS Highflyer*, the base station at Trincomalee, and promptly downed two pints of the delightful lime and lemon served at the wardroom bar. Made from freshly squeezed fruits, with added lemonade, it was to sustain me on countless occasions over the next 18 months.

FIVE

Trincomalee

Trincomalee, invariably known as simply "Trinco" to the Navy, is on the north-east coast of Ceylon, the beautiful island now called Sri Lanka, with a population in 1956 of about 30,000. Together with Jaffna to the north and Batticaloa further south, it is one of the three large Tamil towns in the north and east of that country.

Most of the naval establishment was on a peninsula, jutting out from Trinco town itself into the Bay of Bengal. The huge harbour had an inner and an outer component; taken together, it is probably the largest deep-water harbour in the world and the *Queen Mary* and *Queen Elizabeth* sailed in and out at a rate of knots during World War Two. Trinco served as the base for the East Indies station with the Commander-in-Chief, a Vice-Admiral, flying his flag when at sea in a cruiser and living at Admiralty House when ashore. His considerable staff travelled with him but left the cruiser for the wardroom of *HMS Highflyer*, the base establishment, when in Trinco. One of the principal functions of the station was to maintain a presence in the Persian Gulf, where there were usually four or more *Loch* class frigates at any time. The Admiral would make three cruises each year. One was up the Gulf, calling at Bahrain and Kuwait. The other two were of the "show the flag" variety and involved East Africa, taking in Mombassa, Dar-es-Salaam, Mauritius and the Seychelles, plus another around India, calling at a variety of ports.

The Senior British Naval Officer (SBNO) Ceylon, a captain, looked after things ashore and the Captain of *Highflyer* held commander's rank. SBNO lived on a slightly elevated ridge, together with some of the more senior officers. The houses here were somewhat removed from the stifling humidity and heat and even an occasional sea breeze was not unknown. Some officers had homes overlooking the harbour and one medical officer had an address beginning "Honeymoon Cottage, Passion Point, Trincomalee". Other officers lived near an old Dutch fortification and drove in through the old, imposing gateway of Fort Frederick. This was at some distance from *Highflyer* and they had a more tranquil environment, as well as looking out at a lovely beach and the open sea.

Across the harbour from the naval base was China Bay, not to be confused with the place of the same name in Kipling's poem *Mandalay*. An RAF station was situated here, having few officers and an airstrip which appeared to be used infrequently. The station's main purpose at this time was in relation to the large Sunderland flying boats patrolling between Ceylon and Singapore, thereby fulfilling Britain's international Air Sea Rescue commitments for this region of the Indian Ocean. As in the UK, all the motoring needs of the Navy were provided by Vauxhall. Of course, Vauxhall cars were entirely made in Britain but General Motors, a US company, has owned Vauxhall since 1925. I wondered what Prince Charles would have thought of this with his understandable urge for UK officialdom to "buy British".

In the tropics, naval officers during the day wore white shirts with short sleeves, white shorts, long white stockings and white shoes. No10s was the formal day rig, with long white pants and a white tunic buttoned up at the neck, which I found to be abominably uncomfortable. In the evening, the official rig was mess undress, a white, light cut-away mess jacket worn over a dress shirt with a black bow tie, a black cummerbund and dark trousers. Informally in the wardroom, Red Sea rig was permitted, the mess jacket, dress shirt and tie being replaced by an open necked shirt. Persian Gulf rig was worn in the frigates when up the Gulf, with light white trousers replacing the heavier dark ones. Stripes of rank were worn as shoulder planks, or epaulettes, and one had to be careful about putting them on. The gold material of the stripe going forward to the circular curl had to be uppermost when crossing its other part; if not, the officer was said to be "going astern". Officers were not allowed to buy drinks for their brother officers in the wardroom but an exception was made for officers "going astern", who had to stand drinks for all present if successfully challenged on this dress code infringement. I was surprised to learn that all laundry was done by local men, called "dhobi boys", who would collect all the clothes and take them to the "dhobi pond" (Fig 4) where they would vigorously knead the washing, as well as beating it against rocks. I never succeeded in discovering if any soap or detergent was employed but, like many others, soon became aware of the short life span of most of my shirts!

I now learned that I was to work at the Dockyard Surgery

Fig 4. The dhobi pond, Trincomalee. The vigourous bashing suffered by all the clothing can be imagined.

under a Principal Medical officer (PMO), a surgeon commander, and would assist at RNH only occasionally. I was sure that it beat working at Chatham but there were some problems. My boss tended to take care of the British Admiralty civilians and also practised Opthalmology at RNH. Essentially, I looked after the locally entered naval police, fire service and dockworkers, of whom there were about 4,000. The police and firemen were treated for all their medical problems. The dockworkers, however, would be only treated if they had sustained their injury or illness in the course of working for the Navy; otherwise, they would be given unpaid sick leave and left to find their own treatment. With a crowded surgery and about 100 men to be seen each day, this arrangement forced the physician, invariably myself, to make rapid on-the-spot decisions as to whether or not the patient's condition was in any way connected with his employment by the Navy. This led to considerable disgruntlement among the patients, who would sometimes write to me to plead their case, arguing that their disabilities and problems deserved treatment and, in some cases, financial compensation. Many were illiterate and would pay a professional "writer" to take care of their statements. These efforts were, in most cases, couched in terrible English and were composed, at best, in excessively complimentary and flowery prose. A few months into my appointment, I had grown a beard and received one such letter of appeal. It began "In the name of our Lord Jesus Christ, whom you so closely resemble.......!" In many cases, I had considerable sympathy for the patient, who was invariably very poor, walked barefooted and had no other source of medical treatment but the Navy. However, I was powerless to change the system, to which both the patients and I had to conform.

There were five RN ratings in the Dockyard Surgery, a CPO and four sick berth attendants, and 17 local civilians as well as two young boys called "peons" who ran messages and did odd jobs. In the main, I worked with just seven of these gentlemen. Three were superior employees and, in addition to their clerical duties, they acted as interpreters for me with patients. I could not have functioned without them. One was the dispenser and three drove our Vauxhall Velox car, utilicon van and ambulance. I saw the other ten intermittently about the place. They spoke no English and seemed to avoid me if at all possible, often showing great alarm if I bade them "Good day", when they would make exaggerated gestures of respect. Their precise duties were unclear to me but I imagined that they cleaned the place and took care of the rather shabby garden. I was ignorant of the salary that these workers earned. In the majority of cases, I guessed that it would be very small and that this money would have to suffice for a large, extended family in many cases.

Not uncommonly, locally entered staff in the dockyard would take days off work for religious festivals. The vast majority of these indigenous workers were Tamils, Singhalese being very much in the minority. Most of the Tamils were Hindus but an appreciable minority was Christian. After several months, I began to notice that certain individuals, who had enjoyed days off for the great Hindu festivals, were now claiming similar days for Christian holy days. On taxing them with this seeming paradox, they usually prevaricated, declining to define their religious beliefs. The matter could have been easily dealt with by simply noting these various vacation days but the British Admiralty civilian officials, to whom I brought notice of these practices, clearly did not want to know. It was probable that they feared union troubles and preferred to adopt a policy of letting sleeping dogs lie.

There was a great fear of snakes in Trinco and men always wore long trousers at night in case of inadvertently stepping on one; however, I saw precisely one serpent during my 18 months there. Nevertheless, it soon became clear that snake bites, real or imaginary, were to form a not inconsiderable part of my daily work. The Navy had eight or nine first-aid posts scattered all around the gigantic harbour, some being over 30 minutes or more away by car. These were manned by locally entered workers who had been given some basic first-aid and nursing training. If a patient reported to one of these with an alleged snake bite, an ambulance had to be dispatched from the Dockyard Surgery to pick him up and bring him back, if possible with the dead snake, for examination; this might take 90 minutes or more so there was no chance of early treatment. Also, the snake anti-serum available was a polyvalent type, supposedly effective against many different snake venoms. I was never convinced of this but was well aware of its considerable allergic side effects, with all manner of anaphylactoid reactions, including possible laryngeal and bronchial spasm. Finally, a large number of the so-called snake bites were fictional.

So, confronted with a patient who probably had been bitten more than an hour earlier, I would not administer anti-serum on many occasions. My usual practice was to carefully cleanse the bite area if I could find it, and give the man an oral placebo such as aspirin. I would observe him for a couple of hours. If he were then in good shape, I would discharge him back to work. Anti-serum was reserved for the small minority of patients who showed evidence of the local and systemic effects of the snake bite and I experienced few failures with this philosophy.

Although cobras and many varieties of viper were said to be plentiful in the area, the reported snake bites were, in some 50% of cases, claimed to be due to the "tic polonga". This was said to be a small, slender snake, capable of spitting its venom that could be absorbed from the mouth, eyes and from cuts on the skin. It took me a long time to get a handle on this creature but I eventually concluded that it was, in most cases, a Russell's viper. The venom of this creature has a markedly anti-coagulant action in the blood and was used in the past in medical practice.

In contrast to snake bites, dog bites were usually genuine and were treated very seriously. There were all sorts of feral curs running around Trinco town and its surroundings and the risk of acquiring rabies from a bite was very real. Nearly all individuals who had been bitten by dogs were given a full course of anti-rabies injections, usually administered into the anterior abdominal wall.

All manner of gastro-intestinal diseases were rampant in Ceylon. Many types of worm infestation were extremely common with amoebic dysentery being the most feared disease. More than one death from this resulted in the British community during my time in Trinco. I recall one particular laboratory report which disclosed the presence of ova and organisms representing no less than 12 different parasites, including the dreaded amoeba; and this in the stools of a cook, employed by a naval officer and his family! In the naval community, the problem of these enteric infections was handled by the Dockyard Surgery. All cooks, house boys and stewards had stool examinations before starting employment, after which the appropriate treatment was given for any parasites. The subject then had to have three successive stool examinations reported as being negative before he began duties. This was supposed to guarantee health in the family or community but I found this premise to be seriously flawed. It might work for the naval cooks and stewards who lived and ate within the confines of *HMS Highflyer,* but it surely could not work with civilian staff who were employed by naval families and who left the dockyard each night to live and eat in Trinco town, thereby frequently and quickly becoming re-infected. In my opinion, the scheme gave a totally spurious sense of safety that was quite unjustified.

I drew the attention of both the Surgeon Captain and the Naval Medical Officer of Health (NMOH) to this but obtained no response except being told to keep such opinions to myself. I must confess that, apart excluding all cooks and houseboys who lived in Trinco town from catering to naval families, I could not come up with anything better. This would have been a draconian and unworkable solution, effectively leaving the families without kitchen help. Uniformed naval stewards were employed only in directly serving naval personnel and did not work for the families. Of course, the washing and peeling of all fruit and vegetables, thoroughly cooking the latter, and eschewing salads, shellfish and all dishes containing uncooked eggs and unpasteurised milk, was always obligatory. Incidentally, fresh pasteurised milk was not available in Trinco when I was there; hence tea had to be taken with the dried or condensed variety if milk was to be added. This led to the paradoxical situation of having the finest tea in the world but not having any fresh milk to add to it.

Strangely enough, there was no malaria whatsoever, although we took no prophylactic drugs nor slept under mosquito netting. Although anti-malarial measures, such as widespread spraying, were intense around the dockyard, the entire island in the mid-1950s was malaria free. This happy state was probably due to measures, put into effect by the British over many years, still having an effect. Several years after the complete British withdrawal, this situation had changed dramatically and malaria was endemic once more and a most serious problem.

A few weeks after arriving in Trinco, our cruiser left us for home. *HMS Newfoundland*, usually referred to as *Newfy*, and her officers had been very popular and everyone was sorry to see them go. The entire RN sailing club put out into the harbour to wave goodbye, as well as the RN fireboat, shooting vast quantities of water into the air, and several other naval craft. The Admiral was now forced to fly his flag in *HMS Baron*, a small boom defence ship unused to such honour. To the strains of her Marine band playing *Sussex by the Sea*, *Newfy* gradually pulled away and was then lost to sight as she turned into the outer harbour. Things were now much quieter in Trinco and I experienced a twinge or two of homesickness. The cruisers *HMS Gambia* and *HMS Ceylon* now replaced *Newfy*, both being colony class ships like her. Each remained on station for a comparatively short time only, staying with us en route home from the Far East. Then our new permanent cruiser arrived. *HMS Superb* was a ship with most lovely lines and was more modern than the previous three cruisers. Built as "one of a kind" by Swan Hunter on the Tyne and derived from the *Swiftsure* class, she was commissioned towards the end of World War Two, in which she took no part. She displaced some 8,800 tons standard, had nine 6-inch and ten 4-inch guns, as well as considerable anti-aircraft weaponry. Superb could steam at 31.5 knots, a very fast speed, and had a ship's company of about 800. She stayed as flagship for many months and was, like *Newfy*, a very popular item.

Fig 5. The typical scene at a cocktail party held in the wardroom garden at *HMS Highflyer*. Plain clothes were worn at such gatherings.

The wardroom was very pleasant, being built in the form of a rectangle with a lovely garden in the middle. It had many overhead fans and low walls, only a little over three-feet high. Above these it was entirely open, with a split roof permitting a very free circulation of air. Rattan curtains could be dropped down in the event of severe weather. The central garden of the wardroom was used for parties (Fig 5) and most officers gave one immediately before leaving Trinco for home. The low cost of alcohol made such social events quite cheap, even for a large gathering. On these occasions, lightweight tropical suits were worn by the male guests and all naval officers. Mine had been made by a Chinese tailor in the Trinco pettah, very cheaply and in just 24 hours, and this was obvious when comparisons were made with the much superior suits of other officers, hailing from Gieves, Moss Bros and other established British tailoring houses. However, I had to endure my embarrassment with this dodgy suit until I was able to purchase a better one in Colombo.

All tobacco in the wardroom was duty-free, as were spirits. Gin, brandy and rum drinks were just two and a half pence while whisky was relatively expensive at three pence a measure. Strangely enough, the sodas and cordials added to these drinks often cost more than the spirits. Beer, carrying relatively little duty, was the most expensive drink. Those living in the wardroom were allowed one bottle of spirits a month, "for picnics". I found this reason to be most amusing but never failed to avail myself of it and would frequently use my monthly bottle as a gift when invited out to dinner. This cheap liquor gave rise to considerable friction between the Navy and Admiralty civilians, known pejoratively as "dockyard mateys", which was soon to involve me in an unfortunate and embarrassing incident. The latter enjoyed a status that was, in general, much higher than they would have had in the UK and were given many generous allowances. While naval personnel also received a local overseas allowance, seven shillings and three pence daily in my case, as well as bonuses in the form of housing and duty-free alcoholic drinks, the perception was that they did not do nearly as well financially as their civilian Admiralty counterparts.

For many years, the RN had used "locally entered" men, whose pay was considerable less than that of the the regular British seaman, a great deal. Hong Kong Chinese served as dhobi men on many ships based in the Far East and Maltese stewards were ubiquitous. Our cruiser had Somali seamen, many of them being good athletes. However, I remember them mainly becaue of their involvement in a huge investigation, after several Somalis from *Superb* had been found carrying considerable quantities of gold when disembarking at Trinco for shore leave after the East African cruise. The supposition was that this gold had been acquired in Africa and was to be sold locally for a profit before being transmitted to India, where this metal always commanded very high prices.

The wardroom's stewards were all locally entered and comprised two distinct groups. The Ceylonese were almost exclusively Singhalese and Buddhist, with virtually no Tamils among them. The other group hailed from Goa, at the time a Portuguese enclave in India, and was entirely made up of Catholics. Both groups of stewards were efficient, trustworthy and vastly superior to their British counterparts in most people's estimation. My own steward would lay my day uniform out each evening, as well as the clothes that I would be wearing that night. It was a constant source of wonder to me how he knew if I was "going ashore" or not, i.e. how he knew whether to lay out a lightweight suit or uniform.

Sport played a big part in my life at Trinco and I would play competitive games four or even five times a week. I was introduced to hockey, which was the main team sport in Trinco, and soon became a keen player. I had few skills of the true soccer player but was very fit, could run reasonably quickly and often played for *Highflyer's* second team. As well as playing against the plethora of visiting RN ships that called, some en route to and from the Far East and others which were part of the Admiral's force in the Persian Gulf, there was a very active local competition. It involved teams from the junior seamen, communication ratings, CPOs and POs, RNH, the naval stewards, the naval police, the naval fire service, the Admiralty civilians, the RAF and the wardroom.

Soon after my arrival, I was running all the wardroom teams, simply because no one else was interested in doing this job. We had no problem fielding a cricket team for the matches that were played on matting laid over a concrete strip and were usually of just 20 overs a side. SBNO kept wicket in these and was a reliable batsman and the Admiral occasionally turned out. We could usually manage a decent hockey team, as all regularly commissioned officers appeared to have learned this game thoroughly at Dartmouth; but soccer was another story. I had persistent difficulty in getting a full team on the field and had to resort constantly to arm-twisting and blackmail. The Captain of *Highflyer* was a keen soccer man and kept goal for us. With his permission, I used his name and threats of his disapproval to force reluctant officers to play. We did reasonably well at cricket, not too badly at hockey but were regularly humiliated at soccer, where our defensive corps of not-so-young senior officers, including a couple of portly commanders, often was close to expiring after 20 minutes!

It took me several weeks to become completely acclimatised to the conditions that were not only very hot but also very humid. Because of its close geographical proximity to the equator, Ceylon's only change of season depended on its two monsoons, the north-west and the south-east. For the same reason, an unusual feature of the sporting scene was the rapidity with which the daylight disappeared, this sometimes occuring in a matter of minutes and never much later then 6.30 pm. Because of work commitments and climatic considerations, games rarely began much before 5.00 pm and sometimes might be forced to conclude short of the normal full time period. I remember once in a cricket match, that an over which included several big hits could not be completed before the onset of darkness.

I learned to sail a dinghy and soon became an avid competitor in the weekly races in which the standard, as would be expected, was high. It was necessary to qualify from a sort of second division of competition, sailed on Wednesday evenings, to secure a place in the premier Saturday afternoon competition. 17 clinker-built gaff-rigged RN dinghys were used for these races and were rotated each week to ensure fairness. I usually finished in the middle of the fleet but managed a couple of third place finishes. On one memorable occasion, I was leading by more than 100 yards, with less than a 600 yards to sail, when a motorised fishing vessel (MFV) came out for me. Being on obstetric call that day, I had to transfer to the MFV and hurry to RNH where an officer's wife had gone into premature labour. Arriving at the labour ward, I discovered that the lady concerned was sitting up in bed, drinking a cup of tea and looking very pleased with herself. She was already delivered of her baby and both were in fine fettle. I returned to the sailing club to learn that my young schoolboy crewman had brought in our dinghy first, with no bother at all. However, I was more than a little disappointed to discover that I had been disqualified for prematurely leaving my boat. I thought that the decision, although technically correct, was unduly harsh.

The social scene on the base was pleasant enough, although severely limited by the small British population. There was an efficient and free bus service and many excellent beaches for swimming. The small village of Nilaveli was about ten miles from Trinco and miles of empty, golden beaches stretched away north from here, where decent surfing could be enjoyed. There were open-air movies in the wardroom once weekly, during which one could sip a drink. When the cruiser was in port, there was a regular Sunday evening buffet supper and cinema, to which all *Highflyer* officers living in the wardroom had a standing invitation; this was never anything but most enjoyable. There was also a cinema in the dockyard. Each Saturday, the families traditionally came into the wardroom for a magnificent curried luncheon, during which the Royal Marine band from the cruiser would play light music from the shows. On Sunday morning, many in the naval community went over to the Sea Angler's club, an MFV being provided for this purpose, although many would sail or drive over. This was a private club, mainly serving the up-country tea planters and for which the Highflyer wardroom had a permanent group membership. It was situated on the other side of the harbour, beyond the RAF station, with good swimming and sea fishing and serving wonderful curries and seafood of all descriptions. So there was lots to do. However, one tended to see the same small nucleus of people over and over again. This was nobody's fault, simply an effect of living in a far-from-large community.

Officers, if married and accompanied by wife and family, lived a life that tended towards the idyllic with amahs, cooks, houseboys and gardeners available at a very nominal cost. Single officers, however, had a somewhat less happy time. Occasionally, one felt as if one was living in a prison without bars and the relative absence of female company was most notable. There were perhaps 16 Queen Alexandra naval nursing sisters, half-a-dozen VAD nurses, a couple of civilian teachers and the occasional older daughter. The WRNS, known as wrens, had been in Ceylon during World War Two but were no longer present. Trinco reminded me of the song *There is nothing like a dame* from the musical *South Pacific*, acknowledging sunshine on the sands, moonlight on the sea, mangoes, bananas, volleyball, ping pong and a lot of fancy games but deploring the absence of the fair sex. The situation was considerably worse for single non-commissioned ranks, with sport, movies and the drinking of beer their main pleasures and a traditional lower deck song contained the lines

Send me, send me, send me to sea
but for God's sake don't send me to Trincomalee.

Courts-martial seemed to be held not infrequently in the *Highflyer* wardroom and there were at least four during my time in Trinco. Most seemed to involve the captain and navigating officer of frigates in the Persian Gulf, usually following some navigational error. In several cases, the vessels concerned had run aground. Soon after my arrival, I made a joke about all this at the wardroom bar one evening, suggesting that the Navy should tighten up its navigational training. This went down like a damp squib and I was told that I knew nothing of the nautical problems of the Gulf. Apparently, even in the late 1950s, it was not charted very well and sandbanks, for instance, were continually moving. Quite commonly, I was surprised to see the accused after the court martial enjoying a drink or meal with witnesses and even the prosecuting officer. Of course, the officers concerned had, in some cases, known each other for many years and certainly since being cadets at the Royal Naval College, Dartmouth. Nevertheless, I found this display of civilised behaviour most impressive.

A couple of months after arriving in Trinco, I was invited to make up a party attending a big St Patrick's night dinner dance at the Dockyard club. Rather late in the evening, I joined half-a-dozen ratings and some of their wives for a few minutes after having been asked over by my leading hand from the dockyard surgery. I was served a beer and became engaged in conversation. All naval personnel present were in dress uniform, everyone knew where they stood regarding matters of rank and there was nothing improper in my doing this; indeed, it could have been construed as being unofficerly behaviour had I refused.

An Admiralty civilian, clearly the worse for drink, now joined us, completely uninvited. He knew one of the ratings and began to talk in a loud, boisterous and rude fashion. He suddenly switched his attention to me and commenced to ridicule the Navy, indicating that we officers were of no use and grossly inferior to dockyard mateys. I told him that he was talking nonsense, was also drunk and that he should promptly leave our party and go to bed. At this, he stood up, leaned across the table and aimed a vicious swing at my head, which I had no difficulty in avoiding. However, the drunk's follow-through landed him on the table which, laden with drinks, promptly collapsed. Several ladies in the party screamed and everyone in the room turned their attention to our group. Matters were made worse when one of the ratings in our company disappeared for a few seconds, found the main fuse box and plunged the entire room into darkness. He returned to hiss in my ear "This is your chance, Sir. You can escape now!" After a few moments of indecision, and feeling like a criminal, I foolishly took his advice and felt my way out through the darkness and on to the wardroom and bed.

On awakening, I remembered all too clearly the events of the previous night. I thought that I had been quite innocent in the entire affair, except that possibly my precipitate exit from the scene had been less than wise and might be construed as indicating guilt. I feared the worse and determined that the only course of action was to report the whole matter immediately. I phoned the Dockyard Surgery to tell them I would be late and walked to the office of the

Captain of *Highflyer*. I explained the situation and was told that, technically, SBNO was my boss and he would inform him of the situation. I went to the surgery, until receiving a phone call from SBNO at about 10.30 am, ordering me to report to him immediately. This I did, and said my piece while standing to attention. He listened in silence and then, after several seconds, asked what precisely I had done or said to precipitate the punch being thrown at me. I answered, quite truthfully, that I had not enjoyed this drunkard defaming the Navy and had told him to leave. This seemed to assuage the Captain somewhat who, after further silent reflection, told me to carry on with my regular duties and that he would inform me as to what he was going to do with me at a later date.

The day dragged on without me hearing any more and I remained very concerned and miserable. It appeared that everyone in Trinco already knew of the incident and I felt like a social leper. Having changed for a wardroom cricket match, I saw SBNO arrive being, as usual, immaculately clad in long white trousers, the only one so attired as everyone else wore shorts. He had a good knock and we managed to win the game. I was still feeling worried and this changed to apprehension when he called me over, just before getting into his car after the game. "See you at the house in 15 minutes, Doc. Scruff order", he yelled, before driving off. I had no idea what was going on but ran to the wardroom, had a quick shower and persuaded a friend to drive me to the great man's house.

SBNO was enjoying a drink, sitting with his wife and teenaged daughter in the garden, and I was waved over to join them. Joviality and bonhomie oozing from every pore, he was the perfect host and we all enjoyed a chat over drinks for some 90 minutes. I was still unsure about the lie of the land but felt that things must have improved for me. Eventually, my host rose, indicated that I should leave and surprisingly said that he would drive me back to the wardroom. Once in the car, he wasted no time in telling me that the incident involving the dockyard matey was closed, would not appear in my personal naval documents and that I should forget about it. He added that a potentially very serious situation had been averted by two things, viz. my truthful excuse of defending the RN and my immediate reporting of the incident.

Just before leaving England and increasingly after arriving in Trinco, I began to receive unpleasant letters from my bank manager in respect to a trifling overdraft that I had run up. Unfortunately, I couldn't seem to reduce it very much in spite of my local overseas allowance and very cheap environment. The Navy instituted a new three-year short service commission for medical officers early in 1956. The Army and RAF had this already but the RN had, up to this point, only a four-year short service engagement. I had considered that four years was far too long to serve but three was just bearable, so I applied for this new commission. My Lords at the Admiralty kept me waiting for several weeks before granting confirmation but this was dated from the day of approval, not from the day on which I had applied. So I changed from being a Surgeon Lieutenant RNVR to a Surgeon Lieutenant RN and ended up serving about three years and five months, a most unusual length of engagement. For doing exactly the same work, my salary increased substantially and also I received a small tax-free sum on leaving the Navy.

I now managed to do a deal with a young Admiralty civilian regarding his car, a bright red Singer Nine open sports tourer. As his time for returning home approached, he discovered that he could not sell it for anything approching its real value. Hence I suggested that we did a trade, with a small cash adjustment, for my Riley Nine. I had left this in Crosby with a friend, it was in good running order at the time and I thought that, in all honesty, the swap constituted a good deal for both of us. So I came to possess the Singer sports car and much enjoyed it. Unfortunately, after the Riley had been collected in Crosby, it broke down in the Mersey tunnel as it was being drive to its new home in North Wales and had to be towed out! I was informed of all this by a Admiralty civilian friend of the new Riley owner. I never heard again from the latter and thus had no idea what was the car's problem.

Surgeon Lieutenant Jack London, later to become a GP on the Welsh border near Hereford, was the anaesthetist at RNH. He had been the wardroom food caterer and he bequeathed this position to me just prior to his returning home. It did not involve a great deal of work. One of the two wardroom mess CPO stewards would, at the previous weekend, present me with the menus for the coming week and I would suggest changes where I thought they were indicated. I was careful to listen to the opinions of the officers who lived in the wardroom with me concerning the food, which was generally thought to be of a uniformly high standard. It was purchased either from the Victualling Supply Officer, a senior Admiralty civilian who was in charge of all food supplies for the base, or locally from independent merchants. I had nothing to do with the finances of all this, which were under the control of the naval Base Supply Officer, a commander. I occasionally saw the CPO wardroom stewards in the pettah, deep in discussion with locals, and wondered if they were running some sort of racket with the merchants. The Navy had been infamous for this sort of thing for centuries but as it was none of my concern, and as I was lacking in any kind of proof, I never mentioned it to anyone. My suspicions deepened when, on returning from leave in Goa, one of the CPOs gave me a magnificent present of a very large set of towels of all sizes and colours. Goa was famous for textiles and I used these towels, which appeared to be indestructible, for very many years, despite feeling vaguely like some sort of accomplice in a crime.

As was customary, my predecessor as wardroom food caterer was dined out in the wardroom before leaving us (Fig 6). In addition, Dr London passed on to me his private medical practice in Trinco town. I accepted the latter with something less than alacrity. I suspected that it would cut into my time for sport and other recreations, would generate, at best, a paltry financial income and, most of all, I knew that there would be great diagnostic and therapeutic problems. In addition, the Surgeon Captain was very much against it but, for reasons best known to themselves, SBNO and the Admiral were in favour. So I guessed that the request for permission to engage in this private practise that I submitted to the Surgeon Captain, although likely to be forwarded with a very negative recommendation, would nevertheless be approved and this turned out to be the case.

The key player in this initiative was Ali, a poor Muslim, fluent in Tamil, Singhalese and English, whose precise mode of employment I was never able to discover. He seemed to have detailed knowledge of just about everyone in the town and he provided the patients, whom I saw either in his one-room apartment above a store or in their homes (Fig 7). He consistently refused any payments for his services, stating that it was an honour to work for such a noble Englishman as myself. I took this to mean that he obtained some kind of kudos from associating with me. In fact, the only things that he desired were old copies of various periodicals from the ward-

Fig 6. Officers and guests assembled the *HMS Highflyer* wardroom mess bar immediately before a mess dinner. Surgeon Lieutenant Jack London is centre foreground, before being dined out. The Captain of *HMS Highflyer* is on his right and the author on his left.

Fig 7. My good friend Ali, dressed all in white, standing next to two Ceylon natioanl policemen in the Trincomalee pettah. Next to the teashop can be seen writing in both Singhalese and Tamil.

room, such as the *Illustrated London News, Punch, Tatler*, etc which he used to improve his English and general knowledge and which never failed to delight him. He proved to be a most dependable, willing and very intelligent assistant. For my part, I insisted on no more than two evenings a week and only one if possible. I was not free until 4.00 pm or later, it became dark soon after 6.30 pm and we dined in the wardroom at 7.00 pm. Many of the complaints were impossible to deal with in the absence of radiological and pathological investigations and I could only recommend a visit to Kandy or Colombo. Nearly all my patients were extremely poor and I was correct in my assumption that any earnings would be minute.

Trinco town had a civil hospital staffed by ayurvedic physicians, who had undergone training in traditional Ceylonese Medicine. This hospital had, at the time, negligible diagnostic facilities and was quite unable, for example, to handle surgical cases. Where there was a known condition, I could certainly advise on therapy and I could diagnose the majority of medical conditions and treat a large number of them. Sometimes I was able to make use of drugs that were about to be discarded by the Dockyard Surgery or by RNH. Although the drugs might be very near their expiratory date, or even slightly past it, in most cases it was still safe and effective to employ them a little longer. This enabled me to give medications to deserving cases who would otherwise have been totally incapable of affording the prescription. Frequently, I was very frustrated with clinical problems and often came close to quitting the whole business. At these times, Ali would plead with me to continue as the local people, he said, had little else. This backhanded compliment was hardly a ringing endorsement but was always successful in preventing me from throwing in my hand.

On one occasion, I met with a clearly well-to-do man in Ali's room. He had come from a town more than a 100 miles away specifically to consult with me. I was embarrassed at this, especially when realising that I would be unable to help him without certain investigations, especially a chest x-ray. Ali was particularly anxious that this patient should get maximal help as was a relative of a friend. So I embarked on a madcap course of actions that I strongly suspected I was going to regret and which, years later, would still gave rise to a cold sweat and palpitations. On the following day, I arranged with a CPO at RNH for this man to have a chest x-ray and other films. This, of course, was strictly improper, as the patient had nothing to do with the Navy or dockyard. I had to give the chief a "sweetener", which might have left me open to further charges of bribery. There was now the small problem of getting my patient in and out of the dockyard, the entrance of which was always guarded by Admiralty police.

I met with Ali and the patient at the pier in Trinco town, having sailed there in an RN dinghy. With the patient on board, we then tacked back to a point inside the dockyard where I had left my car, into which I helped the patient. I then drove him to RNH where he had his x-rays while I waited nervously. We escaped from the hospital, drove to the dinghy and took off into the harbour, sailing back to Ali with some difficulty. After arranging to meet with them on the following evening, I pushed off again for the RN sailing club to return the dinghy. I was extremely pleased to have reached this point in my scheme of things without detection and was sure that all was now well, but it wasn't! It was now after 6.30 pm and nearly dark. In many parts of the tropics, the wind dies down after sunset and this was now the case. I had great difficulty in making it back to the boatyard. The dinghy had no riding lights and so there was a small risk of being run down by harbour traffic and the many local ferries.

I seemed to take forever to get to the sailing club where I had to tie up and lower and stow away the sails. After accomplishing this, I drove back to the wardroom where I had long missed dinner. The patient's chest film showed major disease that I was quite unable to deal with. I had to break this sad news to him the next day and felt that I could not charge any fee in the circumstances. Additionally, I had to fend off questions from *Highflier's* irate First Lieutenant about returning the dinghy so late. All in all, it had been a nerve-racking experience that I swore never to repeat.

Because of my daily work with the local dockyard labour force and my private medical work with Ali, I saw a great number of the Trinco town population and became well known to a large section of them. Most of the naval community, including the Admiralty civilians, had virtually no such contact. They lived their lives almost entirely in the dockyard, and in other areas of the penninsula which provided their working environment, habitation and social needs but which were not, in the main, accessible to the Trinco town public. From time to time, they would go into town for photographic supplies, petrol or to take in the local colour but their lives might have been lived on a different planet to the poor locals. This did not indicate any racism on their behalf, or even social superiority. It was simply a matter of the two populations living entirely different lives that were worlds apart.

SIX

Up-country, Lady Edwina

One day, a signal was received from a Japanese fishing vessel some ten miles off the coast. An internationally accepted code had been used but their problem was far from being clear. However, it was obvious that they required medical assistance and I went out to meet them in a launch. They were further away than we had imagined and we had some difficulty in locating the ship. Having found it, I went on board while my launch stood off close by. I was surprised at the very large number of crew and later learned that this vessel, and others like it, were away from home for many months, often much longer than a year, with their catch being transferred at regular intervals to a depot ship. I examined the patient, surrounded by a sea of curious faces. No-one spoke English and the international book of questions and statements in several languages carried by all ships was not very helpful. I did, however, manage to establish that the seaman was suffering from abdominal pain. After my examination, I was concerned about appendicitis but the case was by no means classical. I decided to take him ashore with me and succeeded, with some difficulty, in getting the Japanese Captain to understand this.

After the patient had been admitted to RNH, the Surgeon Commander who was the surgical specialist was also far from sure what the diagnosis was. There was thought to be no clear indication for immediate surgery and the patient was carefully watched. On the following day, however, the clinical picture had changed and appendicitis was now thought to be very probable. This was confirmed at surgery, from which the patient made an uncomplicated recovery. However, his ship was now no longer in our vicinity and the disposal of the patient became a problem. Eventually, after some initial reluctance, the Japanese embassy in Colombo agreed to take him.

A national election was announced for April 1956, with the two main competing parties being the Sri Lanka Freedom Party (SLFP) and the United National Party (UNP). The latter was conservative and vaguely pro-Western, with Sir John Kotelawa as its head.

The former was a coalition of left-wing nationalistic groups headed by Mr Solomon Dias Bandaranaika, commonly known simply as "Banda". Buddist monks, in their bright saffron robes, campaigned openly for the SLFP and were very evident in both cities and countryside.

After a wardroom party one night, I and a number of friends went to a Chinese restaurant situated just outside the dockyard gates, which was regularly checked by the NMOH. There were three men eating quietly in the restaurant, dressed in the very common singhalese fashion of a long white cloth from the waist to the ankles, known as the verti, and a white, long sleeved, collarless shirt; this combination is called the "Arya Sinhala suit". Despite pleas from all of our party, one rather drunken officer insisted on approaching these gentlemen and asking about their political allegiances. "Are you UNP?" he demanded. On being answered in the negative, he proceeded with "Are you SLFP then?" Again they denied this affiliation, whereupon he bellowed "Then what the hell are you?". "PWD" was their reply, which induced gales of laughter and discomforted the rude officer. They were, in fact, from Kandy and were working for the Public Works Department (PWD) on a project near Trinco.

After the SLFP party won the election, Mr Bandaranaika became the Prime Minister and his government proceeded to pass legislation based on its narrow buddhist, singhalese and socialistic philosophy, changing the country's name from Ceylon to Sri Lanka. The "Sinhala Only" Act made Singhalese the official and only language, with both Tamil and English being jettisoned. At the time, about 20% of the population was Tamil and a little more than 70% was Singhalese. However, the government did not wait for signposts, which had always carried three languages, to require repainting. Men were immediately seen on bicycles, riding around the towns and countryside, simply painting over the Tamil and English names on the signs. This action aroused fury among the Tamil populations of the north and east and undoubtedly was an important factor in the aetiology of the dreadful civil war that lay ahead.

A year or so after the election, Banda was assassinated by a Buddhist monk and Mrs Sirimavo Bandaranaika, his wife, succeeded him. She became the world's first female Prime Minister and occupied this position three times. At the end of the second millennium, the President of Sri Lanka was Mrs Chanrika Bandaranaike

Kumaratunga, Banda's daughter, and Anura Bandaranaike, his son, was the Parliamentary Speaker. Many Tamils of my acquaintance regarded these positions held by Banda's family as being little short of nepotism.

A very pleasant young Lieutenant in the Royal Ceylon Navy was stationed with us for several months. I became friendly with him but never quite discovered what he was meant to be doing, imagining that it was some kind of liaison duties. He had spent two years in Britain doing various long courses and was a wonderful cricketer. He had a small, tame mongoose that he used to keep in his pockets which contained peanuts, and caused a great sensation when attending a cocktail party in the wardroom garden one evening. The mongoose, having finished the nuts in one pocket, ran up his master's back to his shoulders, crossed to the other side and headed back down into the other pocket. This was quite a common procedure but, seen towards the end of a party, many thought that they were developing delerium tremens. I and other officers near him stoutly denied to a female guest that we had seen anything unusual, when the animal performed the same exercise a few minutes later, after nuts had been transferred again. It was very perplexing to those not in the know but most amusing to those of us who were. When this officer left us to return to Colombo, he gave me this pet. Unfortunately, the mongoose did not seem to like me and I could not even get him to eat anything in my cabin, about which he raced, trying to escape. I was forced to release him into the wild.

The freemasons on the island had an annual dinner in the *Highflyer* wardroom. I imagined that the three main areas of masonic activity, in an island where the British presence was rapidly dwindling, would be among the commercial men of Colombo, the up-country tea planters and, of course, the Navy. Although not a member of the craft, I was asked if, being the wardroom food caterer, I would arrange the meal for this gathering and I readily assented. I discussed the menu with the Goanese CPO steward, who promised me a different and exciting main course and I, somewhat reluctantly, agreed to leave this in his hands. On returning from a social engagement, I showed my face to the masons, all cabalistic exercises, dinner and the Tyler's toast having been completed. I received fulsome compliments about the food and in particular about the main course, which was described as being "like turkey but much more delicious". Asked what it was but not knowing, I pretended that it was a secret. I was invited to stay and join in some rowdy games that was now being played, these being very similar to the activities following a wardroom mess dinner. I never did discover what the main course had been and really preferred not to know. However, adding up one thing and another led me to conclude that it was probably peacock! I suspected that the acquisition of these birds, held in great regard by Buddhists and possibly captured at a sacred ruined city such as Polonnaruwa or Anuradhapura, was illegal. I kept my head down, said nothing and the matter of the famous meal was slowly forgotten.

A chance meeting with a tea planter, a member of the Kandy rugby team and relative of a Trinco naval officer, led me to begin playing for Kandy. Rugby was not a huge game in Ceylon but there was an active league comprising about nine teams and competition was keen during a relatively short season. Kandy was the most northernly of the league clubs. Although not one of the more successful, it had good team spirit and happy post-match camerarderie, despite a diverse ethnic composition. Singhalese and British players formed the majority of the team, all of the latter except myself being planters, with a few Burghers making up the numbers, and everyone spoke English. Burghers are well recognised in Ceylon as being a small but definite racial group, constituting less than 1% of the population and being derived historically from Dutch and Singhalese intermingling. The league was dominated by two Colombo clubs, one containing a plethora of Australians, and Badulla, an up-country club whose team was almost entirely made up of young British planters.

Our home ground was very close to the celebrated Temple of the Tooth, a famous Buddhist monastery and shrine. One of the tourist highlights of Ceylon was the Perahera, a sort of religious festival when the sacred tooth relic of Gautama Buddha was carried in procession through Kandy by a huge procession of expensively-decorated elephants. The famous Sri Lankan spin bowler Muralitharan, a Tamil who has played for Lancashire and Kent and was neck and neck with Shane Warne of Australia in 2004 for the distinction of having taken the most Test wickets, later emerged from the neighbouring cricket club in Kandy, where Test matches are now played.

The rugby season was quite short and as games did not begin until 4.30 pm on Saturdays, I was able to get to the match from my distant north-easterly domicile in time for the kick-off. My first game was against the Kelani Valley RFC, situated between Colombo and Kandy and very near the site where most of the movie *The Bridge over the River Kwai* had been filmed, with *Highflyer* ratings playing the role of British prisoners-of-war. As well as all home games, many away games required driving through Kandy and then on south through the hill country. I would drive at first through dense jungle on the main but narrow Colombo road, where it was common to see troops of monkeys dashing across in front of the car. The bigger animals would go first and the smaller ones would barely pass before the car was on to them. It was almost as if they were playing a very risky game of "chicken", a sort of "last one across is a Charlie", but I never heard of anyone actually running over any of them. At Dambulla, there are interesting cave temples and the Golden Temple, a World Heritage site. The Rangeri cricket stadium was constructed here at the close of the millenium. It proved to be a place of great humiliation for English cricket, with the touring England team being bowled out for just 88 runs and beaten by ten wickets in a limited overs match here in November, 2003. I would turn left off the Colombo road here and drive the remaining 44 miles to Kandy, which was some 115 miles from Trinco.

I very much enjoyed these occasions. Without exception, I stayed over Saturday nights with one of my teammates, invariably a tea planter. The latter contained a high proportion of men who were either Scots or of Scottish descent. In the years leading up to World War Two, many had joined the Ceylon Planters Rifle Corps and other British regiments and their numbers had decreased spectacularly since then. Some would have young trainee assistants, called "creepers", and many were either single or unaccompanied. There was a widespread belief that, with the inevitable coming of the Ceylonese republic with its associated nationalistic overtones, their numbers could only decline further. Everyone guessed that this situation would arrive in the near future and this proved to be correct. The planters lived in large, sprawling but comfortable bungalow-type dwellings and had many servants; but they worked hard and most were out on their plantations very early in the morning. Each area would have a club, often miles away from individual plantations, where tennis, swimming, bridge, dining and dancing could be enjoyed. It all reminded me irresistibly of Somerset Maugham's Malaya. However, because of the uncertain future and diminished planter numbers, some clubs had closed and others now had only a small membership. I was told frequently by my hosts "if only you could have come here in the good old days".

The drinking habits of the planters were quite different to those of the Navy. Of course, they did not have duty free alcohol and seemed to mainly drink whisky. Although generally intelligent, experienced and otherwise informed, many believed sincerely that this tipple was a cure for all manner of serious complaints, including dysentery and malaria. I was one of a minority who did not enjoy whisky but used to bring some with me for my hosts. The planter's beer also differed from that available in Trinco and included a popular Tiger beer, from Singapore, and a good brand from a Nuara Eliya brewery, with whose young and hospitable manager, a native of Lancashire, I became friendly. In addition, toddy and arrack were present in most planter's houses. Toddy is like a beer, made from the fermented sap of the palm tree, for which I did not care. Arrack is a powerful drink, usually made from distilled coconut milk but sometimes from rice. If triple distilled, it was quite pleasant and not dissimilar to gin.

These rugby weekends and my annual holidays frequently took me to the delightful Ceylon up-country districts. This entailed driving to Kandy again, after which the road would pass through Peradeniya, famous for its lush and lovely botanical gardens, where Mountbatten had his headquarters when South East Asia Supremo during World War Two. The road then climbed steadily through paddy fields to the beautiful highlands further south. Some areas here are over 7,000 feet in elevation, often above the clouds and with a delicious scent of tea on the air. One would frequently pass workers picking tea leaves, often on steeply terraced slopes (Fig 8). These would always be females as they, with their nimble fingers, have much greater dexterity and speed in picking the tea leaves than men. My favourite place among all this great beauty was Nuwara Eliya, pronounced "New Raylia", the tea from here being universally considered as being the very best and truly the "champagne" of Ceylon teas. On the approach to this town was a highly-coloured sign with a rather mellifluous but sincere greeting (Fig 9).

Fig 8. A typical up-country Ceylon scene, with women picking tea from bushes on terraced slopes.

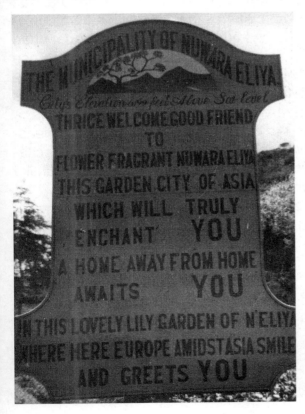

Fig 9. The distinctive but somewhat sugary roadside greeting approaching the lovely up-country town of Nuwara Eliya.

The town had a population of about 14,000 at this time and had long been an English haven, the "Poona" of Ceylon There were several excellent hostelries of which the Grand Hotel was the most superior and the Hill Club was the most fashionable establishment here at this time, being much favoured by Australians including Sir Robert Menzies, a former Prime Minister of that country

Holidays were spent at *HMS Uva* near Diyatalawa, about 200 miles from Trinco, which was an official services rest centre with a nine-hole golf course, tennis courts, etc. The Queen Alexandra Naval Nursing sisters from RNH Trincomalee took it in turns to work there, and there was a permanently based naval physician. One slept under a couple of light blankets and even fires were not unknown in accommodations.

Holidays elsewhere, especially at sea level, were frowned upon. The Surgeon Captain believed, rightly, that time at elevation and in cool conditions was important. However, my bachelor status and car gave me both mobility and freedom and I would leave *HMS Uva* occasionally and explore the southern coast. Ratnapura was the centre of the Ceylon precious stones industry, with a gem museum and many retail outlets, which I often visited. Muslim traders had called the island Serendib, this ancient name of Ceylon giving rise to the word "serendipity". This means the chance making of unexpected and happy discoveries, such as finding a jewel, and was coined by Horace Walpole after *The Three Princes of Serendip*, a fairy tale. I frequently visited the city of Galle, which was both pleasant and interesting. There was an old Dutch fort, a racecourse, occasional cricket of a high standard, good sea bathing and, unlike Trinco, cool sea breezes which could be relied upon.

Occasionally, I would spend a few days in Colombo, where I had many friends, from the rugby field and the Royal Ceylon Navy, en route back to Trinco. Driving, however, in and around Colombo was a veritable nightmare. The streets appeared to be packed with rickshaws, three wheeled pedal taxis, bullock carts, cyclists and cars of all descriptions and ages. There seemed to be no generally accepted right-of-way and I was informed that being involved in any accident, even if clearly the innocent party, could result in hours and even days of wrangling with the other driver and the police, very few of whom spoke English. Government "rest houses" were dotted about the country and provided meals, refreshments and, in some cases, accommodation. I was never certain of the standards of hygiene in these establishments and used them infrequently and then only to drink bottled beverages.

Sid, the Captain of *HMS Baron*, was a Lieutenant Commander promoted from the lower deck. He was a great character and a good friend. His son often crewed for me in the Saturday dinghy races and Sid helped me with the servicing and repairs of my car. Skilled mechanics were in distinctly short supply in Trinco but Sid, who was also in charge of the Boom Defence station, allowed me to use one of his Asian mechanics for any servicing or repairs needed by my car. I would, of course, pay a small sum for this service but I was always a bit uptight about all this, being uncertain as to its legality. However, I used the arrangement for the entire length of my stay in Trinco, with no problems.

Although happy in Trinco, I hankered for some sea time and spent several months trying to wangle myself on to *HMS Superb* for one of its cruises, but to no avail. The Surgeon Lieutenant on board did not wish to exchange positions with me, even for a few weeks, and I could hardly blame him. As a sop, I was given a short trip around the south coast of the island to Colombo. The RAF was about to leave Negombo, its base on the west coast of Ceylon just north of the capital, and was heading for the Maldive Islands in the Indian Ocean. *HMS Baron* was a small ship, far from new and a coal burner. Mainly used for minor salvage work, replacing buoys and carrying out other harbour work, it was going to lay the surface moorings for the RAF marine craft. The plan was for *Baron* to sail under its own steam to Colombo, where its bunkers would be topped up, after which it would be towed by a tug to Gan Island. It was thought that *Baron* could just about make it back to Colombo before running out of coal.

As well as Sid, we had a Flight Lieutenant of the RAF maritime section with us, about eight RN seamen and some 60 local stokers who, working in temperatures approaching 180 degrees Fahrenheit for 20 minutes at a time, kept the boiler fires going. As we left the outer harbour of Trinco, a school of dolphins joined us, playing alongside the ship for hours. It was decided that I would keep the morning watch, from 0400 to 0800, with a CPO of the seaman branch to hold my hand. Of course, he would be the real man in charge but I as an officer, even though not of the executive branch, would theoretically be the officer of the watch. I had no real watch-keeping or navigational skills but the course had been plotted, we were in deep water with no hazards, the CPO was very experienced and Sid was only yards away.

Approaching Matara, on the southern aspect of Ceylon, we saw some distant lights to the east that rapidly closed. It was obviously a large ship that clearly was going to pass well to our south and pose no problems. I suggested that we contact this ship but the CPO thought that there was no requirement for this. I insisted, however, and the communications rating was roused out of his cot and on to the bridge. Using the signalling lamp, he asked "What ship are you, where from and where bound?" or words to that effect. The ship was now about two miles away and, after a few seconds, we received a reply, our signaller soon interpreting this as "SS Chusan, Hong Kong to Tilbury". I got off lightly from Sid on the following morning, although he thought that the stock of the RN with the Peninsular and Oriental Steamship Company (P & O) probably had declined considerably!

Sweeping changes were now introduced into the RN, the result of the first of many subsequent defence cuts. In 1956, Lord and Lady Mountbatten flew around the world in a rather spartan RAF aircraft to explain these at a variety of naval overseas bases and they spent a couple of days in Trinco. Lord Louis was regarded by many naval officers as being a bit of a socialist and rather suspect but he was very popular with the lower deck. I was warned by a friend of a trick that many senior officers, but especially Lord Louis, would pull and we were not disappointed. Mountbatten stopped on two occasions before a senior rating and correctly identified each one. "Didn't you serve with me in *Kelly*?" might be the question, answered in the affirmative by the first rating and with a similar question and answer on the second occasion. The men were astounded at his memory, and pleased as punch to be remembered after all those years. Of course, Lord Louis had merely got his staff to do a little homework and identify men with whom he had previously served. After inspecting the officers and men of *Highflyer* and the Admiral's staff, he mounted a small dais and barked "Break ranks, gather round" which the sailors did with alacrity, leaving the officers very much at the periphery and rear (Fig 10).

That evening, there was a reception for the distinguished vis-

Fig 10. Admiral Lord Louis Mountbatten speaking at *HMS Highflyer*. Vice-Admiral Sir Charles Norris, Comander-in Chief, East Indes station, is seen with hands on hips to the left. The author is in the group of officers to the right, at the front and to the left of the group.

itors at Admiralty House where Richard Thomas, the Flag Lieutenant, heavily involved in preparations for social events, also lived. Richard was a good friend of mine, in spite of me occasionally press-ganging him into wardroom sporting teams, and used to feed me snippets of gossip about the Admiral and his senior contacts. I followed his career with great interest. He became a full Admiral, was knighted and, after retirement, became Gentleman Usher of the Black Rod in Parliament in the 1990s.

I was somewhat surprised to be invited to this reception. No doubt the small number of officers in Trinco had a lot to do with this. I noticed, on arrival, that Lord Louis was busily engaged in talking to the Admiral and SBNO, with Lady Edwina standing alone a little distance away. The Admiral became aware of this out of the corner of his eye, called his Flag Lieutenant across who then approached me. "The Admiral wishes you to engage Lady Mountbatten in conversation" was the command. I wondered for a minute if this was a leg pull and Richard was winding me up but, no, he was quite serious. I took a large gulp of my gin-and-tonic and walked over to Her Ladyship. She greeted me with "Are you the poor man who's been detailed off to look after me?". She was, of course absolutely correct in this which made any reply somewhat difficult. However, she was very easy to talk to, full of interesting information, as one would expect, and seemed to be genuinely interested in my take on Trinco, the Navy and many other matters. To my surprise, no one else joined us and I enjoyed her company, being quite alone with her for fully 45 minutes. I imagine this was because others were intimidated by her status or did not wish to appear to be thought of as being pushy. At this time, she announced that she had better rescue her husband and talk to a few more people. She thanked me for my company and swept off. She was 54 years old at this time, had been flying around the world for a couple of weeks, already had angina according to her biographers Janet Morgan and Richard Hough, and was to die in less than four years time. Yet her beauty, charm and especially her personality were most evident.

A little after this visit, the Duke of Edinburgh came by. He was travelling in the Royal Yacht *Britannia* en route to Melbourne to open the 1956 Olympic Games and disembarked at Colombo. He came on overland to us, visiting Kandy on the way, while *Britannia* steamed around the island. He had intimated that he would like to participate in the weekly dinghy sailing race and one of the 14 foot clinker-built gaff-rigged dinghies had been specially repainted and fitted with a new set of sails for him. Just before the start of the race, we were told that our distinguished visitor was too fatigued to join us and the race began without him. Some 30 minutes later, we saw the Admiral's barge racing towards us, passing very close to some of the dinghies and towing a water skier who was clearly enjoying himself. I wondered if this could possibly be Philip and was later told that, in fact, it was. He didn't stay very long in Trinco and I was not invited to meet him.

One of *Britannia's* medical officers had previously worked in the Dockyard Surgery and he came to revisit it. I met him there and took him up on his kind invitation to board *Britannia* and have a guided tour. The ship's three masts were very distinctive, even unusual, her hull was a very deep blue, not black, and everywhere was immaculate. The sailor's cap band carried the letters *HM Royal Yacht* and I was told that only those with impeccable personal records were selected to serve in her. It was all most impressive but I wondered at the expense of it all and the necessity for having a Flag Officer on board.

Towards the end of September 1956, *HMS Newfoundland* of happy memory was ordered from the Far East to Aden, prior to joining a combined force of British and French ships involved in the Red Sea end of the Suez campaign. *Newfy* made a short stop at Trinco on her western passage and I enjoyed a brief visit with Surgeon Lieutenant Vernon Pugh, a classmate of mine at Liverpool University and an Old Boy of Liverpool Institute, who later became a Dorset GP. *Newfy* subsequently sank the Egyptian frigate *Domiat* in the Gulf of Suez. Some survivors were picked up by the destroyer *HMS Diana*, to which Dr Pugh was transferred by jack-stay. While *Diana's* doctor performed a mid-thigh amputation, a far-from-easy surgical procedure at sea aboard a small ship, Dr Pugh gave the anaesthesia. With no anaesthetic machine available, he had to employ the older technique of "open ether" which involved the dropping of ether onto a gauze mask on the patient's face. Dr Pugh visited the amputee at Djibouti, French Somaliland, at a later date and found him to be doing well. He also came to possess *Newfy's* battle ensign, the last to be used by the RN in a ship-to-ship gun action.

Each year, a very large naval and air exercise was held in and around Trinco. This Joint Exercises Trincomalee (JET) involved the Indian Navy, who would put out more than 20 ships, the Pakistan Navy, with a good deal less, and the Royal Ceylon Navy with just one small frigate. The RN would field a few ships and a submarine. The Indian Air Force and RAF also joined in. In my first experience of JET, the submarine was *Tally Ho*, a World War Two boat that was far from being "state of the art"; in fact, it had operated from Trinco with considerable success against Japanese shipping as long ago as 1943. Nevertheless, it seemed to consistently win hands down against formidable numbers of considerably more modern surface vessels, aided by aircraft. Peter Chapman, the submarine's engineer officer, became a good friend and used my cabin in *Highflyer* to change clothes between afternoon and evening activities.

Sport figured prominently in the JET calendar. Ceylon always won the cricket, with my friend with the mongoose being the star on one occasion. The RN invariably won the soccer and duly did so again, thanks in large part to a young national service member of *Superb's* ship's company who was an apprentice with Everton FC. The hockey was always very keenly contested between India and

Pakistan. There were rumours that these two navies had flown in players who were not partaking in the naval exercise and it was even said that Pakistan had fielded a man who was not even in their navy! I had no way of confirming or refuting these allegations, which were persistent. Volleyball and Tennis were other but less popular JET competitions.

One night during JET, the nursing sister's mess had thrown a party and the place was bursting at its seams. I was helping at the bar and an Indian officer asked for some exotic drink. I told him that we didn't have any but was over-ruled by one of the nursing sisters, who pointed to a top shelf at the back of the bar. There was, by now, dancing going on and the lights had been dimmed. I had some difficulty in reaching the desired bottle, which was at the back of a top shelf, very dusty and clearly not used for years. I was aware of a rustling as I removed it and felt that something had fallen to the floor. I put the lights on in the bar and there was a huge scorpion! It was nearly a foot in length, fat and bloated, with its wicked, stinging tail looking quite deadly. Providentially, I saw a broom lying handy and manoeuvred the creature out of the bar onto the dance floor, switching on the lights at the same time. Some couples were dancing cheek-to-cheek and seemed to resent the increased illumination; on seeing the arachnid, however, they rapidly cleared the floor. Using the broom, I managed to push it out of the room into the concrete monsoon drain outside and thoroughly squash it. Local experts who saw the remains on the following day agreed that it was unusually large and of a really record size. Then I did a little research. It seems that the stings of these creatures are very painful, difficult to treat and can be fatal in young children; but in healthy adults, although spoiling your day, they are very rarely lethal.

As my time for being relieved grew nearer, talk of the base closing down intensified. There was no doubt that the Navy was leaving Trinco, what was uncertain was when this would occur. I was concerned that I might not be relieved and troubled by the prospect of having to stay for an indefinitely longer period. Although I had enjoyed my stay in Ceylon immensely, I had had enough and now wished to get home and on to another posting. However, a large number of very nice bungalows had recently been completed for Admiralty civilians and construction now began on a multi-million pound radio station several miles to the north, which entailed the building of a bridge giving access to the site. I thought this meant that the Navy would not be quitting for several years but was told that I was naive in this view. The know-alls asserted that this splashing out of British money was a sure sign that we were, in fact leaving pretty soon! In favour of this hypothesis was the fact that Royal Fleet Auxiliaries, the ships flying the blue ensign of the Royal Naval Reserve (RNR) and manned by civilians, who transported food, oil and other goods for the Navy, would no longer accept any personal heavy baggage for delivery in Britain. This was a serious blow to my plans of getting my sports car home. I had been very pleased with it but knew I would not get anything like its true value locally. The impending closure of the base would further reduce its value and I doubted if any naval or Admiralty civilian person would be interested in it.

Hence I considered driving home. The Middle East was in its usual turmoil but I thought I could manage to get through all right and drive home. This particular idea was scuppered when I was told that should I do this, my foreign service leave would commence as soon as I left the gates of *Highflyer*. A tough ruling, as the Suez Canal was closed and the troopship would take about a month to get to Southampton, but there it was. So I decided to cut my losses and look for a local sale. My definite date of leaving was soon given to me and the ever-dependable Ali found me a buyer. Although I received nothing like the car's true worth, I was able to hang on to it for a last foray up-country before handing it over in Colombo.

Several Asian Admiralty workers that I knew well, such as those working in clerical positions in the Dockyard Surgery, now asked me "why are you leaving us?" I was unable to give them any cogent reply. They were well aware that their secure and comparatively well-paid positions would soon be terminated, with no alternative employment in sight. In fact, the base was officially handed over to the Royal Ceylon Navy on October 15th 1957 but a British presence was maintained until the dockyard closed finally on September 30th, 1958.

SEVEN

The Fleet Air Arm

During one of my last working days in Trinco, my boss in the Dockyard Surgery presented me with the flimsy of my S206 form. The latter was completed on every RN officer at the conclusion of a posting. Essentially, it was drawn up by the officer's immediate superior and then was counter-signed by a more senior officer; in my case, these officers were the PMO of the Dockyard Surgery and SBNO respectively. The S206 was a detailed evaluation of the officer's performance in many areas and was of critical importance to him regarding future promotion. In my case, as I had no intention of staying in the Navy, it was of largely academic interest. The form itself was confidential and was not shown to the officer, although sections of it could be read out to him. A summary of the findings were presented in the form of a tear-off flimsy, which was given to the officer concerned and on which the senior officer often wrote a short comment.

This flimsy always detailed the dates during which the officer had worked under the command of the senior officer and was followed by the phrase "during which time he has conducted himself........". This latter section often continued with "to my satisfaction", with the final noun perhaps qualified by an adjective. A classic naval joke spoke of a less than outstanding officer whose flimsy had read "during which time he has conducted himself entirely to his own satisfaction". My flimsy read "to my entire satisfaction" but the short note added in longhand by SBNO was somewhat ambiguous and read "Has accomplished a great deal in his life without becoming too bumptious". Nice enough, I suppose, although it implied that I was bumtious at least to some degree. However, this didn't unduly worry me although I wondered how much lay people, even of senior rank and very genial, could know of the true accomplishments and worth of physicians.

The big day for leaving Trinco finally dawned, after I had held a party in the wardroom garden and been dined out at a wardroom mess dinner. I drove off to Kandy and other up-country spots and had a wonderful time while making my farewells to planter chums. In Colombo, I handed the car over to its new owner, a small Singhalese man who spoke no English. However, the ever efficient and dependable Ali had arranged everything and the transfer went smoothly. After enjoying a farewell drink with friends from the Royal Ceylon Navy in the famous *Galle Face Hotel*, the oldest hotel in the country which overlooked the harbour and sea, I then boarded the *Dunera*. This was virtually an identical sister ship of the *Dilwara* on which I had come out. Both ships later were used extensively by schools and other organisation for educational cruises in the Mediterranean. Most of the troops on board the *Dunera* were men of the Royal Welsh Fusiliers (RWF), returning after fighting the communist guerrillas in the jungles of Malaya. The troopship had the usual one doctor and two nursing sisters, all belonging to the Army, and I was told that I must work with them on the way home. I didn't mind this in the slightest and found these colleagues to be very agreeable.

Our first port of call was Port Louis on the island of Mauritius where, by a happy coincidence, *HMS Superb* was at anchor. Having been the cruiser on the East Indies station for many months, I knew her and her wardroom very well. Getting ashore, I wondered if I should pay a call when I met a couple of her officers, keen hockey types and old adversaries of mine. They immediately asked if I would play for them that afternoon. Apparently, several of the regular team had gone on some kind of tourist trip and they were short of players. I agreed, they provided a launch to pick me up from the troopship, which aroused great interest on board, and we had a good game and a narrow win against a Port Louis team. That evening, there was a reception for the *Superb's* wardroom at Government House and, of course, I was told that I must tag along. We finished the evening with a splendid meal in a local restaurant and I got back on board about half-an-hour before *Dunera* sailed at 11.30 pm. I was the envy of all. Most of my acquaintances on the ship had wandered about the capital, some had gone on a boring visit to a sugar plantation whereas I had, once again, landed on my feet. Serendipity indeed!

We crawled on to Capetown, which I enjoyed once again, and then slowly on up the west coast of Africa. There was a certain tension in the air on the ship, which I did not completely understand. Apparently, many of the RWF troops were national servicemen and had endured a far from pleasant time in Malaya. They were anxious to get home, fed up with the slow troopship and getting fractious. I was told in confidence, by a RWF major with whom I had become friendly, that many of the troops had old scores to settle with each other, and more especially with their NCOs and officers, and that there was considerable official concern about this. I recalled my problems with the naval draft on the way out to Ceylon and wondered if this was a normal situation in troopships. I had a cabin of my own, which was much coveted although it was small and hot. My duties were not onerous and my only slight irritation was the slow passage that we were making.

To relieve the tedium, a fancy dress competition was held for the officers. Archbishop Makarios of Cyprus, a leading exponent of Enosis and later to be the first President of Cyprus, had been much in the recent news, having been transported from Cyprus in 1956 by an RN destroyer and placed in exile in the Seychelles. I decided to go as this revolutionary cleric. I borrowed a lady's black gabardine raincoat with red piping and a chef's white hat, which I dyed black. One of the ship's engineers made me an episcopal ring out of a beer bottle top and wire and I fashioned an imposing pectoral cross using stiff, thick cardboard and silver paper, with red fruit pastilles for rubies. I had to admit that, with my beard, I didn't look at all bad in the part. After the grand parade, I was awarded first prize, a bottle of whisky. Dinner followed and then dancing. Some of the RWF officers called me over for a drink with them. It was very hot and my costume made it even more so. I began to feel very queer and excused myself, going down to my cabin to change. No sooner had I begun to undress than I was violently sick and fell to the floor. I was quite unable to rise and abstractly worked out that I must have developed an acute peripheral neuritis and paralysis. I then became doubly incontinent and literally felt like death. With a great effort, I managed to open my cabin door and feebly shout, but everyone was on upper decks and enjoying themselves. I think I must have passed out and the next thing I remember was the officer in the next cabin finding me close to midnight. I was taken to the ship's hospital where I was unable to help my colleague very much with any meaningful history. An intravenous (iv) drip was set up and I drifted off to sleep. I was told later that I was an alarming colour, a sort of deep blue!

Next morning, I felt much better but couldn't move my limbs

and this seriously concerned me. The military police were asking me a lot of questions about what I had drunk, and where, and I couldn't understand this. I gradually improved over the next week and the power in my limbs slowly returned. However, the Army doctor remained very concerned about me, not having any sort of diagnosis, and was all in favour of landing me at Dakar, in Senegal, our next port of call. By now, I was improving rapidly, beginning to walk and vigorously contested this plan. He agreed to wait on this decision until we actually tied up at Dakar, when I made sure that I gave the appearances of someone fully recovered.

Of course, I had been thinking furiously all this time as to the cause of my sudden illness, as had my colleague. I was convinced that I must have drunk something nasty and he agreed with this, suggesting that there was a real probability that a "Mickey Finn" had been prepared for one of the army officers and that I had swallowed it inadvertently. My strange colour was almost certainly due to the haemoglobin in my blood being changed by some agent into methaemoglobin, which does not transport oxygen. A whole host of chemicals will do this but few of these will give rise to an associated paralysis and most would be accompanied by a distinctive taste. I wondered if some strange concoction from Malaya had been employed. The military police on board had been unable to trace my glass from the many scattered about the tables. Most unfortunately, no specimens of my vomitus, urine or stool had been kept by the hospital, so a firm, final diagnosis was never made. I was convinced that I had suffered some form of acute poisoning but had no idea as to the agent or agents responsible.

Finally arriving at Southampton, after a nearly five week trip that had seemed interminable, we were greeted by the RWF families and a military band playing *We'll keep a welcome in the hillside*. Now fully recovered, I was greeted by another of my mother's military relatives but I only had a few minutes with him before having to jump on the special troop train laid on for Waterloo Station. At the very beginning of my foreign overseas leave, I had arranged to see the new Surgeon Captain (Appointments) at Admiralty. This time, I was leaving nothing to chance and getting my pitch in before receiving any posting. A senior officer at Trinco, a friend of his, had already written on my behalf and I was much more confident of achieving a good result than on my first, and surprisingly successful, visit to

Queen Anne Mansions. I was received cordially and asked if I would like some tea. I then requested some form of sea-going appointment. This was greeted with a smile and I was told that, with less than 18 months left to serve and having already had an overseas posting, I should really be given an appointment in the UK. I kept quiet and the Surgeon Captain, after studying a big book for several minutes, looked up and asked if I would like to join an aircraft carrier, HMS Eagle to be precise. I was delighted with this, thanked my host and left his office. Mother expressed considerable chagrin at her poor son again failing to land a posting in Britain. Once again, I laid low and said little.

After foreign service leave of about four weeks, I went off in August 1997 to the Portsmouth area again, specifically to HMS Daedalus, RNAS Lee-on-Solent. This was the headquarters of the Fleet Air Arm and I began the long course in Aviation Medicine there, with eight other Surgeon Lieutenants. Many of the lectures were given at nearby Seafield Park, an institution with the rather grandiose title of "Royal Naval School of Aviation Medicine", which was in a nearby large country house set in sizeable grounds. I found the lectures here to be of excellent quality and uniformly interesting. One morning, we were taken out into the Solent and, wearing life jackets and immersion suits, jumped into the water in turn. We were then picked up by a series of helicopters. The water was not too cold but, having been winched up alongside the cabin, the pilot would not allow me to enter and I had to hang on outside for some 15 minutes, unlike all the doctors ahead of me who immediately enjoyed the shelter of the chopper's interior. My face and fingers were quite numbed from the draught of chopper's blades and I harboured foul intentions towards the pilot. We were then taught about the ejector seat and all had a turn on one mounted against a rig. After the "bang seat" had fired and the passenger propelled upwards, a breaking mechanism stopped his rapid descent; instead, he would be slowly winched down. This mechanism had failed shortly before our visit and a pilot-in-training had descended at speed, suffering severe vertebral injuries. This induced some apprehension in most of us but all went off satisfactorily.

One of the nice things about working at Lee was being able to use the air service, known as "the Clipper", that went around the various naval air stations in the country each Monday and Friday. At this time in 1957, there were still some eight or nine such stations extending from RNAS Eglinton, near Derry City in Ulster, and RNAS Lossiemouth in north-east Scotland, to the south coast. Two planes would make the trip, each going in different directions to cover all the required destinations. One would head west to RNAS Culdrose, in Cornwall and then on to RNAS Yeovilton, in Somerset. The other would fly the short distance to RNAS Ford near Arundel in Sussex, later to become an open prison, then on to RNAS Bramcote, near Nuneaton, and on up north. This was useful for me as RNAS Stretton, near Warrington, was a most convenient drop-off. Most of these air stations, with the exception of Lee, Culdrose, Yeovilton, Brawdy and Lossiemouth, had ceased operations by 1960 and the two latter were subsequently handed over to the RAF. However, there was a big snag with the return trip. Unlike the Divisional Course, I had little difficulty getting the occasional Friday off but had to be present at 8.00 am on Monday; however, the Clipper return service didn't run until later on Mondays and from Lee. So it usually meant an overnight rail trip to Euston, crossing London to Waterloo, another train to Portsmouth, ferry to Gosport and then sharing a taxi to Lee.

Occasionally, I would still drive home for weekends, in an old banger that my submariner friend Peter, now stationed at *HMS Dolphin* at Gosport, had acquired for me. It was another pre-war car, a Wolseley 14, but Peter had ensured that the car was mechanically sound. This gave me the use of a car while I was at home, a night's rest on getting back to Lee on Sunday and was overall much cheaper. Delayed on one occasion, I spent another night at Ratcliffe college. The school Geography society was hosting a lecture evening. Students, with accompanying masters from Uppingham and a couple of local grammar schools, were present and the Professor of Geography at Leicester University was scheduled to speak. I was invited to a small sherry party before the lecture, during the course of which someone entered the room and whispered to the school Geography master. He appeared to become somewhat agitated and had clearly received bad news. After consultation with the Ratcliffe Headmaster, the latter then approached me, told me that the lecturer was taken ill and asked if I would fill in. I readily agreed, stipulating only that I be provided with a map of Ceylon. This was done and I banged on about that island for close to an hour. Of course, I knew my subject and it all went off very well. Both the headmaster and the Geography master were most grateful and a bit of a party developed later. In addition, I got to stay in the house of the music master, without any matrons or small boys about.

My courses at Lee and Seafield Park had all but finished and I was all set to join Eagle in Devonport, popularly known as "Guzz" by the Navy, when an unexpected development occurred. This involved a Surgeon Commander at an air station who had been caught in serious breech of naval regulations; he was suspended from work pending a court martial. A replacement had to be found and the somewhat limited number of people trained in Aviation Medicine were moved around to cover this eventuality. The upshot of all this was that my move to the carrier was put on hold. I became a staff member at Seafield Park for a few weeks, before being sent to *HMS Goldcrest*, RNAS Brawdy. This was in Pembrokeshire, near Haverfordwest, and was a NATO all-weather station, where squadrons were trained before embarking on carriers. The ward-room and cabins were modern and very comfortable and the ship's sporting teams were very active. Unfortunately, there was again an obsession with Divisions on Friday afternoon (Fig 11), which were

Fig 11. The march-past and salute at the end of Divisions, *HMS Goldcrest*, RNAS Brawdy, Pembrokeshire. A pilot with sword leads the parade. The sailors, in best uniforms with white gaiters, look especially smart.

every bit as disciplined and formal as at Pompey Barracks. I had forgotten about all this while in Trinco and my heart sank at the thought of my forced participation. Fortunately, the PMO, a very pleasant Irishman, connived at my absence from these parades most of the time and I was able to get away home at a reasonable hour in the afternoon when necessary.

I enjoyed my ten weeks at Brawdy but was very relieved to finally join *Eagle* towards the end of 1957. Light fleet carriers such as *Triumph, Ocean, Theseus*, etc had been moth-balled or broken up after the Korean War and the carriers *Bulwark* and *Albion* were soon to be converted into commando/assault carriers. *Eagle* and *Ark Royal* seemed to be the work horses of the fleet and a refitted *Victorious* joined them in the late 1950s. *Centaur* and *Hermes* were also operational at this time and several other carriers were in reserve.

A squadron of Seahawks and the Commander (Air), always known as Wings, from Brawdy joined with me so I at once had a few acquaintances on board. *Eagle* was a huge ship of 43,000 tons displacement. Over 800 feet in length, she had a top speed of more than 31 knots. Built by Harland and Wolff at Belfast and launched by Princess Elizabeth in 1946, she was finally accepted into service in 1952 and was a sister ship to the slightly newer Ark Royal, built by Cammel Lairds at Birkenhead. These two carriers were the largest ships in all the world's navies at this time except for the carriers *Forrestal* and *Saratoga* of the US Navy.

Eagle had two full-length hangars, one above the other, served by for'ard and aft lifts, and a five point five degree angled flight deck which was later enlarged to eight degrees, with twin hydraulic catapults, later changed to steam catapults. A mirror deck landing system providing a stabilized visual glide path to the deck and was much superior to the old batsman, with his occasional human misjudgements. It provided for a much more accurately predictable touch-down and so the large number of arrester wires previously employed could be reduced to just five. The mirrors, steam catapults and angled deck were all post-World War Two British innovations which had revolutionised carrier operations, making then much faster, efficient and safer.

The carrier had 14 decks and the ship's motto was *Arduus ad Solem*; after Commander's rounds, many in his party translated this as "hard on the feet". Depending on the mix of aircraft, we never had less than 90 and sometimes over 100 planes on aboard as well as the ship's own flight of three Westland Whirlwind helicopters, usually known as choppers. The ship carried three doctors and a dentist, with a Surgeon Commander as PMO. I shared a cabin with another Surgeon Lieutenant who had a permanent commission and who was, on leaving *Eagle*, to specialise in General Surgery. For much of my time on board, Flag Officer Aircraft Carriers (FOAC) and his staff were with us.

Three chaplains were carried although one was frequently with the cruiser or one of the three or four frigates that usually accompanied us. The two padres that we had in *Eagle* for most of the time were of the Roman Catholic and Protestant persuasion, the latter minister being an Anglican but an Irishman and a member of the Church of Ireland. They were the best of friends and would always go ashore together when abroad. The catholic priest was English and the two would frequently discuss and argue about Anglo-Irish history, often taking somewhat unlikely stances. I would, quite often, win bets and take money from unsuspecting guests by asking them to tell me which of the two was the priest, after eavesdropping on their conversation for a few minutes. The guests were always amazed when given the truth and, before they would pay up, I sometimes had to ask one of the padres to confirm the unexpected answer, which was due to the protestant padre's republican sympathies.

Eagle had provided the bulk of the carrier-based air strikes during *Operation Musketeer*, the Suez campaign which had been a great military success but a political and moral disaster and against which the British Joint Intelligence Committee had strongly advised. Many and various stories concerning this campaign were still circulating around the ship when I joined. The flight deck crew, for instance, were very proud of the fact that, despite one catapult being out of action before the campaign began, *Eagle's* aircraft flew more sorties than did *Bulwark* and *Albion*, the other British carriers present, combined. The Navy had gone to great pains to avoid bombing civilians, with hospitals, schools, etc marked on maps and scrupulously avoided. I was told that *Simon Arzt*, a well-known and popular Armenian tourist shop near the canal which sold souvenirs and curios, was similarly marked.

Another tale that I was told involved an amusing situation

which had developed before I joined the ship when *Eagle* and *Ark Royal* were taking part in a big NATO exercise in the North Atlantic involving many US ships. One night, a US plane was short of fuel and forced to land on *Eagle* rather than its parent ship which was much further away. The aircrews of the British ship were delighted to recieve their unexpected visitor and to exchange views and gossip with him. The American pilot was regaled with drinks in the wardroom before and after dinner, a practice to which he was unaccustomed as all US ships are "dry".

Next morning, now fully sober, the American flew off to rejoin his own ship and to no doubt spread the word about Limey hospitality. It was hardly a matter of coincidence that three or four more US aviators now landed, for a variety of alleged reasons, on the British carriers over the next few weeks. Finally, the US admiral was forced to act and informed all his pilots that the next errant plane would be severly disiplined and possibly court martialled.

A few months after I had joined, one of the ship's officers left us for a great adventure that turned out to be something of an embarrassment both for him and the country. Lieutenant Commander Graham Mann was appointed skipper of *Sceptre*, the Royal Yacht Squadron's challenge for the America's Cup of 1958. The United States, the holder of the Cup, was represented by *Columbia* of the New York Yacht Club, which had defeated some formidable rivals in the trials. The British endeavour was said to be poorly organised and *Columbia* won easily in four straight races.

When all the squadrons were embarked, they and the ship's company comprised 2,800 men and kept the medical department busy. Apart from the usual colds, sore throats, back problems, etc, a medical officer was always required to be on the flight deck during the launching and recovery of aircraft. Usually, he did not do a great deal there but his presence, wearing a red cross on a white background over his normal attire, was said to be reassuring to all. This obligation was very demanding of time, what with early morning take-offs and night flying. Regular naval caps would not stay on heads very long during flying operations and navy blue berets were worn on the flight deck. However, the latter was a dangerous place and sometimes generated its own share of patients. The constant noise of jet engines, together with that of the catapults, tended to cause some degree of dissociation and loss of concentration. If caught in the back draught of a jet on full throttle immediately prior to being catapulted off, an unfortunate man would often be forced to run aft on the flight deck and might have to deliberately fall down to prevent himself from running off the deck altogether.

A specific problem related to the Fairy Gannet anti-submarine aircraft, which had two contra-rotating propellers mounted symmetrically over each other, each driven by its own engine. Often, one engine would be closed down with its propeller stationary while the other engine was running, with its propeller turning so fast as to be virtually invisible. With the cacophony all around, it was difficult to appreciate that one propeller was, in fact, revolving and on some carriers, flight deck personnel had walked into this rotating prop with terrible consequences. Fortunately, this did not occur during my time in *Eagle*.

During the average day, flying would commence at 0700 and continue until 1300. It would usually recommence about 2100 and continue until 0100 or 0200 the following morning. Not to be outdone, the gunners would fire their ordinance each afternoon so any peace and quiet in the carrier was exceptional. There was a good deal of ragging between the ship's officers and the aircrew, who called the former "Fishheads". After a particularly intense and prolonged bout of flying, the Air Division announced a "Grand Sleeping Competition". Lilos were to be used on the quarter deck and notices proclaimed that those with previous experience, especially all Fishheads, were banned from participation. One particular aviator claimed the prize after sleeping solidly for over 15 hours. It was suspected that he had taken sleeping tablets but this could not definitely be established.

A major responsibility of mine was to look after the aircrew. This included ensuring that all their air medical examinations and inoculations were up to date and that they were "fit to fly". Even a mild cold could result in a grounding, if the officer concerned could not perform a Valsalva manoeuve, that is "pop his ears" while forcibly exhaling and holding his nose; this would indicate that his eustachian tubes were blocked. Occasionally, I might be approached by a Squadron Commanding Officer who was worried about one of his pilots. I would then observe this officer closely in his deck landings and also in his general behaviour in the wardroom. The "fear of flying" syndrome could attack experienced aviators and was commonly and unkindly known as "twitch" in the Fleet Air Arm. Landing on pitching and rolling carriers was no joke and, especially at night, called for skills and airmanship of the highest order. A popular and traditional Fleet Air Arm song, written during World War Two, was called after the form a pilot was required to complete after an accident, namely the A25. One verse of this was

> *I fly for a living and not just for fun*
> *I'm awfully anxious to hack down the Hun*
> *But as for deck landings, at night in the dark,*
> *As I told Wings this morning, sod that for a lark*

and the chorus was
> *Cracking show, I'm alive*
> *But I've still got to fill in my A25.*

During night flying in July 1958, there was a terrible disaster with a Sea Venom hitting the extreme aft part of the flight deck, known as the round-down, during landing. The plane somersaulted onto the flight deck and both crew members were killed. The pilot was Lieutenant Geoff Hamon from Merseyside. We were very friendly and had been playing bridge together immediately before his briefing and take-off. I flew off the deck two or three times a month but always during daylight. This was supposed to lead to bonding between me and the aircrew and to be good for their morale.

The Fairey Gannets and Douglas Skyraiders were relatively slow and tended to stay airborne for many hours while exercising their anti-submarine and early warning radar drills. The Hawker Seahawks, of which we sometimes had three squadrons, were single-seaters. So I flew in a two seater de Havilland Sea Venom night-fighter of 894 Squadron and, if possible, with my friend Lieutenant Neville Lockett. He was a Mancunian, the Air Weapons Instructor for the squadron and often referred to as "Wyatt Earp", who later became a Captain with Qantas and Singapore Air Lines. On one particular day, wearing an immersion suit that was commonly known as a "goon suit", I arrived at the briefing room only for Neville to tell me that he had been detailed off for a special task and that I had been switched to the Venom of another officer, with whom Neville and I had a less-than-perfect relationship. Neville told me that this

pilot might try and pull some kind of stunt to alarm me and to be prepared. Duly warned, I climbed into the observer's seat and, assisted
by a naval airman, connected up all my lines and hoses.

I experienced the usual acceleration forces on the catapult,
something like 5g for five seconds, and then we were off and airborne. We formed up on three other aircraft and headed off to blast
Fifla with rockets and bombs. This was a very small, uninhabited
island off the south coast of Malta that the Fleet Air Arm had been
using for target practice for many years. My pilot began jabbering on
the radio but, as usual, I found this practically impossible to understand. He then turned to me and on our own radio channel asked
"Did you get all that?" I hadn't but nodded my affirmation and we
then peeled off from the other aircraft and headed back to the ship.
I thought that my pilot was taking a big risk in doing this just to alarm
me but was happy in what I thought to be my understanding of the
position, as had been explained by Neville. As we passed over the
ship, I noticed that the fire crews were on deck, which I thought a little strange. We then made our approach, very high over the round-
down and with the pilot abruptly chopping power, we hit the deck
hard, bounced up and took off again with full power. There was more
radio chat after this and I was now becoming very concerned. We

Fig 12. The author, wearing an
inflateable "Mae West" flotation
device, being winched down to
the deck of a frigate from the
bread-run Westland Whirlwind
helicopter.

did another circuit and repeated the same manoeuvre; this time, after a short burst of radio talk, the pilot was obviously now happy. I distinctly heard the words "Three greens" as well as the answer from Flyco "Cleared to finals". We made a good landing and I climbed out of the Venom and changed in the pilot's room.

I met Neville, who was wearing a big grin, in the wardroom. Apparently, the Venom in which I had been flying had suffered partial hydraulic power failure soon after takeoff and the pilot had decided to abort his mission and return to the carrier; but he only had two green lights on his panel, for flaps and wheels, the third green for the tail hook being unlit. So he made two heavy landings, the second of which dislodged the hook giving him his third green and a means of arresting his aircraft on landing. If this procedure had failed, a nylon net would have had to be erected on the flight deck as a barrier to stop the plane, with unpredictable results. Neville told me that my pilot had admitted, somewhat reluctantly, that he been very impressed with my composure while he himself had been very worried. Of course, I had been blissfully unaware of the true state of affairs, hence my apparent sang froid.

Another task of mine was to make "house calls" on the frigates accompanying the carrier. The cruiser would have a medical officer but, if part of a task force, the smaller frigates would not. Frequently, my transport would form part of the "bread run" and I would accompany the chopper taking freshly baked bread from the carrier's ovens to the smaller ships that were with us. I would be winched down to a ship (Fig 12), after which my naval cap and medical bag would be delivered and I would see patients. This procedure was quite easy in a calm conditions but with any kind of a sea running, it could be tricky and demanded a good level of understanding between the chopper's winchman and myself, with precise timing being required as to when I should be released. However, I never had any injuries although I did experience a few hairy moments. I tried to arrange matters so that I arrived on board the ship near midday. Examining two or three seamen didn't take long and then I would invariably be asked to enjoy a drink in the wardroom, followed by lunch. I would then chat over coffee for a while before finally calling up the chopper for my ride back to the carrier. This made a most pleasant change to my routine. Neither my cabin mate nor the PMO seemed keen on doing this job and I was always delighted to oblige.

EIGHT

Mediterranean Delights

Eagle visited Gibraltar (Gib) quite frequently (Fig 13) squeezing its hugh bulk through the rather narrow entrance in the breakwater. Sometimes, depending on the weather conditions, prop-driven aircraft positioned in each corner of the flight deck would run their engines to assist in this "pin-wheel" manoeuvere. On these occasions, the aircrews would complain that they even had to assist the Fishheads with steering the ship! These visits invariably included in a "run ashore" in La Linea de la Concepción, a poor, dirty, and run-down town immediately across the border, full of tacky restaurants, bars and brothels. The Generalissimo claimed that British seamen were deflowering the women of Spain and I had to agree with Franco on this particular point. One of the more popular bars here was run by an ex-RN CPO who had deserted his ship, married a local woman and settled down to a life in La Linea. Senior naval officers, in particular, always seemed to call at this hostelry, many of them knowing the deserter from previous appointments. A standing joke was their customary invitation to him to come on across to Gib, visit their ship and meet up with old shipmates. Although the CPO and these officers were always very cordial to each other, had he accepted their invitation he would, of course, have been clapped in irons immediately he had set foot across the border in Gib.

Cheap drinks of all kinds were sold in La Linea and fundador brandy was very popular with the seamen. A particular variety was sold in bird-shaped bottles and was of poor quality. Commonly known as "gut rot", it would make a seaman wildly drunk after he had consumed a relatively small amount, with this invariably being added to much previously consumed beer. The drunk's friends would now have to get him past the Spanish police and custom officials at the border without him assaulting them; then there was a major problem on arriving back at their ship. If the Officer of the Watch saw what was coming, he would make himself scarce in the region of the other ranks brow. The supporting cast would appreciate this and try and get their drunken friend down to his mess deck

Fig 13. *HMS Eagle* about to enter Gibraltar harbour. The rather narrow entrance through the breakwater can clearly be seen. The flight deck appears neat and orderly, in marked contrast to its appearance during the launching and recovery of aircraft.

as quickly as possible. Insulting an officer was a serious offence and striking one would put the offender in major trouble.

I always found visits to Malta to be most enjoyable. At least a couple of RN ships were always in Grand Harbour at this time (Fig 14) and, with more in nearby Sliema creek, official parties could be regularly enjoyed. In fact, I met old friends from Trinco there,

Fig 14. Aerial view of Valetta, Malta, with Grand Harbour in the rear ground, where Castle St Angelo is to the right. *Eagle* and *Ark Royal* are seen together, occupying a large expanse of water.

Lieutenant Richard Thomas, the former flag lieutenant, and Dr Jack London. The Marza club, an RN stronghold, was in full song with much polo being played there; it also had a racecourse and wonderful dining and dancing. The many beaches were delightful and there were some excellent and relatively cheap restaurants. In addition, Peter Chapman, my submarine engineering friend from *Tally Ho* was now stationed in Malta, attached to *HMS Forth*, a submarine depot ship. He lived in a nice naval house in Sliema and I saw a lot of him and his wife Paddy. I also became re-acquainted with John Exworthy, Peter Darby and Dennis McCann, all of whom had been at school with me. Peter was an Oxford graduate and was teaching in the Dockyard Technical School while Dennis was a pilot in the RAF. John, a Liverpool University graduate, was an Instructor

Lieutenant on a cruiser. He took a permanent commission and became a Commander RN before leaving the Navy to run the Careers department of Southampton University. The George Cross Island had not yet been ruined by a plethora of new hotels and tourists and I was far from sharing the very pejorative opinion of Lord Byron that Malta was simply bells, yells and smells.

We now returned to Devonport for a couple of weeks over the Easter period and the Westland Wyverns of 813 Squadron were exchanged for the Westland Whirlwind choppers of the anti-submarine 820 Squadron. These were known as "dunking choppers" as they would frequently lower acoustic anti-submarine gear into the water while hovering above. During this period, the ship's rugby team made a successful tour in Cornwall. I played fullback for the team, which was quite strong. We had one English county player, a trio of Navy players and the inevitable half-dozen accomplished Welshmen. There were often problems, I found, in services rugby involving difficulties between officers and non-commissioned ranks after the game. This was not evident on this particular tour, even when playing at RNAS Culdrose.

After sailing from Guz, we proceeded to the Toulon area where the ship provided facilities for deck landing trials of the Breguet Alize and Fouga Zephyr aircraft of the French Navy, based at nearby Hyeres; this was because no French carrier was available at this time. Six days in Toulon followed, proving to be a wonderful experience. During this period, I visited the French Naval Hospital there, now the Saint-Anne Army Hospital. A friendly French physician who spoke good English showed me around in the late afternoon. My new friend, with a twinkle in his eye, then announced that he would like to show me somewhere else. I demurred, wishing to return to the ship, but he insisted, saying that this next visit would not take very long.

He took me into an anonymous-looking building nearby, passed a doorman whom he seemed to know, and into what appeared to be a luxurious cocktail bar with subdued lighting. It had a rather over-done opulent ambience, with velvet curtains, plush chairs and sofas and several impressive looking pictures and was half filled with men and women who were chatting and drinking. He called one of the ladies over and introduced me. She was attractive, well dressed, spoke excellent English and was apparently a graduate of the Sorbonne. She informed me that she had read English Literature there and, on learning that I was from the North West of England, began to ask me about the Lake poets. I managed to come out with some platitudes concerning Wordsworth but then ran out of information. Both my friend and this lady appeared to be enjoying some huge joke, which I suspected might be at my expense. After chatting rather desultorily, I announced that I really must go and I bid Mademoiselle goodbye. My friend accompanied me to the door, enquired if I knew how to get back to my ship and then abruptly asked if I had any idea of where I had just been. I answered, of course, that I had not and, bursting with laughter at the naive "rosbif", told me that I had been in a bordello! I have no idea if this was officially run by the French Navy or if their physicians simply checked up on the madames. Official brothels were run by the French Navy for many years until the Marthe Richard law of the late 1950s put an end to them, shortly after my visit.

An official cocktail party held on the flight deck was a great success. Two guests were invited for each officer; as we had almost 300 officers on board, over 150 belonging to the squadrons, this meant about 900 people were present. Only three drinks were served, dry sherry, gin and tonic and a sidecar, this being a mixture of whisky and cointreau, and soft drinks were also available. The alcoholic drinks were served from large jugs by stewards, who circled around constantly refilling glasses, making it very difficult to estimate how much one had actually consumed.

Towards the end of the evening, a space was cleared aft of the flight deck and all lights were extinguished. After a suitable dramatic pause, a single spotlight picked out the Marine Drum Major, with the remainder of the band being eventually illuminated, who then "beat retreat". The evening always concluded with the band playing the hymn *Abide with Me* and this polished and highly professional performance never failed to impress the visitors and, indeed, the ship's officers. Experienced officer partygoers on board, of whom there were many, eschewed any flippant social chit-chat and certainly would not waste time entertaining an attractive woman who was alone. They would pick out a married couple of obvious station and concentrate all their efforts for the entire evening on them. This was known in the Navy as "baron strangling" and would lead, it was hoped, to dinner afterwards and to further social engagements during the ship's stay. Of course, if the couple had a charming daughter or some other nice female with them, this would be a bonus.

Most of the ship's rugby was played in Malta but we played the full might of the French Navy in Toulon and the game was broadcast on TV as part of an experimental Euro link-up. As the *Eagle* team had been at sea for several weeks, we were far from being match fit and had played little serious rugby for some time. Our opponents included a host of very good players and we were outclassed as regards ability, experience and, of course, fitness. We lost by a considerable margin but put nearly 20 points on the board ourselves and were far from disgraced. After the game, I was informed that the great Puig-Aubert had been playing opposite me at fullback. I have no idea if this was true or not and, despite contacting the French Navy, was unable definitely to clear up this point, but the rest of the *Eagle* team sincerely believed that he had played. However, I was very relieved not to have known about his possible participation until the game was over. Certainly, the opposing fullback had oozed class and talent and his kicking had been outstanding, but he had played, on the whole, a quiet game. Puig-Aubert is considered by many to have been the greatest RL player ever produced by France. A native of Carcassonne, where he is venerated and where an imposing statue of him was unveiled in the year 2000, his kicking and attacking game were said to be tremendous although his defence was thought to have been considerably less impressive.

After several weeks of intense flying activity, *Eagle* now visited Barcelona to bolster the British presence at a large trade fair. Our jets performed aerobatics before our arrival in the skies above the city and the Marine band played daily in the principal square. Of course, there was another large cocktail party, for which the British Ambassador came across from Madrid. Because of its size, *Eagle* could not come alongside any jetty and moored out in the distant harbour. Three MFVs commanded by midshipmen had therefore sailed over from Malta ahead of us to land and return the sailors going on shore leave. A most unfortunate accident involved one of these, with a rating falling between the carrier and the MFV as he was boarding the latter. The two ships came together in the swell and the poor man was horribly squeezed between them. With some difficulty, he was brought to the flight deck in great agony and I gave him an injection of morphia; there was little else I could do. He clearly needed the services of a thoracic surgeon, so he was quickly flown by one of the ship's flight choppers to a park ashore, near a hospital that was expecting him. He there underwent a thoracotomy and made an uncomplicated recovery although he did not, of course, sail with the carrier.

Barcelona proved to be a wonderful place for a run ashore and *Eagle's* complement all enjoyed themselves. During our stay, a big corrida was held and many sailors and officers attended. FOAC and the Captain of *Eagle* were guests-of-honour and the leading matador dedicated one of the bulls to the Admiral. The seamen, punning on the word "bull", thought that this was most appropriate and wildly funny, clapping and shouting vigourously, to the confusion of the crowd.

On one of the six nights that we spent in Barcelona, it was my turn to be duty medical officer. Only a handful of officers were on board, the rest disporting themselves in the Catalan capital. One of the duty seaman on the aft brow, where all visitors had to pass, presented himself at the wardroom and asked me to help him with a problem. It appeared that a distinguished-looking British civilian had arrived and asked to see the Admiral. I suggested that the officer-of-the-watch should deal with this problem but was told that there had been some semi-emergency in the junior seamen's mess and he was not currently available. I thought that, in the circumstances, I should try and deal with the matter and went up to the brow. I explained to the visitor that FOAC was not on board and that I had no idea what time he might return. I then realised suddenly to whom I was talking and asked him if he would like to join me for a drink, while I tried to get more information. His face lit up and I led him to the wardroom. My guest was none other than the very celebrated star of cabaret, stage and screen, the great Noel Coward. After a few drinks, having been joined by half a dozen other duty officers, I had the temerity to ask if he would give us a few songs. To my delight, he readily assented and we grouped ourselves around the battered old piano in a corner. He asked us to request our favourite numbers associated with him. Fortunately, I had several of his records and after coming out with *A Bar On The Picolo Marina* and *Matelot*, I was able to whisper *Mad Dogs And Englishmen, Poor*

Little Rich Girl and several others to the company. He went through quite a long selection of his more popular items, lasting for nearly an hour, and then suddenly announced that he must leave. I asked for his address to give to the Admiral but was told that he was moving on the following day and simply to give him Coward's best wishes.

During our next visit to Malta in 1958, with the ship moored in the middle of Grand Harbour, a Fairy Gannet of 814 Squadron made Fleet Air Arm history by taking off with the ship at anchor, straight down the deck. There was a strong sirocco wind blowing hard all the way out of the depths of the Sahara at the time. Soon after this, an Italian Naval Squadron called at the George Cross island, this being their first official call since the end of World War Two. An informal lunchtime drinks party was held for the visiting officers and I had the pleasure of entertaining two Italian naval doctors, both fluent in English. They came to notice the ship's battle honours, picked out in large brass letters on a bulkhead at the for'ard end of the quarter-deck, and one commented that his brother had been killed during the Fleet Air Arm's hugely successful attack on Taranto in November 1940. I was able to bang on about Barfleur 1692 and Trincomalee 1782 and move my meredional guests on before they noticed Calabria 1940 and Malta Convoys 1942 among the honours.

The political situation in the Near East became very tense in the summer of 1958. The King of Jordan was assassinated and his son, the great anglophile Hussein, ascended the throne. Mr Mossadegh nationalised the Anglo-Iranian oil company and there was a revolution in the Lebanon. With the Middle East in a ferment, three US carriers were based in the eastern Mediterranean, together with *Ark Royal* and *Eagle*. After several weeks, the *Ark* left to escort a replica of the *Mayflower* from Plymouth into Boston harbour. There was no great love lost between these ships and "Don't nark the Ark" was a familiar refrain, with the crew of *Eagle* believing, not without justification, that the *Ark* always enjoyed the better assignments, as with her trip to Boston, while *Eagle* always seemed to come in for the dirty work, as at Suez and the present situation.

With *Eagle* wearing FOAC's flag and both ship's companies assembled on the flight decks, the *Ark* saluted as she steamed past the flagship and her crew gave three cheers, with caps removed. The Commander of *Eagle* now called for "three cheers for *Ark Royal*" but the effort was very weak. I heard distinctly a sailor near me say "it's all right for those so-and-sos, they're going home and then on for a bit of fun in the States". The Commander, sounding rather embarrassed, called again for another three cheers, adding that we should let the *Ark* really hear us. I thought for a moment that he might add "let bygones be bygones". There was scant improvement this second time and the two ships separated rapidly.

This now left *Eagle*, with her cruiser and frigates, as the sole British carrier on station. One of the three US ships was detached in turn for a week, to such places as the Greek Islands, Naples and Capri, etc but poor *Eagle* had to remain in place. Occasionally, our squadrons would play games with aircraft from RAF Akroteri in Cyprus and their facilities were useful for repairs and servicing our aircraft. Sometimes the ship would stop and, with boats out in case of any emergency, swimming was allowed for 30 minutes. I had been warned about this and did not participate. There were always oily residues surrounding the ship and, worse, enterprising engineers would seize this opportunity to empty certain tanks. However, we would regularly get a treat, of sorts. Cyprus was under a state of emergency at this time and EOKA terrorists were very active. Our marines would go ashore most weekends, ring a beach and guard it with semi-automatic weapons. Some 1500 men from the carrier would then be landed and swim off the beach for an hour or so. I suppose this was better than nothing but it did not constitute my idea of a grand old time.

After being continuously at sea for nine weeks or more, we began to run out of certain items and fresh water rationing came into being. Although there was no shortage of alcoholic drinks on the mess decks or in the wardroom, showering in salt water was not very enjoyable and we began to feel sorry for ourselves. A "sod's opera" was performed on the flight deck to cheer-up the ship's company. The two chaplains, wearing striped shirts and black berets, put on a great act as a couple of Parisian apaches and one of the squadron CPOs was wonderfully amusing as a birdwatcher, with recorded calls. These included the wren, "If you touch me there again, I'll scream", the Devonshire grouse, "This so-and-so ship is getting me down" and the voice of the *Eagle*, "All shore leave is cancelled". The entertainment was first-class and I was intrigued by the ingenuity and skill of the arrangers and artists.

Having signed up for drinks and luncheon with the Royal

Enniskillen Dragoon Guards, I was one of about 30 officers who went ashore in Cyprus one Sunday morning. After disembarking from the ship's launches, we were met by the Dragoon's land rovers and driven inland a few miles to their camp. To our surprise, the whole battalion was living under canvas. We had warm drinks, served under the hot sun with myriads of flies swarming about, and then went into a tent for what was a somewhat less-than-magnificent lunch. The occasion was saved by the anxiety of the Enniskillen officers who, possibly aware of the deficiencies in their food and drink, could not have been more welcoming or hospitable. This visit put an abrupt end to any whinging or complaining about our lot. A week later, two dozen of their officers came on board *Eagle* for return drinks and lunch. They marvelled at our seemingly inexhaustible supply of all manner of drinks, at our superb food and especially at the wardroom's air-conditioning.

With the carrier a few miles outside Israeli territorial waters, our fighters now gave top cover for RAF troop-carrying aircraft who landed soldiers in Jordan, this being too far for the RAF fighters to make it there and back from Cyprus. Talk of evacuating British citizens in Lebanon was now in the air and it was proposed to land a force of marines and seamen from *Eagle* to assist in this. A medical officer was needed to go along and I was selected. I didn't particularly object but thought it might have been fairer and more equitable if my cabin mate and I had drawn lots for the privilege. Friends on board suggested that I had brought this doubtful honour on myself by my exploits with the ship's choppers when being winched down, on a regular basis, to frigates but I couldn't see this myself. However, this landing never came off and I remained on the ship.

One morning, two ratings complained of lower limb weakness after a flu-like illness. One developed some breathing difficulty and I suspected that both might be suffering from polio; I certainly could not exclude the possibility. We got in touch with the British Military Hospital (BMH) at Nicosia and the patients, some of our marines and I were landed by our choppers. The Army provided two Land Rovers and an ambulance, as well as drivers. We were all set to drive off when an Army officer called us back and insisted that I carry a revolver. I talked about the Geneva Convention but to no avail. The Officer Commanding Middle East had issued instructions that all officers in Cyprus must wear a sidearm. So I reluctantly donned one and off we went, myself with the patients in the back of the ambulance, which had large red crosses on its sides, with vehicles ahead and behind containing marines with automatic weapons. After a couple of miles, I heard some loud bangs but thought nothing of it. They recurred a few minutes later, when the soldier driving the ambulance yelled that I should lie flat. I had no idea what was going on and, after five minutes or so, the driver signalled that I could get up. I learned later that the ambulance had twice come under fire, presumably from EOKA guerrillas. So much for the protection offered by the Red Cross! We delivered our patients to BMH where I was delighted to see one of the ship's choppers nearby. It had taken one of FOAC's staff officers to Nicosia and was about to return to the ship. After giving up my revolver, I eagerly jumped in and thereby avoided a return trip in the Land Rovers.

All too quickly, my time in *Eagle* was coming to an end. My relief was announced and I was due to fly home from Malta. I had now arranged a round-the-world trip as a medical officer on the Shaw Savill liner *Southern Cross*, sailing in mid-December, 1958. I paid a quick visit to RNAS Hal Far, the Fleet Air Arm airfield in the south of Malta, making my goodbyes to old friends there. Also, I succeeded in exchanging 200 pounds sterling for the equivalent amount of dollars, which I thought might be useful during my world cruise. This was accomplished with the help of a US officer whom I met in the wardroom. He was a pilot of one of the large Orion four-engined, anti-submarine radar planes of the US Navy, then stationed at Hal Far. A considerable source of concern for me now was whether I could get out of the Navy in time for my ship's departure from Southampton and if my trunk, full of uniforms and other gear, would catch up with me.

FOAC had been consulting me quite regularly for a series of minor complaints. He was a complete gentleman and early one evening, after apologising profusely for troubling me at this time, asked me to stay on in his quarters for a drink. Medical officers were on call 24 hours a day and his apology was quite unnecessary but was typical of the man, a Vice Admiral. We chatted for some time during which he expressed his gratitude for my ministrations. He then went on to add that if he could ever do anything to help me, I should immediately let him know. I took a deep breath and told him about my predicament concerning my baggage and my concern about my actual release date. He was very interested and said that he could promise nothing but would consider it and get back to me. I though that was the end of that. Being summoned to his quarters again a few days later, I learned that this was not to be a medical consultation but for important news. He told me that the Fourth Destroyer Squadron, composed of *Battle* class ships, was returning home from the Far East and, if I was interested, he could fix me up with a berth. Captains were always pleased to have a medical officer on board, he said. He added that this would mean all my gear going with me and also another visit to Barcelona! Regarding my other problem, he told me that this was more tricky but that he was still working on it. I jumped at this wonderful offer, of course, and was delighted.

Dennis, a Lieutenant on the Admiral's staff with whom I often went ashore, was furious with the Admiral's intervention and my good fortune and banged on at length about me using the Navy for a good time and being too lucky by half. Dennis knew all about my change of orders as he himself had been ordered to expedite matters. He had cooled down on the following day and we remained good friends.

Just before leaving the carrier in October 1958, I was presented with my S206 flimsy, which had been written by the PMO and countersigned, together with several glowing compliments, by the ship's Captain. Like FOAC, the Captain had been a patient of mine and knew me well. I was informed that I had done very well in all areas and I was encouraged to think seriously about accepting a permanent commission. Of course, I had absolutely no intention of doing this.

I was given vin d'honneur in the wardroom one lunchtime and then the day of my departure arrived. My time in *Eagle* had been often hectic but it had all been wonderfully enjoyable and I wouldn't have missed it for the world. All my baggage had been sent over to *HMS Barrosa*, the particular Battle class destroyer in which I was taking passage home, named after Sir Thomas Graham's great victory of 1811 in the Peninsula war. I left *Eagle* for the last time in the captain's barge and a Vauxhall naval car took me to Sliema, regarded by many as the Southsea of Malta.

NINE

More sailing, Melbourne

Barrosa slipped her moorings soon after I had boarded and headed north up the east coast of the island, past St Paul's Bay and into the South Comino channel where the squadron did a practice shoot immediately north of Malta. With this completed, we steamed off westward. The ship's stewards were helpful Maltese and the wardroom, very small compared with *Eagle's*, had a nice *Bar Rosa* sign elegantly painted in gilt characters on the dark wood behind the bar (Fig 15).

Fig 15.   The somewhat small, but elegant and cosy, wardroom bar of *HMS Barrosa*. The name of the bar is evident above the spirit measures.

The ship's Captain, a commander, was a younger son of the nobility and I found him to be sociable and charming. I played bridge in his quarters on several nights after dinner and he was a most generous host. Another most enjoyable six days in Barcelona, the beautiful city that I now knew quite well, followed. On our first full day there, I captained a rugby team drawn from the four destroyers against a Barcelona team. We led by 18 points at half time but our lack of fitness was acutely demonstrated in the second half and we lost the game by 5 points. On my last night in Barcelona, I was returning to the ship with some new friends when we heard some lovely singing and saw a crowd around a bar up ahead. We soon recognised the tune and words of an old, traditional British sailor's drinking song and as we grew nearer, I realised that, to my considerable surprise, the singing was coming from a dozen or more of Barossa's seamen. They were sitting outside a tavern, singing a most appropriate shanty, the first verse of which was

> *Farewell and Adieu to you, gay Spanish ladies*
> *Farewell and Adieu to you, ladies of Spain*
> *For we've received orders to sail for Old England*
> *But we hope in short time to see you again*

At the completion of this number, they were given a huge hand by the surrounding Catalans. My companions and I thought that this song would have been much more likely to have come from Dartmouth cadets or midshipmen. In fact, we were amazed that the sailors even knew the shanty, thinking that it was far more likely that they would sing the latest pop numbers. This same song was featured, many years later, in the movie *Master and Commander*. I thought of this incident when reading of trouble that English soccer fans had created in mainland Europe.

A few days later, we were in Gib. The Captain turned out for the ship in a hockey match there, after which the wardroom put on their last party of the ship's commission. I was informed that I could ask a couple of guests and I decided, after some thought, to ask two Christian Brothers whom I had known in the past and who were currently teaching in their school on the Rock. As is usual in RN ships, the Captain was not a member of the wardroom but on this occasion he received the guests there. I met my guests at the head of the brow and escorted them for an introduction to the Captain. I thought a brief spasm of annoyance crossed his face when he saw my guests in clerical garb, perhaps because he did not think men of religion, often called "sky pilots" in the Navy, would contribute to the gaiety of the occasion. However, being a complete gentleman, he made them welcome, saying that they didn't have too many priests as visitors. I quickly pointed out that they were not, in fact, priests but lay brothers of a religious order, and we moved on to make way for other arriving guests. The Captain later came over and spoke to us and I was quite sure that this was in the nature of a "duty visit". The conversation was originally about Gibraltar and the two Brothers brought him up to date with various developments. Then the subject turned to Sport, about which the visitors were very well informed. Having been in the Far East for more than two years, the Captain was not altogether cognisant about what had been happening in the world of rugby and the conversation waxed on famously. Then the First Lieutenant came up and whispered in the Captain's ear. He clearly had to go and speak to some VIP who had just arrived but promised to return to us very soon.

In fact, he was not able to do so but we chatted merrily with many of the ship's officers. After a most enjoyable evening, my guests thought that they should leave. However, the Captain spotted us as we were making our way aloft and rushed over. "Surely you're not going now, are you?" he demanded. They replied that the party seemed to be breaking up and that, in fact, they were leaving. They were implored to remain and to give him ten minutes to say farewell to his guests. So we returned to the wardroom, where he soon joined us, only to insist that we accompany him in his day cabin. He was eager to have further sporting news and rang for his steward to produce more drinks. I could have done without any more alcohol and craved a reasonably early night; but it was not to be as the conversation was now about cricket! Finally, close to midnight, our host reluctantly admitted that we should call it a day, after thanking me for bringing such interesting guests along.

He accompanied us to the upper deck and then a thought seemed to strike him. "How are you getting home?" he asked the Brothers. They told him that they would easily grab a taxi at the dockyard gate. "Nonsense", replied the Captain, "our Land Rover will take you". Now this had been secured prior to our sailing, so the duty driver had to be roused from his bunk and the First Lieutenant instructed to winch the vehicle ashore. Neither of these gentlemen appeared too pleased and the guests were clearly embarrassed. The Captain, however, was quite unperturbed and never stopped talking about Sport. So off went the Land Rover, with the First

Lieutenant and a couple of sailors forced to remain on deck to secure it on its return.

The next morning, I felt tired, jaded and slightly hung over. I met the Captain, who thanked me again for the pleasure of meeting my friends and invited me to join him on the bridge as we left harbour. He seemed to be in the pink and in great form. He was, for most of the time, leaning over one wing of the bridge, smoking a cigarette through a long holder and issuing seemingly off-hand orders to the helmsman, such as "Left a bit, midships, now right hand down a little". As we approached the breakwater, I saw a big ship about to enter the harbour. This was *HMCS Bonaventure*, a Canadian aircraft carrier, not nearly as large as *Eagle* but much bigger than *Barossa*. A strong sea was running in the straits and there was a fierce and gusty wind. The carrier's bulk shielded us from the wind for some time, then we were exposed to it again very suddenly as she cleared us by what appeared to be only a few yards. Then we were out into the straits of Gibraltar proper, turning west for home. One of the ship's executive officers, who had also been on the bridge during the leaving of the harbour, later told me that the whole business of passing *Bonaventure* in wind and sea, close to the breakwater, had been very tricky and that he himself would not have cared to do it. He was full of admiration for the nonchalant skill of the Captain.

We were now heading for Pompey. Whether by accident or design, the squadron arrived off Cape Trafalgar on October 21st, the glorious anniversary of Nelson's great victory in 1805, and the four ships formed a square. A chaplain read some prayers, a wreath was laid on the water and we were off again. It all seemed very rushed to me, even indecently so, but I was informed that the weather was deteriorating rapidly in the Bay of Biscay and, with a firm arrival time and date to keep at Pompey, we had to get a move on.

The weather forecast was remarkably accurate on this occasion. The wind freshened and we were soon in rough waters as we headed north. Along with three other officers, I was living back aft in the ship, most of the officers living further for'ard near the wardroom. The First Lieutenant warned we four that the upper deck would be placed out of bounds at nightfall, and probably for a good part of the next day, making it impossible to travel between our cabins and the wardroom. Hastily, we had a few drinks when the wardroom bar opened, then made our way cautiously aft, where sandwiches and cordial awaited us. I was always a good sailor and did not suffer from mal de mer. I was fatigued and slept soundly for 11 hours. The others were not so fortunate, two being very sick. On waking up, I phoned the bridge and was told that the deck was still closed. The weather soon moderated a little and we were able to rejoin our fellows about lunchtime. I was ravenous by then but a hearty appetite was rare at that meal. We arrived only an hour or so late at Pompey and the ships, after being more than two years away from their home port, came alongside to cheering families. I had only been part of this squadron for a couple of weeks but had been treated extremely well and felt most fortunate to have made the passage home with them.

After a few weeks leave, I returned to Pompey in mid-November for what was basically a few weeks of general practice, looking after wrens and naval families. I was then notified that my official date of release would be at the end of December but that, in effect, I could leave on December 2nd. This would enable me to join the Southern Cross at nearby Southampton in time for its sailing ten days later. So FOAC had come through for me again in a big way. Now it was time to leave the Navy, I realised what a marvellous three years and a few months I had enjoyed in the service. However, it was the end of a chapter in my life and time to move on.

I was home again for a few days during which time I had to get my RN uniform suits changed, with Shaw Savill buttons and straight gold stripes without any curl. Then down to my new ship at Southampton in mid-December 1958, exchanging the Grey Funnel Line for the Merchant Service, the white ensign for the red duster. I joined the day before sailing and went that night with most of the ship's officers to a pub on the Beaulieu River, where I was introduced to my new shipmates and enjoyed a pleasant evening. I had a senior colleague and there were two nurses, both trained in London teaching hospitals, to assist us.

The *Southern Cross* (Fig 16) had been built by Harland and Wolff at Belfast and launched by HM Queen Elizabeth II in 1954, this being the first merchant ship ever launched by a reigning monarch. She was of 20,000 tons and carried 1160 one-class passengers. However, accommodation varied from elegant suites on the promenade deck, complete with bathrooms and day cabins, to more cramped six-to-a-cabin accomodation on "B" deck, in the bowels of

Fig 16. The *Southern Cross*, about to pass under the Sydney Harbour bridge. (Printed with permission of the Furness Group).

the ship. Although perhaps somewhat behind P & O in the social stakes, Shaw Savill at this time was a very prestigious company, especially in Australasia. The young Queen Elizabeth and Prince Phillip had made a long and highly successful tour of both Australia and New Zealand in 1953-54 aboard the Shaw Savill ship *Gothic*, accompanied by the band of the Royal Marines, Portsmouth, and this had really put the company in the news. I soon discovered that the ship was loaded with Australasians, mainly females, returning "Down Under" after they had "been home". I very much doubt if this concept of "going home", implying a trip to the UK, is still in vogue today among Australasians and those that do choose to visit would now fly. A few passengers used the ship virtually for a cruise, either flying home from a point of interest or, less commonly, travelling with us around the world.

After some rough weather in the Atlantic, a very nice Englishman suffered a mild heart attack. I wanted to land him at Trinidad but he pleaded with me to let him stay on board. He had one of the most comfortable suites on the ship and was doing well clinically, so I agreed to this, after he had promised to obey my orders strictly and without question. In Port of Spain, Trinidad, the ship's officers had a permanent membership of a country club. I went there with the nurses and a few others for a swim, after which we reclined in the sun and enjoyed cool drinks. I got into conversation with a barman and the conversation turned to cricket. Sir Leary Constantine was pointed out to me, sitting in the shade and apparently asleep. The barman urged me to approach him and introduce myself. I was loathe to do this but as the great man arose and walked passed us, the barman called out to him and told him who I was. So Sir Leary and I moved away to sit down on deck chairs and enjoy a lengthy chat. Constantine had been, of course, an outstanding cricketing all-rounder for the West Indies, after which he had played for Nelson in the Lancashire League and then for Bootle in the Liverpool and District league during World War Two when well past his prime. He asked me about many Merseyside cricketers, few of whom I had even heard of, which was very embarrassing. He struck me as being a very unassuming and friendly man.

Curacao was our next stopover, at that time comparatively unspoilt and a genuine small piece of transplanted Holland. Then I was fascinated by the engineering marvel that was the Panama Canal and wondered about the thousands who had died, mainly of yellow fever, during its construction. After a few hours at Panama City on Christmas Eve, we celebrated Christmas at sea. A long stretch of the Pacific now followed until we reached Tahiti, a most colourful stop. This became a popular tourist destination in later years but few ships called there in the late 1950s and I was told that several crew members signed on specifically for the brief four-a-year visits here. Then south to Fiji where I was entertained by Dr Tony Eslick from the year ahead of me at medical school, who was now working for the Southern Pacific Health Service. Wellington, New Zealand's Windy City, soon followed and then through the Cook Strait to Sydney and its impressive harbour.

Edgar Knight, the former Liverpool University rugby player whose mother was Australian, had migrated to that city with his family after his father's retirement and had been very unfortunate not to win a place on the Wallaby team. I had known his sister Valerie when she attended the Liverpool Art School and she and her husband, together with Edgar, met me at the ship and showed me many of the tourist sights during our three whirlwind days there. Then came beautiful Melbourne, after which we crossed the Bight to Fremantle and Perth.

While at Perth, I watched South Australia playing West Australia at cricket at the latter's lovely ground by the Swan River, with a trotting track adjacent. This was on January 26th, Australia Day and a very big national holiday. The game was entertaining, in front of a large crowd. The Sheffield Shield, later to be called the Pura Milk Cup, had been won by Western Australia in the 1947-48 season, somewhat surprisingly as this was their first year in this competition. However, they were still relatively new to this form of cricket and were finding the eastern states a real handful. Graham McKenzie, that superb Aussie bowler of the 1960s, had not yet made his debut and the England test cricketers, Tony Lock and Colin Milburn, were still to join the team. Ian Meckiff was a leading Australian bowler of the time although his action was thought by many to be highly suspect. Playing in this game for South Australia, he was at one stage fielding deep on the boundary. He made a smart pick-up and return, sending the ball very quickly into the wicket keeper's gloves. There was polite applause for this, interrupted by a loud shout from a man near me of "well bowled, Meckiff", followed by roars of approval from the home crowd.

A few days rest crossing the Indian Ocean was most welcome before visits to Durban and Cape Town. I had been to the latter city before, en route home from Ceylon, but again enjoyed its wonderfully scenic environs. Then came the long haul up the West coast of Africa to Las Palmas and home. What a fantastic voyage, the trip of a lifetime! Around the world in 88 days, at 18 knots.

Meanwhile, the heart attack victim turned out to be a high-ranking mason, my second close encounter with the craft, and a succession of masonic brothers visited him at each port of call. Originally, he had strict bed rest and I made a point of asking his visitors to leave after a short period. After a couple of weeks, we began gradual ambulation and I relaxed my social strictures. He did very well overall and made an uncomplicated recovery although, of course, I strongly recommended that he consult a cardiologist on arriving home. Just after leaving the Cape, he told me how grateful he was at not being put ashore and how he firmly believed that his stay in the ship had been better treatment for him than any hospital. He then said that he wanted to repay me and he knew no better way of doing this than to arrange admission for me to his lodge. Clearly, he meant this as a sincere and considerable compliment but I did not wish to take him up on his offer. I had to explain, politely but firmly, that I had no desire to become a freemason. He found this very hard to swallow but reluctantly accepted it, asking me what I would like instead. A highly successful businessman, he lived in a large house and spread in Hertfordshire where he was a near neighbour of Lord Salisbury, the then current Leader of the Tories in the Lords and Chancellor of the University of Liverpool, who had presented me with my degrees in 1954. My patient was a real entrepreneur, being involved in many different ventures, one of which was a theatrical ticket agency in London. The musical *My Fair Lady* had just opened in the West End and tickets were extremely difficult to obtain, so I asked him for two front stall seats, thinking that these would be impossible to procure and the matter would be closed. However, my patient's daughter met her parents at Southampton and I was introduced. She thanked me profusely for looking after her dad and handed me an envelope. I stuffed it in my pocket and went off to clear customs. Waiting for the London train with one of the ship's nurses, I came across the envelope and opened it. There were tickets for two excellent seats for the outstanding musical that I had nominated and the nurse and I hugely enjoyed the show a couple of weeks later.

In 1970, air transport was forcing shipping economies and Shaw Savill discontinued round-the-world services from Southampton. After seven cruises out of Liverpool were undertaken, Shaw Savill withdrew the *Southern Cross* from service in 1971. After being laid up for some time, she was sold in 1973 and then several more times. She was finally renamed *Ocean Breeze*, a name under which she continued sailing for the Imperial Majesty Cruise lines. Approaching her half century, and after several refits, she still cruised out of Port Everglades, Florida, well into the twenty first century before sailing off to the breakers yard in Bangladesh at the end of 2003.

I had been thinking, on and off, as to what I was going to do with the rest of my life. I thought some time as a medical registrar was the best bet until I had definitely decided on my future plans.

However, although conscious of having spent nearly four years in a non-hospital setting since my house jobs, I still hankered for one more period of employment overseas before settling down. I had been very impressed with Australia and with the many Aussies I had met so I contacted Shaw Savill again and enquired about travelling one-way to Australia. I was told that I was in luck and could sail on a small cargo ship, leaving London in about three weeks and sailing non-stop to Melbourne. With a crew of less than 50, a medical officer was not legally required but Shaw Savill would always give one a trip. They were obliged to pay him and I was going to receive exactly one English shilling for my three weeks aboard. Mother was, of course, aghast at this but I promised to be back in about six months. I had no job arranged in Melbourne but I had friends there and was confident of finding employment.

I joined the *Alaric* in the early Spring of 1959 in the London docks. I had a few drinks ashore that evening with the Mate, who filled me in on the ship and our trip. Built in Hamburg less than two years earlier, serious problems had developed with the engines and an extra Chief Engineer had come on board "just in case". We sailed about noon on Sunday and, after clearing the Thames estuary, I had my first patient. One of the ship's company, who looked at least 70 years old but assured me that he was much younger, had acute retention of urine. This was a surgical emergency and I hurtled up to the bridge to try and get him ashore on the pilot boat but was told that it had just left! I was very annoyed and asked my patient why he had falsified his age at signing on and why he hadn't sought medical help earlier, receiving no real answer. I was very concerned about how I was going to manage him and began with a hot bath and an injection of morphia, which had no effect. With great reluctance, I now had to pass a catheter into his bladder to relieve his distress. The catheters available were old, made of rubber and very large. Leaving them in place for too long would seriously risk infection, but I had little choice. I started the patient on antibiotics and removed the catheter after a couple of days. The man was still unable to urinate and I had to replace it with a new catheter.

I wondered about putting him ashore at first Gibraltar and then at Malta. The Captain was a real Job's comforter now. He had sailed during World War Two as an RNR officer and gave every indication of not having been appreciated as much as he had anticipated; in fact, he clearly had no great love for the Senior Service, with which he seemed to closely associate me. Of course the patient could be landed, he said, but I should realise that it would cost the company thousands of pounds in tug and docking fees. I decided to press on as best I could and wondered if I might place a supra-pubic catheter, going directly into the bladder from the exterior, without traversing the urethra. This would have eliminated many of the problems posed by the continued presence of the large catheter, but unfortunately, I was entirely lacking in the instrumentation needed to perform this procedure, which I had never carried out previously.

Port Said was the next possible port-of-call but the Captain forcibly indicated that he could not contemplate landing my patient there, after the damage the Navy had inflicted on the town a few years earlier! We passed through the Suez Canal and I was most relieved when we reached Aden and I was able to take the patient, who was in good condition, ashore to the RAF hospital there. Ironically, apart from a few patients with flu, this case causing me considerable anxiety was virtually the only medical problem I had to deal with while on board.

A few days out from Aden, with Melbourne still 11 days away, the ship's engines had to be stopped for recurring problems. The engineers, including the extra Chief, worked on them for 48 hours while the ship drifted in the Indian Ocean. Repairs were finally completed and we eventually arrived at Port Melbourne and sailed up theYarra River to the city. Being more than two days late, I was keen to be on my way but had to accompany the captain to the shipping office to be "signed off" in approved fashion and to receive my 12 pence wages.

As anticipated, I had no difficulty in securing employment and worked for the Victorian State Railways for a few days, doing routine medical examinations. Soon after this, I joined a family practice in the suburb of Moonee Ponds, close to the home of Dame Edna Everage. Her creator, Barry Humphries, had lived as a boy in the more up-market suburb of Camberwell but had placed his fictitious Dame Edna in Mooney Ponds because the name amused him and also because it was a rather "everage", the Aussie pronunciation of "average", suburb. I lived with the principal partner and his family and enjoyed the work, although it was quite onerous. I would spend more than an hour doing house calls before breakfast each day, an exercise that was quite new to me and not entirely enjoyable, and then take morning surgery and complete the patient visits. I might have a few hours off after lunch before evening surgery. The practice schedule was complicated by the fact that the senior partner, who had acquired much surgical experience in World War Two, worked at several hospitals as a general surgeon, where he was much respected. He asked me if I would like to act as anaesthetist for him, an offer that I speedily declined; but I did take care of pre-natal examinations and normal deliveries of our patients at a large down-town maternity hospital belonging to a teaching hospitals group. I found this system intriguing and very different to the British setup. It has now changed completely, with family practitioners no longer working as part-time specialists.

One of my first patients, seen at the evening clinic, was an elderly, charming and highly intelligent academic. He told me that he had contacted Hard Pad a few years earlier and now had a recur-rence. This startled me as I thought this disease only occurred in dogs. No, the patient assured me, the Australian variety involved humans also. I could see little amiss with the patient's skin, admitted that I knew absolutely nothing about this disease, promised to find out and asked him to return in a couple of days. At dinner that night, I asked my principal about it. "You must have seen Dr Smith", he replied. "Just carry on with his psychiatric drugs which you will find detailed in his notes". Dr Smith was well known in our practice, and in others, as a relatively harmless and mild psychotic.

There was a ridgid ban on buying drinks after 6.00 pm in operation in Victoria at this time although alcohol could be served with meals in most restaurants. This meant that workers emerging from offices and factories at about 5.00 pm would endeavour to sink as many drinks as possible in the remaining 60 minutes. Beer appeared to be the most popular drink by far, especially in the hot summers, and this was squirted from a nozzle into glasses that had been kept in a fridge. The resulting drink was thus ice cold and lack-ing in any taste. This "six o'clock swill" as it was called had little if any beneficial social result. On the contrary, many would be thoroughly intoxicated after an hour's hard drinking and it was abolished in the mid-1960s.

Anne, a friend from the *Southern Cross*, was very helpful in my early days in Melbourne. She showed me around the town and gave assistance in many ways. A graduate in Physical Education from the University of Melbourne, she was herself no mean athlete. She had held both the Melbourne and Australian Universities Women's long jump titles, as well as running in sprint relays, and had competed for Australian Universities. Anne introduced me to the great Austrian coach, Franz Stampfl, at the university track. Having left England where he had coached many successful athletes, including Thelma Hopkins, Roger Bannister, Chris Chataway and Chris Brasher, Stampfl was now the University of Melbourne coach but also helped many other athletes. These included Merv Lincoln, the outstanding multi-world record holder Ron Clarke and, somewhat later, Ralph Doubell, the gold medallist in the 800 metres at the Mexico City Olympics in 1968. When my schedule permitted, I would occasionally get in some jogging on this track and see Stampfl in action. His technical knowledge was more than confirmed and his enthusiasm most obvious.

By sheer chance, I discovered that the UK Trade Commissioner for Victoria and South Australia was an Old Boy of my school and an acquaintance. In July, Basil Harries took Anne and I to Flemington to see the Australian Grand National. He had a box, champagne was laid on and we all had a great time. He also hosted a cocktail party for the touring British Lions, at which I assisted him and his staff with the drinks. Alan Ashcroft, a Waterloo, Lancashire and England player from St Helens, who later became the Art master at Liverpool College, was one of the guests. Alan was highly amusing company and I was delighted to see him. A few days later, the Lions played Victoria and I took several bets, giving the takers very high odds against a home win. Victoria was, at this time, a state where Australian Rules football was King and rugby was not widely played. However, Victoria had one man on their team who was a Wallaby and he was their kicker. Aided by a one-eyed referee, this man slotted over six penalties in the first 20 minutes of the match and the Lions were 0-18 down. I started to feel nervous about the truly astronomical sums I might have to fork out if this continued, but it didn't. The Lions clicked into top gear, after scoring a try with the movement beginning behind their own posts, and eventually won very easily. Ten days later, I flew to Sydney to see the Lions play the first Test. I managed to get into their dressing room, something that would have been impossible a few years later, and saw Ashcroft again and a few others whom I now knew, before the kick-off.

I was determined to get back home by September so that I could begin a hospital job in Liverpool. Shaw Savill again proved very helpful and I was to sail home on a ship that was to call at Trincomalee. The RN had now left this port, which the Sri Lankan government was trying to develop for commercial use, especially for the export of tea. Later, I heard that this sailing was going to be delayed and I was offered the *Dominion Monarch* instead. This ship had been built by Swan Hunter at Newcastle and launched in 1938 by Lady Essendon, wife of the Shaw Savill chairman. Although old, she was extremely well furnished, with elegant cabins and public rooms. She carried only 350 first-class passengers and was the largest refrigerated ship on the Australasia-Britain run. I would be the only medical officer and would have the assistance of a nursing sister. I was sorry not to see Trinco again but the change of ship was going to be better for me. We left Melbourne and called at Fremantle for a day. Visits once more to Capetown and Las Palmas followed before arriving back at Southampton. I felt that I now knew all these ports intimately and could manage without seeing them for a while. The comfortable and stately *Dominion Monarch* was withdrawn from service in 1962. After being used as a hotel ship at the World Fair at Seattle, she was broken up in Japan. She was replaced by the *Northern Star*, a slightly larger and improved version of the *Southern Cross*. Shaw Savill became part of the Furness Withy group, although always operating independently with its own house flag, but disappeared in 1986 after the integration of independent groups within Furness Withy.

TEN

Medical Registrar

I had missed all the interviews for hospital positions beginning in September 1959 but was, nevertheless, successful in securing an appointment at the Liverpool School of Tropical Medicine. Once again, an important officer at Trinco, the new Surgeon Captain who had arrived shortly before I had departed, was critical in this appointment. His cousin was a senior clinician at the Tropical School and this had enabled me to be appointed as the resident medical officer, without any interview, in the school's clinical unit. This position was, in fact, only rated as a house physician but I would get every morning off to take the Diploma of Tropical Medicine and Hygiene (DTM&H) course, for which there would be no charge, and I would take care of the in-house tropical patients at Sefton General Hospital, where I had worked during my second house job a few years earlier. There were never more than a handful of such patients but I had to give lectures to the nurses doing a tropical nursing course and also look after general medical patients. The course lectures and laboratory sessions were superb and I hugely enjoyed my six months during this appointment.

During this time, I became friendly with David Marsh, a house surgeon at the hospital. A Cambridge graduate who had chosen to do his clinical training in Liverpool, David was an outstanding golfer and after gaining a blue and playing many times for Lancashire, he went on to play a staggering 75 times for England. He was English amateur champion twice, played in two Walker Cups and was non-playing captain in another two. He is a past captain of both the Lancashire Golf Union and the English Golf Union and was captain of the Royal and Ancient Golf Club of St Andrews in 1990. As well as these distinctions, he was never anything less than tremendous company, always very modest and hugely entertaining. His "stag party" at the Southport and Ainsdale golf club, just before being married, was a memorable occasion.

After completing my six months on the Tropical Unit, I had some problems getting a good medical appointment. After being unsuccessful in one particular interview, a friendly consultant surgeon took me aside and told me, very much "off the record", that my travels and especially my DTM&H qualification had counted against me, with most of the interviewing committee thinking that I would be off out of England again very soon. I thanked him for this disclosure, which left me wondering what I might do to overcome such small minded parochialism. Of course, I was very conscious of having been out of mainstream clinical hospital medicine for more than four years and realised that I had to make up this time as quickly as possible.

Dr Ronald Finn, for instance, had been in the same year as me in medical school, after he had completed his National Service. A pleasant and very smart student, although somewhat shy, he was now way ahead of me in his medical career. He was already a member of the Royal College of Physicians of London (MRCP) and was part of a group working at the Liverpool medical school with Professor Cyril Clarke, who had replaced Lord Cohen as Professor of Medicine, became President of the Royal College of Physicians of London and was knighted.

In 1963, this team published their important paper on the prevention of Rhesus haemolyic disease in pregnancy. Many felt that the Nobel Prize would have been very probable but for there being more than three research workers involved in the work. However, the team was given the Lasker Award, a most illustrious prize known as the American Nobel Prize in Medicine. Dr Finn, a lifelong traditional Jew, later referred to this work as "giving back some of what the Holocaust took". Ron was soon awarded an MD and became a consultant physician in Liverpool in 1966 when 36 years old. Years later, following a Nile cruise, he investigated the deaths of Howard Carter and Lord Carnarvon, concluding that radon poisoning was more likely than any curse of Tutankhamen.

I now worked for a few months as a locum registrar in Medicine to Professor Clarke and Dr Baker Bates, widely known simply as "BB", at the Liverpool Royal Infirmary. BB was a colourful and a rather "larger than life" physician, not only in a literal sense. His diagnostic tools, such as patellar hammer, tuning fork, stethescope, etc were all of enormous size and he had scores of pamphlets on all sorts of conditions and diseases that he would hand out to patients. He was full of pithy and humorous maxims and would, for instance, inform obese patients that they were "digging their graves with their teeth". An anecdote circulating in the hospital at this time alleged that BB's father, a GP and a member of the St Helens town council, had been informed by the mayor that a railway station in the town required more urinals. The story had it that his father, being of gentle birth, had asked the mayor exactly what a urinal was. On being informed, BB's father then suggested that the station could also profit from more arsenals!

I had quite a few Irish friends and frequently visited the Emerald Isle at this time. In the summer of 1960, I flew into Dublin and, after hiring a car, headed westward. I was due to meet up with friends that weekend in Galway but stopped to look in on the South of Ireland golf championship. This is the oldest provincial golf championship in Ireland and is played at the Lahinch club, on the coast of County Clare, where Percy French famously claimed that "the sea shines like a jewel" in his song *The West Clare Railway*. Just as I arrived, the holder of the title was leaving the course. This was Geoff Roberts, a member of the Southport and Ainsdale club, who had won the title at his third attempt the previous year but had just lost narrowly in matchplay to Paddy O'Sullivan of Kinsale, who went on to win the title. After watching the golf for some time, I retired to the drinks tent where I got into conversation with a genial, very friendly man who told me that he was Paddy, a GP from nearby Milltown Malbay. He seemed to know everyone. More of Paddy's friends joined us and we had a great old time. I had planned to go on to Galway that night but, with time passing quickly and considerable quantities of alcohol having being consumed, I decided that it was best to stay the night locally.

Declaring that I really had to leave and seek hotel accomodation, Paddy rubbished this idea, insisting that I go home with him to his house at Spanish Point. He told me that this small town was so-called as a couple of Spanish galleons, remnants of the Armada, had foundered nearby and some of the survivors, after being rescued, had remained and married locally. After dinner, I succeeded in avoiding any further drinks and managed to get off to bed. Next morning, I awoke rather early and, feeling tired and not too clever, decided that I must be off at once to avoid any further delays and to meet belatedly with my friends further up the coast. Arriving in the kitchen, I asked for coffee and some toast and, with great difficulty, managed to convince the female servant that I could not possibly stay until mine host descended for breakfast. I asked that she give Paddy my thanks for his hospitality and apologies for my leaving without personally saying farewell. I resolved to write, thanking him for his hospitality, but did not do so because of my ignorance as to his address. On the point of departing, I asked what Paddy's surname was. With a very strange look, I was informed that it was Hillary. It seemed as if Dr Hillary was active in Fianna Fail political circles, was prominent nationally and was well known to my friends in Galway. Over the years, I stayed abreast of Dr Paddy Hillary's career. He became a very good Minister of Education and was later President of Ireland from 1976-1990!

I had just been appointed as a medical registrar at Whiston hospital near Prescot in September 1960, where coal mining still continued nearby, when mother died. Her death was not completely unexpected but I took it very hard, thinking of all the time I had been away in distant lands. I comforted myself with the thought that I had, at least, been at home with her during her last twelve months.

I was in Dundalk for the following New Year's Eve and was invited to a men's club by Jack Flanagan with whom I was staying. He was Chairman of the Dundalk League of Ireland soccer club and was widely known and respected. When things had warmed up and singing had commenced, I was prevailed upon by the members to join in with a solo number. I knew quite a number of humorous Irish ditties, especially those of the great Percy French, but for perverse reasons, probably related to the considerable alcoholic load I had taken on board, I chose to sing *The Old Orange Flute*, the words of which, for some obscure reason, I happened to know. This was a ridiculous choice and my chum blanched visibly as I began. Fortunately, the assembled crowd knew that I was with my popular companion and perhaps he had told them something of me. The song passed off without mishaps but to very muted applause. Some ten years later, sectarian conflict had erupted in Ulster, with Dundalk in the front line and adjacent to South Armagh. In fact, the town was commonly referred to as "El Paso" after the once wild and dangerous town on the Texan/Mexican border. There was a considerable and active IRA presence in and around it and being unable to complete my ballad would have been by far the least of my troubles had I been so silly as to try and sing it in the 1970s.

A year later, I became registrar to Dr Cyril James Williams at Walton Hospital, which had been established as a workhouse in 1868 and became of one England's Poor Law hospitals. At the inception of the NHS in 1948, it was the largest comprehensive hospital in the UK, although grossly under-resourced, and even had an internal railway. CJ, as everyone called him, was enormously respected. The son of a national school teacher in North Wales, he had graduated in Medicine at Liverpool in 1938 and after wartime service in the Royal Army Medical Corps, had secured the MRCP qualification when working as a GP. In 1949, he had opted to take the MD degree by examination and in the specialty of Neurology. Professor Henry Cohen much preferred aspiring MDs to take the degree by thesis, although the regulations did allow for an examination. In addition, Neurology was the Professor's own specialty and he could be expected to give anyone choosing it a difficult time; but CJ sailed through the exam in great style.

I was always very busy when working with CJ. He was responsible for two very large wards, each containing more than 50 patients, and ran four out-patient clinics each week. One of these was for diabetics and we would regularly see more than 100 patients. Another was for pregnancies where there was a concurrent medical condition, such as a cardiac abnormality. Then there were two general medical clinics. In most of them, CJ would see the new patients and I would take care of the follow-up visits. Dr Williams was an excellent teacher and I learned a great deal during my time with him. He was a very concerned and conscientious physician and visited his wards every Sunday morning to check on new admissions. Usually, I joined him in this, after which we would go off for a drink in a country pub. If he had a fault, it was his reluctance to publish anything that was fractionally less than rare or outstanding. This was due to his very high standards but meant that I had few if any publications while working with him.

I was on-call one night a week and on every fifth weekend. These duties were onerous and usually very demanding. Invariably, they kept me very busy and I and my fellow registrars never enjoyed much sleep. During these on-call nights, I would often interview the relatives of patients in our wards prior to their discharge. The main purpose of this was to ensure that the patient's home conditions were satisfactory and that relatives would be able to take care of the patient. One night, I met a quiet, middle-aged Scottish couple. The wife's elderly father had been in the ward for a couple of weeks. I was told that he lived with them and thus there would be no difficulties after his discharge. I discussed his illness and prognosis in broad terms and said that we would see the patient in the clinic a few times after his discharge. As they were leaving, the man asked if I followed soccer. Replying in the affirmative, I received a card from him which I was told to present "at the gate" any time I wished. I did not understand what he was suggesting and asked for an explanation, reading the card simultaneously. The man was Bill Shankly, who was Manager of Liverpool FC and was about to take the club back into the First Division of the Football League and to many other honours, including two FA Cup wins and three First Division Championships. He was inviting me into the Liverpool FC boardroom section of the grandstand for all home games, this including hot refreshments at half time and drinks after the game. I took him up on his offer with celerity but did not overdo it.

Some of the junior resident staff lived in a building called "the Creche", this presumably being its function in the past. It was just inside the main gates of the hospital, from which it was separated by a distance of nearly 200 yards and a soccer pitch. The bar downstairs in the Creche was the site of hospital parties that were not always quiet or respectable. I was told that a certain registrar, long since having emigrated, used to drive a Rolls-Royce hearse and tour the streets of Liverpool, selling tickets for these parties to any female who caught his eye. George was a Polish Neuro-Surgical registrar, quiet but very popular, who worked at the hospital in the early 1960s. His country was under the rigid control of the communist party at this time and he had encountered great difficulties in managing to arrange this period of training; of course, his wife and young family could not accompany him. On the evening of his departure, a small informal party was held for him in the creche at which a good deal of alcohol was consumed. There were several sincere, but rather incoherent, speeches and George became very emotional. I then burst into the Polish national anthem, when George dissolved into tears and began to hug every person present. Now realising the power of my voice, I desisted from further singing and after more lachrymal farewells, we drove him to Lime Street station and the midnight train to London.

Dr Sandy Skene, a Scot, was the Medical Superintendent of the hospital and had a somewhat difficult role. The concept of Medical Superintendent was very outdated and, at the time, few of these positions remained. He had to take care of much administration, with the bed situation being chronically difficult. Dr Skene was also a consultant physician so his hands were always very full. A very large hospital, Walton had a big catchment area and many clinics, as well as housing the regional neurosurgical unit. The Merseyside bed bureau, who had to place emergency admissions for GPs, were never off the phone and we rarely disappointed them. There was a strong tradition in the hospital that requests for emergency admissions should not be refused. This led, especially in the winter when many bronchitics became ill, to beds being erected in corridors quite commonly.

One evening in a hotel bar, I was introduced to Simon Mahon, the Labour MP for Bootle for many years. He was very much a right-wing socialist and was a great friend of my father's but I had never met him previously. Simon's brother was Peter Mahon, who was the Labour MP for a Preston constituency. Peter's son Phillip had been several years behind me at school, had played for Waterloo RFC and Lancashire at rugby and went on to become a master at Stonyhurst College, near Clitheroe. Simon and I talked about many things, including affairs at Walton Hospital. Believing in free speech, I enunciated some of the beefs of the junior medical staff but mentioned no names and was not, I thought, in any way disloyal. I met Dr Skene the following morning and mentioned to him my meeting with Mr Mahon MP. This produced a violent reaction close to panic and I was immediately interrogated as to what I had said. Of course, I refused to tell him but instead did some gentle "leg pulling" which worsened Dr Skene's concern. There is no doubt that he was quite perturbed by my story and I was surprised at the degree of this. Possibly he had visions of headlines in the press, other forms of bad publicity and even questions in the House. Dr Williams was most amused when Dr Skene complained to him about the matter.

Walton hospital was quite close to the famous Aintree racecourse and many jockeys were admitted there, usually to an orthopaedic ward and occasionally to the neurosurgical unit. I had been to the racecourse as a young boy, with father before World War Two on "Jump Sunday". At this time, the course had been open to the public, who could stroll about it, on the weekend before the big race. Prince Monolulu was one of the attractions on this day. Basically, he sold racing tips but in his colourful Zulu garb, shouting "I got an orse", he was quite a character. I had also been just once to the race itself but did not really enjoy this visit. It was difficult to acquire a good position without considerable expense and the poor weather and my lack of winners contributed to an unmemorable day.

A motor racing circuit was opened at the course in the late 1950s, when Aintree's stock, reputation and popularity were in decline, and the British Grand Prix, an international event, was run there on five occasions. However, the cost of providing facilities for motor racing was high and soon proved to be prohibitive, with the last Grand Prix being held there in 1962. On this occasion, Jim Clark in a Lotus was the winner and Phil Hill, a leading American Grand Prix driver of the time, was involved in a crash. He sustained a pneumothorax, or collapsed lung, and was treated medically, being admitted under the care of Dr Williams to a private ward where I got to know him quite well. I would visit him socially very regularly, helping to dispose of his mountain of fruit and chocolates. As he was very bored, he was always glad to see me and we became quite friendly; he even gave me his address in the USA, urging me to look him up should I ever get over there. A government subsidy was granted to the Aintree racecourse in 1968 and after changes of ownership and modernisation of facilities, the 2.3-mile course with its 16 fearsome jumps were saved from oblivion.

Whenever possible, which was not very often, I would escape from the hospital and spend 60 minutes or so at the nearby Bootle stadium, where for a few pence I could run and use the ramshackle changing rooms and shower facilities. This arena was held by some to have great site potential and, it was claimed, was certain to be developed in the future by the Liverpool or Everton football clubs; 40 years later, these predictions have not come true. A Liverpool Police soccer league operated there on Wednesday afternoons and I would sometimes share the changing rooms with these teams. Having been in the Royal and Merchant navies, I was no stranger to bad language but the Liverpool police variety was far worse than anything I had previously come across and was really something else! The chronic use of four-lettered words, the many obscenities and the general foulness of speech employed by the policemen never failed to disgust me. Ludovic Kennedy, that consistent critic of the British police, would have been in his element here!

I was a member of a quiz team, playing in the Merseyside and District league for the *Derby Arms*, a West Derby hostelry where my uncle was publican. There were four in a team and we had a good reserve. The other team members were academically undistinguished but their general knowledge was truly formidable. At that time, two points were given for a correct answer and one point if the team member asked did not know the answer but a colleague was able to give the right reply. It was agreed amongst our team that I would answer on questions on Sport, Geography, Science and Medicine However, the other team members were much better informed than I on a host of other subjects, including Music, Literature, Greek Mythology, Politics, History, Astronomy, etc. We performed consistently well and were among the honours every year.

This knowledge of many diverse subjects was not confined to our team. I was constantly amazed at the high level of answers in our league and cup encounters. The old joke about a docker, on being asked "Who painted the Mona Lisa?" and answering "Lairds, they do all the Isle-of-Man boats", was highly misleading, even if mildly amusing. Cammell Lairds, of course, were once famous ship builders in Birkenhead and many Isle of Man ships sailing out of Liverpool had the word "Mona" in their name, she being a legendary Manx Queen. There was a nondescript pub in Kirkdale, a working class area between Liverpool and Walton, whose quiz team consisted mainly of dockers together with some manual workers. They regularly showed an amazing level of general knowledge and never failed to give us a very hard time in competition. Without in any way being patronising, but rather being full of admiration, I thought they were in the very best tradition of working class self-improvers. They seemed committed to a life, or at least a good slice of it, in the pursuit of knowledge for its own sake. What drove their dedication I must leave to better social historians than myself. A cynical friend proposed that the spur to many of these people was the ability to win an argument in a bar or quiz game, but there was a good deal more to it than that! I read somewhere that it would not have been surprising to find another Alan Sillitoe emerging from among these quiz players and I had to agree.

My uncle, a devout Evertonian, had an oil portrait of Dixie

Dean that was, he claimed, the only one in existence. I am not certain if this was correct but he certainly valued it highly. William Ralph "Dixie" Dean set a Football League record, which is highly unlikely to be ever equalled, by scoring 60 goals when playing for Everton FC in the 1927-28 season. He was a superb header of the ball and for many years was included in most people's "best ever" team. At the start of the season, or on the occasion of a great Everton triumph and especially when the Blues had beaten their Liverpool rivals from across the other side of Stanley Park, the picture of Dixie would be set up on the corner of the main bar. Evertonians would come in and genuflect before it while Liverpudlians would pretend to spit and curse!

All this time during the early 1960s, my salary was about 5,000 pounds annually. I had a new car, a pretty much bottom of the heap Ford Anglia, and lived with father in the house where I had been raised. Although having no acute financial problems, I had very little in the bank and so took evening surgeries for GPs several times a month. I was still spending two weeks with the Navy each year for RNR training. This was a most welcome break, which was in addition to my four weeks annual vacation, with duties that were anything but strenuous; and the small amount of money that it generated was most welcome. The RNR and the RNVR amalgamated around 1960, after which I held a commission in the RNR; so I had, in fact, been commissioned in all three branches of the Navy.

I could usually choose the location of my annual RNR training and went most frequently to RNH Gibraltar, usually doing a locum for the vacationing medical specialist. I never considered, however remotely, going to La Linea again but would often take the ferry across the bay to Algeciras, a moderately large port from which ferries ran to Tangier and Ceuta in North Africa. The hotel *Reina Cristina* was here, a most lovely establishment and rated by Ian Fleming as being, in the 1960s, one of the top hotels of the world. A delightful half-day could be had, swimming in the afternoon and then enjoying a wonderful but surprisingly affordable dinner in the evening. There was continuing disagreement with Spain about the status of Gib and the border would frequently be closed, with the ferry to Algeciras suspended. However, if one was prepared for the expense and time, one could still enter into Spain by going from Gib to Tangier and then back to Algeciras on a Spanish ferry. Strangely enough, the Spanish authorities did not object to this stratagem as long as the place of direct entry into their country was not Gib. At RNH, I met Lieutenant Tom Skuse, a popular Irishman who was the fifth generation of his family to serve in the RN. He was the Supply Officer for the hospital and ran the wardroom mess bar. Being tee-total himself, he also served most of the time behind the bar and ran things with charm and efficiency. He came from West Cork and I came to know that area later through him. On one occasion, I did my training in Malta, at the Families Clinic in Sliema, and was accom-modated in *HMS St Angelo*. This was now a shore establishment of the RN but little changed from when it had been the famous fortress of the Knights of St John which had withstood the might of the Ottoman Empire in The Great Siege of 1565, one of the most deci-sive actions in the history of the Western World.

A battalion of the Royal Irish Rangers was stationed on the Rock during one of my visits there. I met the Commanding Officer at a party and he kindly invited me for drinks and lunch at their depot. He was, I believe, Anglo-Irish himself and his Adjutant who lunched with us was from the Republic. They told me that the Rangers had a mixture of men from both sides of the border and this caused no dif-ficulties whatsoever. The Royal Irish Rangers amalgamated with the Ulster Defence Regiment in the early 1990s to become the Royal Irish Regiment (RIR). I remembered this in 2003 when Tim Collins, a Lieutenant Colonel in command of the first battalion RIR, was accused of impropriety in Iraq following allegations by a US Army Reserve Major who had been placed under arrest by Collins for insubordination. After Collins and his actions had been investigated by the Royal Military Police, he was fully vindicated and all charges were withdrawn. This was followed by news that the regiment was to be considerably reduced in size, this announcement being handled is a particularly inept manner. So the RIR, a great example of Pan-Irish harmony which I thought resembled the Irish RU team in this respect, was to be severely pruned. Shortly after this, I read that Tim Collins had resigned his commision.

In the late 1960s, a general election was under way while I was on the Rock and anti-Spanish sentiment was running high. Four London metropolitan policemen were drafted in on a temporary basis to assist the local force during this period of tension. A senior officer of the Gib police, who had devoted his life to serving in a variety of British colonies including Palestine, was more or less running things on a day-to-day basis and was under great pressure. During one of the few public rallies held by a pro-Spanish candidate, a large crowd heckled this man unmercifully and then, with the female members of the mob very prominent, began throwing things. A large number of local police stood by doing absolutely nothing and the scene became ugly. The principle here was that all candidates should be free to campaign without harassment. The four London coppers and the senior officer tried to help the speaker but were overwhelmed by the angry crowd. By the skin of their collective teeth, they managed to escape with him.

Next morning, I was asked to see this senior policeman. He would normally have consulted his civilian practitioner but the situation was extraordinary and it was felt best for him to be treated by the Navy. He was in a very bad condition, severely shaken from his ordeal of the previous day and fearful of what lay ahead for him. In layman's terms, he was physically exhausted and close to a nervous breakdown. I admitted him to RNH, where he was heavily sedated and allowed no visitors. I refused to allow either the Governor or the Admiral to see him and they complained to the Medical Officer in Charge of RNH, a surgeon captain. The latter remonstrated with me but I refused to budge, telling him that he could take over the patient's care if he wished but that, while I was the police officer's physician, he must have no more aggravation, including visitors; of course, this offer was not taken up. I managed to persuade the authorities to give the poor man two weeks leave and, after four or five days, he was discharged to enjoy this holiday.

Playing rugby regularly for Waterloo RFC at this time, I was also managing to fit in a good deal of squash at the Northern Cricket Club in Crosby. A member of the latter was an executive of CP ships, affiliated to Canadian Pacific Railways, and through him I managed to get an appointment as a relief Surgeon on one of the beautiful White Empresses that sailed to Montreal from Liverpool every Tuesday. Once again, I had to change my naval suits, now adding CP buttons and no less than three gold stripes on my uniform sleeves.

My first trip was in May 1963, aboard the *Empress of Britain*, built by the Fairfield shipyard of Govan, Glasgow, and launched by Her Majesty the Queen in 1955. She had a length of about 640 feet, a beam of 85 feet and a displacement of 25,500 gross tons, her short foredeck and low profile giving her a very distinctive appearance among trans-Atlantic liners. Her cruising speed was 20-21 knots, which was twice as fast as the *Dilwara* and *Dunera*. There was a ship's company of about 470 of whom some 290 were in the catering department.150 first and 900 tourist class passengers could be carried, as well as more than 10,000 tons of cargo. These lovely White Empresses also undertook cruises to the West Indies and Mediterranean, but were not altogether suitable for this. They had been designed for trans-Atlantic crossings and had much enclosed space, with only a small amount of open deck. My accommodation included a surprisingly large day cabin as well as a bedroom and bathroom. I had my own personal steward and discovered that I had certain social duties to perform, for which I was given an allowance. As well as my own table in the first-class dining room, I had been given a list of medical and scientific people travelling with us and also the names of "frequent CP passengers". I was expected to invite the latter, in groups of four to six, to my cabin for drinks before dinner. My steward, a real scouser, was a very willing servant but his handling of these guests sometimes bordered on the hilarious.

Having sailed from the Pier Head at Liverpool, we called in at Greenock to take on passengers from Scotland and Northern Ireland. We did not go alongside and I was put ashore in one of the tenders used to transport passengers to the ship. CP operated what I thought was a quaint, almost bizarre, system. The ship's surgeon had to make sure that all the boarding passengers had the appropriate inoculations and were not obviously ill. At the main point of embarkation, namely Liverpool, this was taken care of by the CP office. There were no facilities for a proper physical examination and I was not advised as to what the position would be if a passenger was lacking in jabs or health. However, all appeared to be in order and, with the last of the passengers in the tender, we set off for the ship.

I sat down early for lunch and was enjoying my soup when one of the pursers rushed in. He said that I was urgently needed in the ship's hospital and, arriving there, I found a family of four and my nursing sister. The mother had, immediately on arrival on board, gone to the hospital and asked if she could have something for her two children who had chickenpox. I had no recollection of seeing these children when meeting the passengers ashore and wondered if they might have been smuggled past me. I examined both children, who were not pyrexial but certainly had a rash. The parents told me that the children were now both recovering from their infection and that their GP had told them that they were fit to emigrate to Canada. I was horrified at this, tried desperately to remember how long chickenpox patients remained infectious and, after some consideration, told the parents that they could not travel with us and must go ashore at once. At this, the mother broke down completely and cried loudly, with her two children soon joining in. The father now informed me that they had disposed of their house located far from Glasgow, where they had no friends or relatives, and that they had very little British money. I was in a real quandary. I suppose that I might have been able to contact some local social service if I had time but the ship was about to sail. In addition, it could be argued that the family had already infected the ship. I decided to let them stay on board, confined to the hospital, and extracted a promise from the father about this. I felt far from happy about the situation and was seriously worried about the ship being granted pratique at Montreal.

After sailing, we made a 90-degree turn to port just after Gourock and, now heading due south, passed Rothesay and Kilchattan Bay to starboard and Great Cumbrae Island to port. Leaving the Sound of Bute behind, we entered the Firth of Clyde and turning to starboard, passed the Isle of Arran and soon cleared the the Mull of Kintyre. I had not seen this part of Scotland before and found it all most interesting. Now in the Atlantic proper, we passed Inishtrahull, a small island off the northern tip of Donegal which is the traditional leaving point and landfall for the great circle routes to and from the mouth of the St Lawrence. The sea had become progressively rougher as we left the enclosed waters of the Clyde and many passengers began complaining of sea sickness. The routine operating on the ship, established by the regular ship's surgeon and CP, was to give an intra-muscular injection of an antihistamine for this complaint. If the surgeon made a visit, a fee of two US dollars or one pound sterling was charged but, for reasons that were unclear to me, the same treatment from the nurse alone was free. There were all manner of jokes about the surgeon bribing the officers to take in the ship's stabilisers and to make course deviations in search of rough weather, but this was seldom necessary for generating patients with sea sickness.

This matter of sea sickness soon involved me in a serious medical emergency. All the ship's more senior officers and the nursing sister were invited for drinks in the Purser's cabin before lunch on Sundays, a custom that was irreverently termed "communion". On my first Sunday on board, the nursing sister was called away and soon returned for me. I was informed that an elderly female had been vomiting blood and was now in bed in the hospital. She was clearly very shocked and I immediately set up an intravenous (iv) drip of saline and passed a naso-gastric tube into her stomach. I managed to elevate her blood pressure slightly and then learned that she had a radiologically proven benign gastric ulcer and, feeling sick, had taken some Alka Seltzer, which had clearly caused her ulcer to bleed. I now received a serious shock. I had begun the voyage with six bottles of saline, six of glucose and six of plasma but I had to jettison two bottles of plasma as they were clearly "off". There were no facilities for typing and cross matching blood on board, not even the out-dated and despised tile method. The patient's blood pressure and general condition now worsened and aspiration of gastric content via the gastric tube confirmed continued bleeding. I set up a second drip and she improved marginally. Leaving her with the nurse, I went up on to the bridge and informed the Captain of the situation. By now, just about everyone on board knew about this emergency and there were many offers of blood from willing donors. When I thanked them but admitted that I could not use their blood, I received puzzled looks which were most embarrassing. I slept in the hospital with the patient and took my meals there. This did not particularly help matters but I thought it would not look good if I continued with my normal routine. I managed to get a second opinion from an elderly, retired American physician, who agreed with what I was doing and couldn't add anything.

After two nights during which I had little sleep, the patient's condition had improved only slightly. Despite taking down the second iv drip, I was now rapidly running out of intravenous fluid. After a consultation with Peter Roberts, the First Officer who was to become a friend, we approached the Captain and suggested contacting the US Coastguard Service. The Captain was not very keen on this, for reasons that were unclear to us, but I insisted. Contact was established and our position, course and speed given, after which we were informed that a Royal Canadian Air Force plane would perform a blood drop. Several hours later, with less than two bottles of intravenous fluid remaining, a Shackleton aircraft emerged from the clouds over the Grand Banks and dropped a package on a parachute into the sea. A boat was lowered, the package recovered and I had two pints of O negative blood, usually universally compatible. After another 24 hours, the pilot boat came alongside at the entrance to the St Lawrence River and took the patient off to Quebec City. I later learned that she had continued to bleed in the hospital there, was eventually operated on and died about a week later.

I was far too tired to enjoy Belle Isle, Anticosti Island and the St Lawrence River and slept for a few hours until the Port Health Authority medical officer came on board early in the morning at Quebec. I had filled in the appropriate forms and, to my surprise and delight, no interest was shown in the chickenpox cases, who had fully recovered and were free of rashes. He was, however, very curious about my management of the haematemesis patient and I had to give him the whole story. There was no problem with pratique and I gave the Captain this glad news. I now made a beeline for my cabin and, after a shower, went to back to bed where I slept for more than 12 hours.

Arriving back home, after a very welcome medically quiet trip, I began to see a good deal of Peter, the ship's First Officer. He lived in Southport and was a keen private pilot. Because of his interest in this activity, I joined the Southport Aero Club to which he belonged. This club used the facilities at RAF Woodvale, a splendid airfield for light aircraft, now operated by a commercial company and mainly used by the air squadrons of Liverpool and Manchester Universities. I learned to fly on an Aircoupe, an American plane having a tricycle undercarriage that was incapable of stalling and was generally not very challenging. I went solo after five hours, and then made the required solo navigational triangular trip to Leeds-Bradford and Wolverhampton airports and return, landing at both fields. After this, I was awarded my Private Pilot's licence and was free to fly with passengers.

A few months later, I spent an enjoyable week at the British

Executive Air Services field at Kidlington, near Oxford. As well as further flying training, now in a Piper Colt, I received instruction in radio, meteorology and navigation and lived on the airfield in an old but comfortable Nissen hut. On the Thursday of that week, I was asked to leave a class and was told that I had an urgent phone call. It was from the man who lived next door to my home, telling me that father had been found wandering, dressed in pyjamas, in a busy shopping street near our house. He was very confused and had been admitted to Walton hospital and, indeed, to my own ward. I hurriedly packed my things and drove to the hospital. My father had clearly suffered some kind of cerebro-vascular accident and the senior registrar, who had taken care of his acute admission, explained matters to me. Father did not really know me and, with a heavy heart, I went home for the night.

Each morning, Dr Williams, the house physician and the ward sister went to see father at the end of the wardround but I did not accompany them. Dad had now been moved into a private room and CJ explained to me later that, although the future was uncertain, it was most unlikely that father would make a full recovery. Although he had no gross paresis, his mental condition was poor and waxed and waned alarmingly. I had thought it best to move on from Walton hospital, enjoyable and satisfactory as it was, but my father's presence there held me in place. After more than a year, I asked CJ how long father could remain in a private room of an NHS hospital. I knew that dad was getting superb medical and nursing care but I was concerned about how long the present situation could continue before he was transferred to less intensive, long-care accommodation. I simply did not have the financial means for a private nursing home and hospices were not yet in place. Dr Williams asked for Mr Cope's case notes and then, thrusting them into my face and pointing to the large letters "Dr CJ Williams" on the front, asked me what that meant. I answered, of course, that they signified that he was the consultant in charge of the case. "Exactly", he replied "so I'll decide when and where he is moved, if at all". I took this to mean that I was not to worry about matters and that CJ would take care of things. His show of annoyance was entirely contrived and I felt enormous gratitude to him.

Shortly after this incident, I had the opportunity to make another trans-Atlantic trip with CP in May,1964. I was worried about leaving father and discussed this problem with Dr Williams. Having been told that he could die any day, or live for several more years, I decided to go. I alerted uncles of both my maternal and paternal family and sailed again for Canada, now on board the *Empress of England* (Fig 17) that was similar to the *Britain*, although somewhat newer. It had been built by Vickers Armstrong at Walker-on-Tyne and launched in 1956 by Lady Eden, wife of the then British prime minister. There was a maitre d'hotel who stood at the entrance to the first-class restaurant and greeted the incoming diners. To my considerable surprise, I learned that this was Lord Vivian, the son of a former gaiety girl, who was an Old Etonian and had been a partner of the great CB Cochran, with whom he had put on many West End productions. However, in 1954 he had been shot in bizarre circumstances by his lover, Mrs Mavis Wheeler, the former wife of Sir Mortimer Wheeler, the famous archeologist, Head of the London Museum and star of the TV series *Animal, Vegetable or Mineral*. After this incident, Vivian lost control of Cochran Productions, which he had gained after his partner's death, and went into catering. This career change was not successful and he had been obliged to take up a position with CP that could only be described as "a real comedown".

The vast majority of the crew were scousers and I was told that they made his life a misery. Vivian was not classed as an officer and lived with the other ranks below decks. Although not generally cruel or vindictive by nature, the average steward, seaman or engine room artificer found the idea of a peer of the realm living among them irresistibly and hugely amusing. The poor man was subjected to incessant leg-pulling and worse, with a certain degree of feral behaviour. So much so that Vivian, friend of the likes of Sir Alan Herbert and Augustus John, would often miss meals to avoid scorn and derision. I felt sorry for him and would occasionally buy him a drink after dinner. Sitting in the first-class lounge with the ship's Surgeon, a man from a modest background who was currently earning the miserable sum of just 5,000 pounds per year, gave this dispossessed aristocrat a little peace and helped him forget his troubles for a while.

A few hours before arriving at Montreal, I received a ship-to-shore cable telling me that father had died. I felt very bad at not being there at the end and had a very quiet visit. There had been no

Fig 17. The *Empress of England* in the Clyde. The ship's clean and graceful lines are well displayed, with only limited open upper deck space. (Reprinted by permission of the Canadian Pacific Railway archives).

great problems outward bound but, returning home, a young girl presented with what was clearly an acute appendicitis. There were no other medically qualified doctors on board although the Purser found me a musician, physicist and mathematician from the passenger list, all calling themselves "doctor", as they were entitled. Acute surgery in the circumstances was not an option. I was not trained in surgery and had no anaethetist. I put the young patient on large doses of intra-muscular antibiotics, set up an iv line for hydration and gave her nothing by mouth. After several anxious days, the infection localised with abscess formation and she was landed at Liverpool in good condition. She underwent successful surgery some time later.

By this time, the jet aeroplane was rapidly eroding steamship passenger numbers and the ship had been far from full, especially in first-class, on both legs of the trip. The *Empress of Britain* made her last voyage in October 1963, just a few months after I had sailed aboard and only seven years after her maiden voyage. She was initially chartered by the Travel Savings Association and was then sold to the Greek Line in 1964. After 11 years of service as *Queen Anna Maria*, she was sold to the Carnival Cruise line. She was renamed *Carnivale* and became their first cruise ship. The *Empress of England* was sold to Shaw Savill in 1970 and renamed *Ocean Monarch*. The *Empress of Canada* was the sole CP passenger ship after this and passenger services were terminated in 1971 when she, too, was sold to Carnival Cruise Line and renamed *Mardi Gras*. General cargo ships known as Beaver boats and container ships continued to fly the red-and-white checkered CP flag.

ELEVEN

Changing Horses

The acquisition of the MRCP qualification had been exercising me for some time. The written exams for this were held in Queen Square, London, in the same large room used for the Conjoint qualifying exam. In the 1960s, the exam consisted of two written papers, each of three hours and including a translation from either French or German. My schoolboy French was insufficient for this task and many others found the same problem, as well as wondering why any language test was necessary. The test was later dropped.

Then, after a week or two, candidates would return to London to one of the teaching hospitals there for a very thorough clinical examination. This consisted of a "big case", where the candidate would have 45 minutes to examine a patient in detail before giving his diagnosis to the examiner. Invariably, he would be required to demonstrate the important physical signs, to discuss them and their significance and to suggest the correct treatment. Now followed a rapid parade of "small cases" and I tended to enjoy this part of the exam. The examiner would wander about a large ward or room filled with patients, most of whom had been brought in specially for the exam. He would then bark out a series of commands, such as "Look at this lady's optic fundi", "Listen to that man's heart", "Palpate that patient's abdomen", "What do you make of this patient's leg reflexes?", "What of this patients skin and what investigation would you order?" etc. The examinee would have only a very short time to carry out these tasks before being grilled by the examiner. If successful, the membership candidate still had to get through two more vivas successfully before being able to write MRCP after his name. This qualification was essential for the aspiring medical specialist and was a very difficult exam at this time with a pass rate of about 16%. The trips down to London, always requiring an overnight stay in a hotel, were expensive and the exam itself was quite stressful. However, as a classmate of mine had said of some of his medical school exams, I must have enjoyed this London membership exam as I sat it a number of times. On one occasion, I surmounted successfully the first part of the exam, as described above, but was failed in the following viva.

Finally, I managed at last to get some study leave and attended the membership course in Edinburgh in 1965. This 12 week refresher course in the Scottish capital was most useful and I sat the Scottish membership soon afterwards. The pass rate for this was only very slightly higher than for the London exam, from which it differed in requiring a specialist subject, with a whole raft of additional written papers, clinical and oral tests. Having never worked on a specialist unit, I had no obvious specialty and, after deep thought, opted eventually for Renal Physiology and Renal Diseases. I hung about the Renal Unit at the Edinburgh Royal Infirmary at every opportunity and studied books on these subjects with great determination. Another difference with the Edinburgh qualification was that examinees were often compelled to travel for the clinical exams. Lacking the plethora of teaching hospitals possessed by London, there simply was not enough clinical material in the city of Edinburgh for all candidates, who therefore could be sent off to Glasgow, the Borders, etc. I was given a ticket to Dunfermline and had my clinical examination there in General Medicine. It was all very relaxed and seemed much less impersonal and rushed than the London exam. I had no problems with any section and was soon informed that I was now a Member of the Royal College of Physicians of Edinburgh and could write MRCP Ed. after my name.

However, I was now feeling very uncertain as to my future. It was very doubtful if I would be considered for a senior registrar position in England without the London membership qualification but I was not even certain that Internal Medicine would now be my career choice. Consultant positions, even those in less attractive locations, were extremely competitive and difficult to secure and so much of General Medicine had become geriatric in nature, with little opportunity, it seemed to me, for much exercise in diagnostic acumen. In short, my initial enthusiasm for this specialty had considerably waned. However, I didn't wish to do anything rash and decided to accept a position at Aberdeen Royal Infirmary as a medical registrar and see what, if anything, this led to.

Immediately before taking up this position, I spent two weeks at RNAS Lossiemouth in Morayshire, undergoing my annual RNR training. An old friend from my service days was there as Senior

Pilot in a second line squadron, which was working up prior to embarking on a carrier. We flew together one day in a two-seater Meteor towards the Shetland islands. Because of the planes dual controls, I had charge for the first 30 minutes or so and then my friend announced that he would now take over and that we would perform some aerobatics. I had always enjoyed these and had never previously experienced any discomfort. We did the lot - tight turns, loops, barrel rolls, etc. I felt distinctly queasy and light-headed for a good deal of the time and concluded that I was growing old.

In the words of the classical song, the *Northern Lights of Old Aberdeen* were, if not Home Sweet Home to me, at least tolerable. Overall, I enjoyed the city, with skiing at Mar Lodge and Aviemore at weekends. After the first snows, I usually managed to make use of the rather primitive tows set up by enterprising farmers around the city, on hills on their land. This gave some pre-season practice and the requirement of holding on tightly to the rope attached to the powered drum while being pulled uphill was good for strengthening the hands. On one notable occasion, I was skiing midweek at Aviemore around Easter in glorious conditions. There was a great deal of good snow, the day was warm and sunny and there were only a few skiers. Travelling up the mountain on a lift with a Frenchman, the latter remarked on the excellent conditions and promised to tell all his friends back home to ski henceforth in Scotland. I assured him that the current conditions were virtually unique but my companion dismissed this as English prejudice, babbling on about the Old Alliance. I could only shudder at what a Frenchman would make of the more usual conditions, with lots of old fashioned T-bar tows, biting winds and a marked paucity of snow.

Some locals became firm friends and I particularly remember watching Celtic FC on TV becoming the first British club to win the European Cup, in Lisbon against Inter-Milan in 1967. I was pleased to find that many supporters of Glasgow Rangers FC were also happy with Celtic winning this coveted trophy. I discovered, however, that many Aberdonians were rather dour and I was not overwhelmed with hospitality. In general, they were honest and straight but somewhat parochial in outlook. However, I certainly did not agree with Martin Amis, who called the Silver City "the epicentre of gloom" and "one of the darkest places imaginable, like Iceland". This highly pejorative verdict was given in an interview in September,

2002, in connection with an untitled story inspired by pornography and sex. Amis confessed to having never visited the Granite City, which made his pronouncement even more extraordinary.

Two classic stories, told to me by Scots who were not pulling my leg, initially seemed confirm my impression as to Aberdonian parochialism. Both were said to have appeared on the front page of the principal local newspaper, the *Aberdeen Press and Journal*. After the sinking of the *Titanic* in 1912, with more than a thousand deaths, a headline was said to have read "Aberdeen man lost at sea". Then in 1945, after the dropping of the atomic bomb on Hiroshima, the headline was alleged to have been "Giant turnip found at Turrif", this being a small town in the north-west of Aberdeenshire, some 35 miles from the city of Aberdeen. The first story about the *Titanic* is certainly a long running myth, having no truth in it. The second, about the giant turnip, has proved more dificult to run down but probably is also untrue. In addition, I suffered countless jokes on my surname. All these referred to Sir John Cope, the English general defeated in 1745 at Prestonpans by Bonnie Prince Charlie. A classic Scottish folk song dealt with this and alleged that Johnny Cope had quit the battlefield at an early stage and galloped with the news of his own defeat to Carlisle. I considered that I put up with this ribbing for the most part with equanimity but it became very wearing on occasions.

Dr Cecil Kidd, an Ulsterman, and I became friendly. We both had an RN background but did not always agree about the divisions and goings-on in the Red Hand province. At the time, he was a Senior Lecturer at the prestigious Ross Clinic, well known for Psychiatry and giving an excellent course leading to a specialised postgraduate degree in that subject. I was desperately searching for a suitable study that would lead to the MD qualification, something that I would be able to develop without access to specialised facilities. Dr Kidd persuaded me to explore the relationship between Hypertension and Depression, which he believed were intimately linked. I started this study, mainly using patients from the Ross Clinic, but could not finalise it because of later moves.

I found that my disillusionment with Internal Medicine and my concerns about career prospects in that discipline persisted and I became increasingly attracted to Radiology. After much hard thought and discussion with informed physicians, I decided to switch to that specialty. I was interviewed at Edinburgh by the Chairman there, Dr Eric Samuel, and started the Edinburgh course for the Diploma of Diagnostic Radiology in September 1967, fully 13 years after my graduation. I bought a pleasant flat at Corstorphine, out on the Glasgow road and quite near to Turnhouse Airport. I joined the local Flying club, of which King Hussein of Jordan was patron, and flew a Cessna 150 whenever time and funds would allow. The first year of my Radiology training was not very taxing and I enjoyed living in Auld Reekie, as its inhabitants called the Scottish capital.

During my previous stay there while taking the membership course, I had become friendly with Maeve and Bill Christie, husband-and-wife solicitors. Bill had since become Secretary of the Hibernian (Hibs) Football Club, largely because the majority shareholder was a client of his. This would have been a fulltime post in England but, probably with the exception of Glasgow Celtic and Rangers, this was not the case in Scotland. Bill could attend all the Hibs games, including the away matches, and I frequently accompanied him, thus getting to know the boardrooms of many of the more successful Scottish clubs. I played a good deal of squash at the Edinburgh Sports Club and became a member of Edinburgh Wanderers RFC, having known them previously through their fixtures with Waterloo RFC. At the time, they played their games on the back pitch of the Murrayfield International rugby ground and had a very strong team. Later, and especially after the advent of professionalism in RU, they suffered a marked decline in both revenue, players numbers and success, as did many other clubs. In addition, I enjoyed watching Scotland's home rugby games at Murrayfield, tickets for which were easily procured through the Wanderers club.

In the second year of the Radiology course, two of the five trainee registrars were required to leave town, one going to Aberdeen and another to Dundee. All those on the course had to compose a letter to Dr Samuel stating their preference and giving reasons for it; of course, everyone wished to remain in Edinburgh. I wrote a short note asking not to be removed. I pleaded my age, recent apartment purchase and especially the considerable moves that I had already made in my life. Some of my colleagues wrote huge essays, detailing at great length the absolute necessity for remaining in Edinburgh. Perhaps their voluminous content impressed the chairman as I had to move on to Dundee for my second year, a fact that did not please me at all.

Dr and Mrs David Asbury kindly accomodated me for a couple of weeks in Dundee. David was an Edinburgh graduate and an Old Boy of St Edward's College, Liverpool. Like me, he had been shunted off north of the Tay a year before my move up there. Later, he became a well known radiologist at Withington Hospital, Manchester. I was only in Dundee for a year and can't say that I enjoyed it very much. Many weekends I would go down to Edinburgh, staying in my apartment which I had rented out to a senior registrar in Radiology on condition that I could use it occasionally. Sometimes I would ski at Glenshee. Eventually, I instructed my friend Bill to sell my apartment in Edinburgh.

I put in two weeks of RNR training at *HMS Sea Eagle*, Derry City about this time. This was a big NATO anti-submarine base, run jointly by the Navy and the RAF. Many groups were continuously passing through for training, including Germans, Dutch and other NATO allies. About twice weekly, a group from the wardroom would sally out into Donegal in a collection of cars, to sample the wares of the restaurants and pubs of the Inishowen Peninsula. We would rarely drive beyond Redcastle and nearby Muff was the favourite for purely drinking, with Buncrana, situated on beautiful Lough Swilly, best for dining. Crossing the border, these cars filled with serving officers and clearly originating from Sea Eagle, would invariably be stopped by an unfriendly Royal Ulster Constabulary. Everyone would have to get out while the cars were searched. After crossing a few yards of no-mans-land, we would arrive at the Irish border post. Typically, a guard would stick his head in the window of the first car, recommend a bar where the Guinness was particularly good at that moment and wave us on. On returning, the Irish border guard would ask if he had been correct about the Guinness, once more wave us through and we would all then exit the cars at the Ulster customs. We never patronised any of the establishments around Derry itself, which I was told were generally bleak and unfriendly.

After obtaining my Radiology diploma in Edinburgh after two years, I secured a position in Bristol and moved there, staying initially with my cousin John Farrell and his family. Professor Howard Middlemiss was the Chairman at Bristol and ran a Radiology department that was very popular with trainees and considered by many to be the best in the country. Middlemiss became the first

President of the Royal College of Radiologists and was knighted. He was prominent in the World Health Organisation and was away visiting foreign countries on a regular basis. Registrars and radiographers from third world nations were usually in evidence at the Bristol hospitals. I bought a pleasant garden apartment at Westbury-on-Trim and enjoyed living in Bristol. There was a nice indoor swimming pool at the Bristol Royal Infirmary (BRI) and also a squash court.

The United Bristol Hospitals ran two teams in the Gloucester and Somerset Squash league. The first team was potentially very strong, with a county player and a Cambridge blue, but players were not always available because of clinical commitments; hence the team tended to yo-yo between the first and second divisions of the league. I ran the second team for four years. We played some club second teams, university halls of residence, Army and RAF teams and tended to be too good for the fourth division of the league but were not always able to maintain a position in the third division. Our second team had a pool of seven or eight players. I would pick the best possible five for the toughest fixtures and rested our better players during easier fixtures. I always played at number five and often dropped myself for the more taxing fixtures. This sheltered selection resulted in me suffering only two defeats during my entire time on the team. Having only one court was a nuisance but meant that we were able to support our teammates in their play. After games, we would take our visitors to a nearby hostelry for sandwiches and beer. Happy times indeed!

Another RNR training stint at nearby RNAS Yeovilton, near Ilchester, Somerset, saw me meeting up again with Tom, my Irish friend that I had met in Gibraltar. Neville, my pilot friend from *Eagle*, was also there and we had some high jinks together in the Tiger Moth of the gliding club. I got to know many in the wardroom and was always invited to the annual Air Day, which never failed to be anything less than a hugely entertaining occasion. As well as the aerobatics, with visiting teams and pilots from the US and other NATO air forces, it was great to meet old friends from the Fleet Air Arm and to reminisce over a drink.

After being promoted to senior registrar, I started to work at the United Bath Hospitals two or three days a week. Professor Middlemiss had so many junior staff on the books, many from overseas, that this rotation was necessary for the full employment of his

Bristol registrars. I met Frances in Bath, a senior radiographer who had trained at the Derby Royal Infirmary and who became my wife. After some time at Addenbrooke's Hospital, Cambridge, she had then spent two years in Australia, from where she had recently returned. She was related to the great Steve Bloomer on her maternal side but, unfortunately, few of his sporting genes passed to her or to our daughter Helen. Bloomer was the most prolific goal-scorer in English football before World War One. He scored over 352 league goals, most of them for Derby County, and his 28 goals for England stood as a record for nearly 50 years until being surpassed by Nat Lofthouse.

Meanwhile, I had transferred to the Severn Division RNR and initially joined their headquarters ship, *HMS Flying Fox*. I was asked if I would accept a transfer to the Royal Marine Reserves (RMR) as they were in need of a second medical officer, of which *Flying Fox* had rather too many. With some mild reluctance, I agreed and henceforth carried out my medical duties at Dorset House, a large and classical building in Clifton. Although I was never quite as comfortable and "at home" with the Marines as with the Fishheads, one major spin-off of this change was that Frances and I were able to host our wedding reception in May 1972 in Dorset House, the elegant RMR officers mess. However, I was rather put-out when, just a couple of days before the wedding, I was asked abruptly by a permanently commissioned Royal Marine officer if any wedding guests would be coming from Ireland; if so, I was informed, it would create a major problem. All this was, I suppose, in response to renewed IRA activity in England. In fact, I had invited an Irish physician but he had been unable to accept this invitation.

After this, Frances and I spent two weeks at Rosyth, where I fulfilled my RNR training. A young Midshipman was keen to show us round his ship and we accepted his kind offer. *HMS Rapid* was a very old destroyer but was, in fact, still one of the fastest ships in the fleet. Used now just for training purposes, her only armament was a small saluting gun. We also visited a minesweeper that was in dry dock, her Captain and I playing squash together most evenings. It was nice to see old friends in Edinburgh again but Rosyth did not represent my best ever RNR experience. The following year, we went to Gib where I worked now as a radiologist but was not too busy. I was determined to show Frances a typical, working, naval vessel. However, the only ship we managed to visit was *HMS Matapan*, an experimental vessel full of secrets and with lots of civilians on board, many being Americans. So Frances had seen only a very atypical sea-going Navy. Nevertheless, we had a most entertaining and enjoyable visit overall, which included the annual cocktail party of RNH Gib. Frequently, I managed to join my wife in late morning at Rosia Bay, where the crippled and largely dismasted *HMS Victory* had been towed by *HMS Neptune* after the battle of Trafalgar, with Admiral Nelson's corpse on board, pickled in a large cask filled with brandy. The swimming here, off a quay, was not particularly good but the bar-restaurant was outstanding and served excellent calamari.

Dr John Roylance was one of the consultant radiologists at the BRI at this time. He was a superb teacher, jovial and very popular. He helped me with several published papers and he and his wife attended our wedding. He later became very involved with administration and was appointed Chief Executive of the United Bristol Healthcare Trust. In the late 1990s, it became clear that the paediatric cardiac surgical results at the BRI were very poor and grossly inferior to the rest of the country, with unacceptably high mortality rates. An anaesthetist who had moved to Australia was the first to blow the whistle. The enquiry of Professor Kennedy, lasting three years and costing 14 million pounds, established that between the years 1988 and 1995, the Bristol mortality was double that of other hospitals operating on similar cases. In 30% of children, some 550 in number, the report found that there had been "less than adequate care". The two thoracic surgeons involved were deemed to have been guilty of serious professional misconduct and their names were struck off the medical register. Unfortunately, this punishment was also meted out to Dr Roylance. Many physicians, not merely his friends, thought that he had been treated very unfairly as his involvement was of a purely administrative, not clinical, nature.

I went off now to London to sit the External Certificate for Foreign Medical Graduates, an essential requisite for physicians entering the USA. At that time, I had no intention then of doing the latter but thought that possession of this certificate just might, at some time in the future, be useful. The exam consisted of multiple-choice questions and I found it quite easy. At the end of this section, there was an exam in English that, unexpectedly, I found quite taxing. Some words would be read out and the correct one had to be circled on the exam paper out of four possible choices. The difficulty was that the enunciator was a man with a strong Texas accent, sounding as if he had chronic sinusitis and a severe cold. I had great trouble in making up my mind about various specific words but all was well. I passed both the scientific and English papers with ease.

Just after this, Professor Middlemiss asked if I would go to Southmead Hospital, an excellent institution and part of the Bristol teaching group, as a locum Consultant, taking the place of a radiologist who was in the West Indies on sabbatical leave for two years. I jumped at the opportunity. I would get a much larger salary and have virtually no "on call" duties. In fact, I really enjoyed my time there but it did have a downside of which I was not aware when accepting the position. Early in 2003, I was amazed to read that the North Bristol Trust, comprising Southmead and Frenchay hospitals, which I remembered as both being excellent institutions with high clinical standards, now had a deficit of some 44 million pounds, which was expected to rise further by years end. About this time, I sat the fellowship examination of the Royal College of Radiologists (FRCR). At breakfast at the hotel in London at which I was staying before the exam, I met a friend from my medical school year. Ron Todd, whom I had not seen since graduation, was an Old Boy of MTS Crosby and a consultant surgeon. He was an examiner for the FRCS, a higher qualification in Surgery, while I was still a struggling examinee! In fact, I was unsuccessful on this occasion and never acquired the FRCR. My appointment at Southmead, pleasant though it was, had removed me from the teaching main stream of the BRI; and my marriage during this time created another major, but happy, distraction. I had a few months to serve as a senior registrar after finishing the locum appointment and I asked Professor Middlemiss if I could study Mammography during this time. I had missed tuition in this important modality because of my locum stint at Southmead Hospital and very much wanted to acquire at least some basic skills. Middlemiss pooh-poohed my request and, instead, I did three months of highly specialised Neuroradiology, a sub-specialty that I was never to engage in again. I felt very uncomfortable about my lack of mammographic knowledge and future events proved that I was correct to do so.

A few weeks later, I met up with Dr Scarrow, the Chairman of

Radiology at the Liverpool Royal Infirmary, who kindly offered me a position there. I was not keen to work again in Liverpool and did not accept his offer. A consultant position in Radiology was advertised at the Southport and Ormskirk Hospitals. I found this very attractive, having worked previously at Ormskirk, but all of my friends believed that I was crazy to turn down the soon-to-be-opened Liverpool Teaching Hospital for Southport and Ormskirk, where I would have no registrar assistance. Some of my reasons for this choice involved the facts that private practice in Southport was said to be very good and that a new hospital would shortly be opened there, in which I could have a large input regarding the design of the Radiology department. In addition, with the boundary changes instituted by the Heath Government due to take effect on January 1st 1974, Wrightington Hospital would come into the Ormskirk district. This had a famous Orthopaedic unit where the great Sir John Charnley, a leading pioneer in total joint surgery, worked for many years. I was greatly excited at the prospect of being associated with he and his team.

So Frances and I moved to Southport at the end of 1973 and I began work there and at Ormskirk on January 1st, 1974. We lived in a large, older house, with lovely moulded ceilings and a huge garden. It was, in fact, far too big for us but Frances and I had fallen in love with it and I though it possible that, at some future time, I might install an x-ray unit in one of the many cellars. I now renewed my acquaintanceship with many old friends in the area and certainly enjoyed my social life. I played squash at the Southport and Birkdale Cricket Club, where the Lancashire County Cricket Club played at least once a season and where, on one of these occasions, I lunched with the Red Rose team, courtesy of a friend. I joined the Hesketh Golf Club whose first tee was a mere 300 yards from my home. There, I met and played snooker with Curtis Strange during the preliminary rounds of the British Open in 1975, after he had failed to qualify for the final rounds which were played at the nearby Royal Birkdale club. Curtis went on to win many USPGA events, two US Opens and to appear in six Ryder cups, in one of which he was non-playing captain. The arrival of Helen, our daughter, greatly added to our happiness.

However, things were not so good as regards work. There were serious personnel problems at Southport and no news of the opening of the new hospital. In fact, Prince Charles performed this in 1988, many years after the date that I had been promised at interview. In addition, Wrightington Hospital did not, in practice, come into the Ormskirk District clinical setting although it was technically in that District. The reason for this I was never able to discover and this was a grievous disappointment to me. Also, I was finding it difficult to make ends meet on my salary. I had opted to be a "maximum part-time" consultant and so received only nine-elevenths of the full-timers' salary. I did this to be free to examine private patients in my own time but these were in decidedly short supply. It would have been better, in retrospect, to have gone full-time initially and to then have changed to maximum part-time later.

The Ormskirk Medical Society was an all-male institution that met on a regular basis, either at the Buck i'th Vine pub or at the Ormskirk golf club. Lectures alternated between purely medical subjects and those with a non-medical but intellectual content. The members were friendly and gregarious and the meetings never less than enjoyable. Dr David Marsh gave a lecture on one occasion on the anatomical basis of the golf swing, followed by an interesting account of the Lancashire golf team's tour of Rhodesia and South Africa. As a new member, I was invited to lecture, which I did with a scientific subject. It was preceded by drinks and dinner and it was long after 10.00 pm when I rose to commence my talk. The West Lancashire Medical Society was later formed to accommodate female physicians and to satisfy the new regulations regarding seniority payments to GPs, which were linked to attendances at accredited meetings. Regular meetings of this society were held in a new and impressive post-graduate centre in the grounds of the hospital. Unfortunately, this soon led to a decline of the Ormskirk society which I am told now carries on in a very limited way and virtually involves social events only.

I continued to discharge my RNR training obligation of two weeks annually and, to supplement my dire financial situation, I also did locums for a large Radiology group in Winnipeg, Canada, for a couple of summers. They were arranged for me by Gwillam Evans, a friend who had been a year behind me at medical school. Neither my RNR training nor my Manitoba locums were very onerous but, done in the same leave year, they accounted for all my holiday time. Of course, because of financial considerations, my family could not accompany me. Although I continued to enjoy living in West Lancashire, my professional and personal situation became more and more intolerable. I saw an advertisement for a staff radiologist for the Cleveland University Hospitals, wrote off about it and had a most encouraging reply. I was not yet ready to leave England, however, and did not follow up. In the following year, with things no better, I again went to Winnipeg to do a four-week locum. While there, the Cleveland radiologist who had earlier written to me, got in touch again and I flew to Ohio for a mutual "look see" for two nights, with all expenses paid. The set-up there had many attractions but salary was not discussed and no promises were made on either side. I flew back to Winnipeg, and later to England, far from convinced that I should emigrate to the New World.

Unfortunately, my professional situation in Southport and Ormskirk continued to deteriorate. My exiguous salary was frozen, even though it was below the level at which the government pay freeze was supposed to begin. The Regional Board justified this on the grounds that, had I been employed as a full-time consultant rather than a maximum part-time one, then my salary would have been above this critical level. However, I wasn't in full-time employment, my salary was not above the threshold and the ruling was both curmudgeonly and totally irrational. In addition, I now found difficulty in scheduling private patients who were referred to me, being told on one occasion by one of my technical staff that this constituted "queue jumping". Such private practice was, of course, part of the NHS, for participating in which I gave up a considerable part of my fixed salary. Finally, a request to the central NHS authority in London for a registrar had been approved after a long delay but only if I could myself provide the salary from some source! This was the last straw and I decided that I couldn't continue in this hostile environment until distant retirement and I determined to take up the Ohio offer.

I wrote to Cleveland, announcing my firm intention to join them, and was relieved to learn that there was no problem with this plan. However, I received a serious shock when applying for a US visa. Despite firm evidence of a definite job offer, I had great difficulty in actually gaining one. I began the process in early 1976 and had not laid my hands on the coveted document by the end of that year. I was now extremely anxious as, should I enter the USA after midnight on January 7th 1977, I would fall foul of new legislation making my subsequent stay there difficult and perhaps even impossible. This legislation was based on the premise that the USA no longer needed the many foreign physicians who were entering the country. Their admission would, in future, be much more severely controlled and new examinations would be mandatory.

So Christmas and New Year saw me on tender hooks, very uncertain as to my immediate geographical place of residence. Eventually, I received a call from the US embassy, went to Grosvenor Square, London, and was handed the precious visa. The delay was largely due to the large number of visa applications, many from physicians, prior to the procedural changes. I then had precisely 48 hours before flying off to Cleveland. I had taken two weeks leave and a locum was in place for this period at Southport. I now sent off a letter of resignation but was unable, of course, to give the customary and courtesy three months notice. I did whatever I could before my very rushed departure and left my wife and daughter at the gate at Manchester airport. Eventually, suffering from a bad dose of flu and after delays caused by an IRA bomb scare and a blizzard in New York, I arrived at Cleveland thoroughly exhausted. The next few days were spent filling in forms, meeting my future colleagues, being introduced to other British refugees from the NHS and recovering from my flu and jet lag. There were several new radiologists other than myself, the majority from South Africa, and I was told that more were on the way; clearly, a big recruiting drive had taken place. The weather was bitterly cold, with six inches of snow on the ground.

At this stage, I began to wonder if I might be able to go back home for a few weeks. I had departed in such a hurry and was, among other things, concerned about not giving much notice as to my leaving. I discussed this with my new Chairman, who was most obliging. He agreed that I did not have to begin work immediately and even gave me a salary advance that enabled me to fly home. So, five days after leaving my family at Manchester airport, I was reunited with them; then I suffered another blow. The Mersey Regional Health Board agreed that I could carry on working at Southport but the Lancashire Regional Board would not permit me to resume work at Ormskirk. They took the view that I had resigned and that was that. My going home, involving a return flight of more than 7,000 miles, was done largely to discharge my responsibilities to the hospital. However, this reasoning was ignored by the bureaucrats in Manchester, as were pleas from several of the Ormskirk consultants, who pointed out that the hospital would now have only 50% of its previous radiological cover.

TWELVE

Ohio and Oregon

I worked back at Southport for about eight weeks, a leisurely schedule but one bringing in precious little salary. I was able to sell my car, leaving Frances with hers for disposal closer to her later departure, and many other items. The radiographers presented me with a farewell gift and I then was off west again. This time, I was in good health and suffered no delays. I arrived back in Cleveland and began work at the Metro General Hospital, on the west side of the city in a tough, working class area. I lived in an old but pleasant three-roomed suite for which no charge was made. I could eat three meals daily at the hospital dining room, these being nutritious, cheap but not very exciting. I thought that I could stand this form of existence until the family arrived. I noted that many workers, including those in offices and many other occupations, began work at 8.00 am. This was the case in the Radiology department, with some examinations being scheduled earlier than this. There would be resident conferences daily at 7.00 am and the whole day was far more structured and busy than were comparable days in the UK. I had always thought that I had worked hard when a registrar in the NHS but had never had early morning conferences and few midday lectures. The US residents did approximately the same amount of "on call" duties as their British counterparts but they seemed to have much better back-up from senior residents, fellows and consultants.

I was employed with a provisional license that did not permit me to work at any other institution. By US standards, my salary was modest as I had neither a state license nor certification of the American Board of Radiology. However, compared to my exiguous earnings in England, I was now being paid at a truly princely rate and had definitely arrived on board what many British medical expatriates called "the gravy train". I led a relatively quiet life, awaiting the arrival of Frances and Helen. This occurred after another five months, with little Helen, who had refused to sleep during the long journey, charging across the tarmac into her dad's arms at the Cleveland airport. July 4th dawned soon afterwards and two small girls from the house next door knocked and asked if Helen could play with them. Helen accepted the invitation with alacrity and, proudly waving her Union Jack, ran into the road. She had acquired the flag just before leaving England, during the celebrations of the Queen's Silver Jubilee, and I could only persuade her to give it up, on this uniquely American day, with great difficulty.

We lived in a rented duplex on the west side of town and I enjoyed showing the newcomers all the sights. In the following year, the city of Cleveland defaulted on loans from six banks and became the first US city to do so since the Depression. The city's bond rating on Wall Street plunged downwards and increased interest rates on bonds and loans were now felt by Cleveland and many surrounding suburbs and towns. The Cuyahoga river, flowing through Cleveland into Lake Erie, now almost unbelievably caught fire because of its grossly polluted state and, with crime on the increase, the city became known as "the mistake on the lake". Dennis Kucinich, the Mayor of Cleveland, was said to be at loggerheads with many city councillors and there were even stories that he had ordered that the precincts of some councillors should not be ploughed after heavy snow falls. I have no idea if this was correct or not but he certainly appeared to be a divisive figure. He appeared on a larger stage in 2003 when emerging as one of the many hopefuls for the Democratic nomination in the 2004 US Presidential election.

There were countless differences between this New World and the older one now far behind us. I found the absence of any Boxing Day and the short Christmas and New Year holidays very unusual and disconcerting. Like Isaiah Berlin, I discovered a marked reluctance among many Americans to accept any quibble or nuance in answer to a question, however complicated it might be; a simple "yes" or "no" was required. Club ties and blazer badges were very rare and little if any equivalent to the rugby or cricket club bar appeared to exist. I could never appreciate why so many American males felt it so important to wear caps and hats indoors. This occurred not only in gymnasia, sports arena, etc but in libraries, homes and even at dinner.

Another striking feature was the strident, shrill tones of many females. This was especially noticeable with women on TV, in many ladies who were otherwise attractive and no doubt very pleasant people. I wondered if it was a cultural or environmental phenomenon but could never find the answer to this query. When asking colleagues about this, including an ENT surgeon who was deeply interested in speech pathology, they professed complete ignorance as to what I was describing. Of course, there were very many positives, not merely my work satisfaction and financial situation, but especially the courtesy and consideration shown to the customer in a shop or to a patient at a hospital.

We had to endure considerable "culture shock". In particular, this included the abuse of the English language, from which I never completely recovered. There appeared to be no knowledge of the difference between adjectives and adverbs, with the former being very frequently employed incorrectly in place of the latter. I would frequently hear on TV the boast "CNN. The most trusted name in News". Clearly, this trust clearly did not extend to English grammar, as the phrase "CNN. Real news, real fast" soon followed. Nouns were similarly misused, usually as verbs as in "to dialogue", "to party", "to transition" and "to medal", as in the Olympic games. Finally, prepositions were inappropriately overused, as in "listen up", "visit with" and "cancel out". "Two times" was employed rather than "twice" and the word "fortnight" was vitually unknown. I heard a fierce altercation going on one day in the hospital. One enraged individual called his adversary "a cretan". I could not understand why representing someone as hailing from an island in the eastern Mediterranean should be so bad; after all, El Greco had hailed from there. It was some time before I heard this word used again and then realised that the word "cretin" was intended. Many years later, I read Fritz Spiegl's most interesting book *"Contradictionary: An A-Z of Confusibles, Lookalikes and Soundalikes"*, which deals with malapropisms and other linguistic howlers. I agreed with all he wrote and ranted against but though that, should he have penned the book in the USA, he could have doubled its length!

However, when on holiday back in Britain, I was frequently very disappointed with the English spoken by native Britons. I recalled George Bernard Shaw's complaint that "the English have no respect for their language and will not teach their children to speak it". Then, in the early years of the third millenium, came multitudinous complaints from GSCE examiners and university lecturers in Britain as to the gross deficiences in spelling and grammar of a high proportion of students. A new form of attack on the English language was disclosed in 2004 by the Assessment and Qualifications Alliance, the largest examination board in the UK. This was the increasing use of abbreviations in writing, based on text message language and mobile phone shorthand.

John Humphrys, anchor of the *Today* programme and feared BBC interviewer, published his book *The Mangling and Manipulating of the English Language* in the same year. In it, he deplored the split infinitives, greengrocer's apostrophes and other syntactical monstrosities that were now so commonly encountered in the UK. Humphrys blamed academics and politicians for this situation whereas I would lay the blame, at least in the USA, on the gobbledygook of the media, with a variety of TV anchors, all making obscene salaries for reading out the news, contributing to this grammatical jungle. Anthony Burgess had said that "only in England is the perversion of the language regarded as a victory for democracy". This could be taken as being a reflection on what had become common by the end of the millenium, namely that verbal barbarians had taken over, with glottal stops and rising inflections. These would include, many felt, a whole mass of BBC broadcasters and even the Prime Minister. Hence I wondered if perhaps I was being too hard on the Americans that I encountered.

Although many Americans were avid runners and keep-fit merchants, I was amazed at the amount of sheer obesity that I saw around me on a daily basis; this was especially noticeable, I thought, in females. Another surprise was the number of people who sported tattoos. Quite a substantial minority of these were females, this trend probably owing much to show biz personalities such as Cher. I remembered being taught in medical school that any patient with a tattoo should have serological tests for venereal disease. Of course, this was in the immediate post-World War Two period when many men had been far away from home for long periods. No doubt this advice would horrify Americans today and produce angry cries of protest. It certainly represented an earlier time and a different society.

In 2001, the American Alliance of Professional Tattooists claimed that one-in-ten of the US population now had a tattoo, compared with just one-in-a-hundred in 1970. Personally, I think the practice has nothing to recommend it, that a large proportion of tattoos are crude and ugly and that many later wish they had never been mutilated, with some paying large amounts of money to have the tattoos removed. For many years, I have had a great respect for the intelligence, knowledge and sheer industry of Paul Johnson. He is, of course, especially informed an matters of Art. Writing in *The Speccie* in December 2003, in connection with the publication of his huge *Art: A New History* book, he stated that there are now more magazines devoted to tattooing than to the fine arts. He went on to suggest that in 100 years time, the most highly esteemed and paid artists may be body decorators. On reading this, my immediate thought was "I hope not!"

There was a great deal of amateur Sport shown on US TV and this, almost entirely, involved the Universities. All varieties of college Sport were followed very closely by the general public and this was entirely different to the situation in the UK. College football (i.e. gridiron, or American football) and basketball filled the screen from late August to March and commanded huge audiences. Several college football games were shown on TV every Saturday and the University of Notre Dame had a unique nine game contract for football games every year with the National Broadcasting Corporation (NBC), one of the three major US TV networks. A national collegiate basketball tournament, known as "March Madness" lasted for more than two weeks and involved 64 teams competing initially in many widely separated sites. Practically every game was shown on TV and every office and work place seemed to run a betting pool on the competition, for which there was gigantic public interest. Of course, there was even more professional Sport on offer, especially on Sundays, when football and golf coverage, in particular, would frequently over-run its allotted time and lead to various programming, including the main evening news on the major networks, being shown either late or not at all.

I do not have a high regard for US sporting journalism. In general, I find a marked lack of oratorical and literary skills with little humour and far too much statistical information. The idea of someone like John Arlott, EW Swanton, Brian Johnston or, of course, Neville Cardus, appearing as a US sporting commentator is impossible to imagine. However, to be fair, the like of Cardus, a friend of both Sir Thomas Beecham and Sir Donald Bradman, has not been seen in England for many years and Johnners was similarly unique.

In the medical school, I soon realised that the title "Professor" did not indicate the Head of department, as it did in the UK. It was simply an academic rank, above Assistant and Associate Professor. Not uncommonly, the departmental Chief might only be an Associate Professor as many full Professors had no interest in tackling the many administrative headaches and financial battles associate with being in charge. I was also shocked as to the degree of evaluation carried out in academic Medicine. Medical students were constantly being rated, as were residents and faculty also. Even departmental Chairmen were scored as to their abilities, these numbers being asked for in a multitude of areas. I have no doubt that much personal bias crept into these and personal grudges and dislikes would often determine a rating. No doubt this sort of thing has crept into British medical schools by the third milennium but it was all new to me in 1977 and I did not care for it at all.

As a matter of priority, I had to secure the Flex examination. This was a qualifying exam for US students, such as those trained in the Caribbean or elsewhere, and for physicians from overseas, like myself. There were no clinical or oral exams as in the British equivalent and the only problem for me was likely to be in the Basic Sciences, which I had not studied for many years. So I drove down to the state capital, Columbus, and on a very cold morning, joined many others at the Ohio State Fair Grounds. I found some of the questions very tricky, especially those relating to Anatomy, Microbiology and particularly Biochemistry. However, I thought I had done well enough overall and this was confirmed by the results. I now had an Ohio license and was qualified to freely practise Medicine in that state.

I still had to become certified by the American Board of Radiology. This was not absolutely essential for a radiologist but was highly desirable. It would be unusual for a reputable University department, for instance, to employ anyone who was not board certified. So I went off once more to Columbus and sat the multiple-choice papers of the exam. I had done little if any preparation because of my new environment, my family's arrival and the Flex exam. I was especially concerned about the Physics section, this being a subject that I had not studied for many years, and I was correct in my surmise. I passed the main part of the written exam but was "referred" in Physics; this was a gentle way of telling me that I had failed. However, at this time, I would not be delayed in completing the exam but I would have to take an additional exam in Physics at the later oral examination.

My family and I were happy enough in Cleveland but found the winter months very harsh and the urban sprawl unattractive. I had resolved to escape as soon as I had pased my Boards and could find a pleasant alternative. So now I began searching the radiological journals for vacant positions and soon found one in Portland, Oregon. I applied, enclosing my curriculum vitae, and was delighted to be invited to University Hospital and the medical school of the University of Oregon, for an interview.

I flew there, changing planes at Denver, and had two full days in the Radiology department. All travelling and hotel expenses were, of course, paid by my hosts as this was and is the normal procedure in the USA. I gave the usual didactic lecture to the residents and faculty and dined with the Chairman on the second night. I mentioned that my family and I were shortly taking a vacation in Virginia and intended to visit the battlefield at Gettysburg. The Chairman promptly pulled out a book about Colonel Pickett's famous charge at Cemetery Ridge in that epic battle, thrust it into my hands and told me to read it prior to my visit. I wondered as to how I could return it to him but said nothing. I had little time to explore Portland but the medical school had commanding views of the Cascade mountains to the east and the Coastal Range to the west. It all looked most attractive.

On my way back to Cleveland, I found myself hoping that I might be offered an appointment in such a beautiful region. I explained all this to Frances but emphasised that nothing was yet definite. Then, a couple of weeks later, I received a formal offer of employment in the mail, which I accepted with alacrity. On the day of our departure, Frances took off with Helen in the back of her car. I remained behind while the contents of the rented house were checked and then followed. Our late start meant that our first day's mileage was modest and we stayed that night at a hotel in South Bend, Indiana, just to the east of Chicago and right on the campus of the famous University of Notre Dame. The next day, we drove around Chicago and on to Waterloo, Iowa. The following day saw us in Ogden, Utah, north of Salt Lake City and just east of the Great Salt Lake. On the fourth day, we drove along the south bank of the lovely Columbia Gorge and on into Portland.

We had arranged via a friend in Portland to rent a house and lived there for just under a year. Early in our stay, a family of raccoons would press their noses to the glass sliding doors opening on to the patio each night when we were eating dinner. Helen was fascinated by them and they remained about the house for months. Unlike many Americans who purchase homes in a new location immediately after deciding to relocate, we did not wish to buy a house until we had a feel for the area, schools, shops etc. Eventually, we did buy very close to the rental home and moved our furniture ourselves, with the help of a faculty member and a couple of residents. Portland proved to be a clean, exciting city with lots to do. The beautiful Oregon coast and majestic Mount Hood were both less than 90 minutes driving away.

Soon after taking possession of our new home, a severe bout of cold weather hit the Pacific North West, beginning with a big snow storm and then what was locally called an ice storm. The fridgid conditions, which were atypical for Portland, lasted for more than a week and we and many others were without electrical power during this time. This was due to the power cables, suspended from poles above ground, collapsing under the weight of snow and ice. Fortunately, our water heater was gas powered, as was a stove top, and we had a fireplace in the family room. Nevertheless, we had to endure an unpleasant existence for six or seven days, using oil lamps in the house and frequently eating out. For the last 20 years or so, most US cities have been placing their power lines underground.

Mount St Helens was slightly to our north in Washington State and its spectacular and explosive eruption in May 1980 caused much damage in the region and many deaths. The volcanic mountain had been first sighted by Europeans in 1792 when Captain George Vancouver aboard the sloop *HMS Discovery* christened it in honour of Lord St Helens, the envoy of George the Third to the Spanish Court. The mountain had a high, rounded peak reaching to 9,677 ft, was said to be comparable in appearance to Mount Fuji in Japan and had been inactive for the previous 123 years. Warning tremors and shocks began in the early Spring of 1980 and showed dramatic increases up to May, when they no longer had much news value. On Sunday morning, May 18th, an earthquake of magnitude 5.1 on the Richter scale involved the summit, which slid away in the largest landslide in recorded history. The top 1270 feet of the mountain disappeared and more than one cubic mile of material was discharged into the air. The eruption column, comprising gas and ash, rose 15 miles into the sky within 15 minutes (Fig 18). Prevailing winds blew the ash towards Spokane, a town in eastern Washington state 250 miles away, where almost complete darkness ensued. There were 57 human deaths, most being due to asphyxiation from ash. These unfortunate people com-

Fig 18. Mount St Helens erupting. The huge mass of smoke and ash is obvious, arising from the crater. The dome of the mountain has disappeared (Reprinted by permission of the United States Geologic Survey).

prised loggers, rangers, local inhabitants and tourists. There was also great loss of wildlife, with more than 7,000 big game animals killed and 12 million juvenile salmon lost. The total economic damage to the area was estimated at $1.2 billion. Some 120,000 acres of forest were laid waste by the eruption and the subsequent flooding, with 3.3 billion board feet of timber destroyed. Initially, winds took the ash to the northeast but a wind change soon drenched Portland in the stuff. Roads, gutters and gardens were full of ash and some cars had their electrical systems affected. Relatively minor eruptions continued until October of 1980, with further atmospheric pollution, and extrusions of lava occurred over the next six years until a lava dome was finally built over the crater.

Dr Charles Dotter was the Chairman of the Radiology department at University Hospital in Portland, who had been appointed at a young age. He was a somewhat eccentric figure and his specialty was angiography. He achieved lasting fame by developing the very widely employed procedure, called "angioplasty", in which a catheter is passed into an artery and advanced beyond an area of narrowing. A balloon is then inflated on the catheter tip and the catheter withdrawn across the area of stenosis, thus dilating it. This procedure can be repeated several times, if necessary. The technique has been refined over the years and is now used extensively in other anatomical situations including narrowed coronary arteries. It represented a quantum advance in the management of vascular disease.

A few weeks after arriving in Portland, I had to fly to Chicago to complete the Radiology Board exam with the oral. To my surprise, it was conducted in a large hotel, specifically in the bedrooms of the various examiners. These Board exams were similar to the British FRCR examination but were rather more detailed. They consisted, after the written papers had been successfully surmounted in a number of locations, of a 23 minute oral exam in each of about ten sub-specialties, such as Chest Diseases, Ultrasound, Nuclear Medicine, Musculo-Skeletal Diseases, etc; so the examination of each candidate was comprehensive. Although I had engaged in practically no Nuclear Medicine nor Neuro-Radiology for several years, I had enjoyed some intensive coaching in the latter specialty from Helmut, a charming German fellow in the Portland Radiology department. I encountered no problems with any of the radiological specialty sections and found the examiners to be universally courteous and gentlemanly.

The Physics viva, about which I was rather concerned, was completed last and was rather more difficult. The examiner had nine or ten cards spread out on a table, each bearing the title of a radiological topic having a physical angle. I was invited to pick several of my choice and talk about them in turn. I spotted one card with "Modulation Transfer Function" (MTF) written on it, this referring to a complicated and difficult aspect of x-ray image quality. Of course, I avoided this like the plague and carried on selecting easier topics doing, as I thought, quite well. Then the bell sounded outside the room we were in, signalling the end of my viva session. I thought that I was home free but the examiner now thrust the dreaded card at me and asked me to tell him about this. "Don't worry about the bell", he said "this will only take a few minutes". I came out with a definition of MTF, repeated my answer using different words in a different order, and was about to dry up when the door burst open and a senior examiner announced that I must leave at once and make way for the next candidate. So I had been saved by the bell, literally, albeit after a severe scare. I thought I had done well enough overall and a letter a few days later informed me that I was now "boarded" in Diagnostic Radiology.

One of the slight reservations I had about my new position was that it involved me working largely in Gastrointestinal Radiology. I was fully competent at this but it was not my area of prime interest. However, I thought that accepting the position would get me out of Cleveland into a nicer part of the world, which it certainly did. As well as this work, I had to take my turn in the reading room, dealing with all manner of films. All the Radiology faculty did this in rotation but Dr Dotter was often unable to fulfill his obligations in this area for a variety of reasons, including ill-health, and invariably called on me to substitute for him. I was also in charge of student teaching. Batches of medical students would rotate through the department doing elective periods. In addition, there was an unusual, but very effective, system of Radiology teaching in place for all students. Classes would be held each Tuesday night at 7.00 pm for one hour. Groups of eight to ten students would discuss films with a radiologist, many non-university radiologists participating. The students would have been given the films a week before this discussion and would acquire new films each week. This scheme was thought to be superior to didactic lectures and there was some justification for this belief. I described the whole process in a published paper, to which I added Doctor Dotter's name.

Formal exams for medical students, again employing film sessions and not written questions, were held once or twice a year. I had to organise these and created a stir when I had two residents in the large room with me during the projection of the films. This was because widespread consultation, or cheating, invariably went on and it was impossible for a single person to deal with this and act as projectionist at the same time. In April 1982, Dr Dotter asked me to substitute for him, at rather short notice, at a big radiological conference at Spokane. He was to have spoken on angioplasty, of course, but I spoke on several musculo-skeletal topics. I was delighted to be involved in this venture. My lectures went off well, I received a generous honorarium and it was all most enjoyable.

Holidays involved trips into California, where young Helen hugely enjoyed Disneyland and the Universal Studios, and up into Canada where we met up with old friends on Vancouver Island. We skied a good deal, which was thoroughly enjoyable and hugely superior to skiing in Scotland, often at nearby Mount Hood, which was relatively close to Portland. We also used Mount Batchelor, near the town of Bend, if we had more time. The snow conditions here were said to be superior and Bend made a serious but unsuccessful attempt to host the Winter Olympics. The bid failed because of poor communications and lack of sufficient infrastructure, such as accommodation. All in all, we thoroughly enjoyed living in Oregon.

A few months after arriving in Portland, I spent a week in the Radiology department of the University of San Francisco Hospital. I was able to live in quite pleasant resident accomodation and to learn how this busy and efficient department did things. The Chairman of Radiology there was Dr Alexander Margulis, originally from Yugoslavia. He was a very senior and respected figure in US Radiology and, before leaving, I asked him if he would come up to Portand for a few days, advise us on our proceedures and give a few lectures. He readily agreed to this and also was happy to stay with the Cope family, rather than in a hotel. His visit was a great success, in spite of young Helen charging into his bedroom at an early hour after his first night in our home, to inform him of all her many discoveries and questions.

I became Secretary/Treasurer of the Oregon Radiologic Society and was an enthusiastic member of the Pacific Northwest Radiologic Society, which met alternatively in Portland, Vancouver, Seattle and Victoria. Attendance at these meetings confirmed an impression that I had long held, that a large proportion of Canadian physicians would gladly give their right arm for the chance to practise Medicine in the USA. The society was active and the social gatherings were most enjoyable. I met up with some old friends at these meetings, notably Dr Danny Sinclair who had trained in Edinburgh a few years before me. He and another Edinburgh-trained radiologist jointly proposed me for the fellowship of the Royal College of Physicians of Edinburgh and this was successful. So I was now FRCP(Ed). Two proposers had earlier been unsuccessful on my behalf when I was living in Southport.

I rediscovered my love of running soon after arriving in Portland and started to run on a regular basis. I learned to ignore the very frequent rain and to appreciate the joke that Oregonians do not tan but rust! Running was a huge sport here and the Cascade Runoff, held each year in Portland, was a major race in the US running calendar with many thousands participating. The US Olympic Track and Field Trials, and many other big events, were frequently held on the track of the University of Oregon at Eugene, some 120 miles south of Portland. When work permitted, I would run at lunchtime, joining hundreds of others on a hilly course near the medical school. I joined the Oregon Road Runners Club and became a regular competitor. I gradually increased my mileage and began planning to compete in a marathon. I ran my first at Snoqualmie, in Washington state, finishing in a respectable 3 hours 32 minutes, although I found the last few miles incredibly tough. The great interest shown in all forms of running in this part of the world was reflected in the big crowds along the route of most marathons. Groups of people would often yell "looking good" at me and, if not suffering too much, I would respond with "feeling terrible". I ran another four marathons, including the celebrated Nike marathon that began and finished on the university track at Eugene, with runners from all over the world taking part. My best race was at Seaside on the Oregon coast where I finished in 3 hours and just 20 minutes. Aged 52 years, I was very pleased with this time as I was rarely able to get in much more than 40 miles of running each week.

When competing, I often met with a man who was 16 years younger than I and slightly taller, with massive shoulders and upper torso, a physique not ideal for a runner. We often ran together, at least at the start of a race, but I invariably moved ahead of him in the later stages. He complained to the mutual friend that had introduced us that, although he quite liked me, he was irritated my constant chatting while running, when he was suffering. It took me quite some time to realise who this man was. He was, in fact, Don Schollander, who had won four Olympic gold medals for swimming at the Tokyo Olympics, where I remember him beating Bobby McGregor of Scotland by a touch in the 100-metres freestyle. He was an 18 year old Yale student at the time and was described as "gliding effort-lessly to his victories". He won another gold and a silver medal four years later at Mexico City and set 13 individual world records. He was a really nice guy, a superb athlete and a striking example of the fact that one cannot always shine at multiple sports.

We finally visited Tom Skuse's lovely house overlooking the harbour in Union Hall, a small fishing village near Skibbereen, County Cork, after having had multiple invitations over several years. I knew the latter town as being one of the very worse centres for mortality during the great Potato Famine of the mid-nineteenth century. I knew also that its onetime newspaper, now long defunct, had achieved world fame on a certain day in that century. This paper, with a respectable although modest circulation, had run a front-page headline of *The Skibereen Eagle* warns the Tzar "Hands off Turkey" and, because it was what is known in journalistic circles as "a slow news day", this was picked up by a host of news agencies all over the world and quoted in London, New York and many other capital cities. We had a truly marvellous holiday and I wondered about the possibility of purchasing a small property there at some future time.

While there, we went a couple of times to Castletownsend, a neighbouring village. Admiral Somerville had lived here and was the main reason for many local men enlisting in the RN. The Admiral was shot and killed by the IRA during "the troubles". *Marianne's* was a popular pub here and we had a great night of singing with the crews of the "Round Ireland Sailing Race". We went back a few days later for the rowing regatta. Rowing is very popular, it seems, all along this coast, from Cork City in the south-east right up to Kerry in the west. One race was announced as being for the "four old ladies" and we thought that this was rather rude. Clearly, our ears were not attuned to the local brogue; the race was, in fact, for "four oared ladies". Nine year old Helen had a marvellous time, as we all did, and we vowed to return soon. According to the *Sunday Telegraph* a few years later, growing numbers of British and American residents have arrived in the area, attracted by the peace and beauty of the countryside and not put off by the high price of gasoline, groceries and real estate, even of the derelict variety. These newcomers include David Puttnam, the movie producer, and Jeremy Irons and his wife Sinead Cusack. The latter couple bought the ruined Kilcoe Castle on scenic Roaringwater Bay, which was restored and painted a terracotta rust, the colour of which some, including the local newspaper, strongly disapproved.

We seemed to have lots of British visitors in Portland. My friends Gainor and Dai Morgan stayed with us for a few days and we enjoyed their visit. I had lived near Gainor in my youth, hence knowing her and her family, and met Dai through Waterloo RFC. A proud Welshman and native of Neath, Dai was the Physical Education master at MTS Crosby for many years and an outstanding wing forward who had captained the very successful Lancashire team of the early 1950s. We later stayed with him on two occasions at his lovely home, close to the Royal Birkdale Golf Club. Other visitors included Marjory and Howard Ballance. Howard was a dentist who had held sessions at the Ormskirk District Hospital where I had met him. He was, in fact, the only non-medical member of the Ormskirk Medical Society and had been the society Secretary. Gregarious by nature, he was excellent company and loved to tell stories and to reminiscence over a glass of wine. He was a Justice of the Peace, Chairman of the local Magistrates Bench, an Ormskirk Town and Lancashire County Councillor and Chairman of the Lancashire Police Authority. He died a few years after his visit to us and his funeral was something of a news-maker. The main car park in Ormskirk was closed so that mourners would have only a short walk to the parish church. Traffic paralysis ensued and chaos resulted. The Chamber of Trade complained to the police, who said that the Town Council had asked them to do it. The incident was an expression of the regard held by many for Howard Ballance and the power of the 11 masonic lodges in Ormskirk.

The work situation for me in Portland began to deteriorate

after a few years. Some physicians with whom I worked tended to be very aggressive and demanding and even seemed to try to use me as a resident rather than a consultant. Changes in faculty then occurred so that I was doing much of the musculo-skeletal, as well as the gastro-intestinal, work. In a sense, I did not object to this as it was my preferred area of interest; but it did lead to problems and greatly increased my workload. Dr Dotter became ill and was out of the department for many weeks, making it impossible for me to be granted tenure. An acting Chairman asked me to handle the mammography, an area in which I had literally had no formal training despite attempts to remedy this in Bristol. My objections were brushed aside and I had to struggle with this difficult task, frequently requiring assistance from other radiologists. Fortunately, the absurdity of the situation soon became obvious and I was relieved of this responsibility.

Dr Dotter's absence continued and several faculty members resigned and went elsewhere. These departures were, in some cases, coincidental but the faculty situation became very critical. I was working hard, covering many areas, and trying to look after the medical students also. My relationships with some residents suffered because of all this. Often, I would invite a couple of them home after work on Friday afternoon and we would sit on the deck, have a few drinks and generally shoot the breeze. Frances and I enjoyed these occasions and I think the residents did. However, relations between myself and other residents worsened and their evaluations of me were probably not flattering. There was also serious thought that the medical school, or at least the hospital, would close. This did not occur but such talk was very worrying. I had some more thinking to do!

THIRTEEN

Missouri

I was certain that the situation in which I found myself would never have occurred had Dr Dotter not been ill but this was scant consolation. With considerable reluctance, I decided that a move was indicated although I knew that I would be very sorry to leave the Pacific North West. Colleagues assured me breezily that they had moved several times, that this sort of thing was quite common in American university life and that they were sure things would work out well for me. I began looking at the advertised vacancies once more and finally applied for one in the Mid West, at the University of Missouri (MU) at Columbia, often known simply as "Mizzou". I had no idea where this town was and found it on a map only with some difficulty, located midway between St Louis and Kansas City. I remembered that Jackson Scholtz had been an MU student when winning the 200 metres and running second to Britain's Harold Abrahams in the 100 metre final at the Paris Olympics of 1924. All this was featured in the movie *Chariots of Fire* in which the first Earl of Birkenhead also appeared. I duly made application, was invited to visit and stayed for the usual two days, giving a lecture, meeting the faculty and residents and being shown around University Hospital. Columbia turned out to be an attractive, small town with about 80,000 inhabitants but was the site of the main campus of the University. It was also home to two other colleges, was known as "Collegetown USA" and was virtually free of any industry or pollution.

I decided to take up their offer but when I informed ten year old Helen, she burst into tears. This made me feel very uncomfortable and added to my concerns about moving. With a somewhat heavy heart, we left Portland in August 1984 after six happy years. Again, we traversed the Columbia River gorge and left the beautiful Beaver state at Ontario, passing into Idaho. We drove on to Denver, where I gave an invited lecture, and then to Iowa City, Iowa. Here I gave another lecture and we were ensconced in very comfortable accommodation in the university club. In Columbia, as was our prac-

189

tice, we rented a house for 12 months before purchasing our definitive new home.

I found the first year troublesome. I missed Portland dreadfully and kept comparing my new situation with the former one. I found our first Missourian late summer and fall to be very hot and humid and had some problems getting a Missouri medical licence, although this was soon satisfactorily resolved. In addition, I had developed a painful and intractable inflammation of an Achilles tendon which did not respond to conservative measures, including the liberal application of dimethyl sulphoxide. This was a by-product of Oregon's timber industry and, at the time, was widely held by runners to be a sure cure-all for musculo-tendinous problems. My painful tendon had become a chronic problem, prevented me from running and increased my depression. Eventually, Dr Bill Allen, the Chairman of Orthopaedic Surgery at University Hospital, who was soon became a good friend, operated on me. He cleaned out the tendon sheath under local anaesthesia, removing much fibrous tissue and debris, and obtained an excellent result.

After moving into a new home, situated a few yards from a lake in which we could swim, fish and sail, I felt much better. We were now quite settled and enjoying the delights of this small college town. Columbia had an abundance of trees, for which it garnered several awards, and was especially attractive in Spring when the blossom of magnolia, forsythia and Bradford pear, the latter developed by the MU Agriculture school, made a brilliant sight throughout the town. It lacked some features of the much larger metropolitan Portland but it had a good deal of other advantages. These included low housing costs and property taxes, relatively cheap food and gasoline, very good walking, running and cycling trails and an absence of crime. The schools were generally excellent and a very large shopping mall was built soon after our arrival. In addition, the medical school and University Hospital were situated right on the campus of the main University, with all the sporting facilities of the latter being immediately adjacent, not over a 100 miles away, as in Portland. We tailgated at every home football game with a group of friends, eating and drinking about a van prior to the game. Drinking before the game took a little getting used to but we soon took it for granted. So it was no great surprise to my family when our new city was voted number five in the nation for "livability" by *Money Magazine* in its annual survey of 1990. Two years later, this magazine rated Columbia number two, with only Sioux Falls, South Dakota listed as being superior.

By mid-western standards, the winters were generally mild, with perhaps one big snowfall each year, when cross-country skiing on the university's 18 hole golf course was a popular pastime and Helen could enjoy skating on our neighbourhood lake. However, we did suffer the occasional very cold spell and I remember vividly enduring a temprature of -20 degrees Fahrenheit, more than 50 degrees below zero, for a short period. This inclement weather always came from Canada and was often referred to as an "Alberta Clipper". I certainly did not miss the incessant Oregon rain.

As in most of the Mid West, the summers could be extremely hot and for three or four weeks each August, an associated high humidity could make for unpleasant conditions. During pre-season football training in August 2001, a student on the Northwestern university team in Chicago collapsed and died, as did a professional member of the Minnesota Vikings; both deaths were said to be due to heat stroke. Our house was to the west of my place of employment, as it had been in both Cleveland and Portland. I was again bothered severely by the bright sun when driving to work each morning and, usually to a lesser degree, when returning home in the late afternoon. Especially in winter, a low lying early morning sun could be quite dazzling, making drivers almost blind, despite the use of sun visors on the car and driver's sunglasses. I was reliably informed by a police officer that this phenomenon was a cause of several road accidents each year. At least three friends told me that, for this reason, they always bought houses to the east of their workplace.

The Katy trail was a source of much enjoyment for us and we used it several times a week throughout most of the year. Built on the old Missouri-Kansas-Texas railway, which terminated its services in the mid-1980s, the main trail extended nearly the entire width of the state, from St Charles, just west of St Louis, to Clinton, 40 miles south-east of Kansas City, with much of it adjacent to the wide Missouri River. A spur from this runs some seven miles into Columbia, right into the downtown area, and is a highly popular walking, jogging and cycling facility. There are trees on either side, providing shade in the hot summers, and many creeks cross the trail on their way to the Missouri River. Deer are frequently encountered and a plethora of birds and a rich variety of flowers makes it a delight for the ornithologist and naturalist. Even in the winter, with snow on the ground displaying animal tracks, it remains enjoyable to use.

We went to Ireland again in 1987 for another wonderful vacation although we did not visit Union Hall. I gave a lecture in Limerick and another in Galway City, where two of the consultants had worked earlier with me in Britain. We went on to County Mayo and called on Dr Vincent and Angela O'Sullivan, who were friends of friends. Vincent was English with his sister a radiologist in London. He was a GP with a dispensing practise far from any town. He owned a Rolls Royce and was in great demand for miles around as he was always willing to drive brides to church for their weddings. The O'Sullivan children were going to a dance on Sunday evening which began at 11.00 pm. Apparently, this unusual start and day were traditional in these parts, and indeed in much of Ireland. They pleaded with us to allow 13 year old Helen to accompany them and then to stay the night. Somewhat reluctantly, Frances and I agreed and, leaving Helen behind, went off to Belmullet to a small hotel. Frances then became increasingly uneasy at leaving her only child with virtual strangers in the wilds of a foreign country! Next morning, we were informed that our hotel bill had been settled via the phone by Mrs O'Sullivan and no money would be accepted. Arriving back at the O'Sullivan's house, Helen enthusiastically told us that she had enjoyed a wonderful time. The cost of the hotel was again refused as we left this hospitable and generous family. After a mile or two, Helen began waving at a youth driving a tractor in a field and asked me to sound my horn. We were informed that this was Sean, whom she had met at the dance. We then stayed on Achill Island, where the Irish themselves go on holiday. There we met up with Niall and Mary Tierney and their family, Niall and I having worked together years earlier at Whiston Hospital. Niall had become a medical administrator and had risen to great heights in the Irish Health System. Helen practised her flute each day and on one occasion here, quite a crowd of visitors had gathered outside our bed and breakfast establishment to listen to her, thinking that this was part of the town's entertainment.

After returning from this vacation, Frances took a part-time position in a travel agency situated in the heart of the Mizzou campus. "Ticket Qwick" sold airline tickets mainly to students and faculty although other forms of transport were also catered for. The offices were sited inside Brady Commons, a large building containing the university bookstore, cafeteria, bowling alley, several shops, etc. The work was varied and generally interesting although many students had little idea of what they wanted and no idea of how much it would cost. For instance, two students enquired about going to Australia for Spring Break, but had absolutely no concept of what was entailed in getting "Down Under". The periods just before university holidays were obviously the busiest with Spring Break, a time when American students flock in their thousands to the southern beaches, and especially to those in Florida, especially hectic.

On one occasion, a tall, good-looking young man called Freddie, who was obviously English, enquired about the cost of flying home for Christmas. At this time, one could fly directly from St Louis to Gatwick on TWA and charter flights were also available, often requiring a plane change in, for instance, the New York City area. It appeared that Freddie was an exchange student from an English university and his father had promised to pay for this trip, provided he managed to obtain a cheap ticket. Using a travel company that specifically dealt with students, Frances obtained such a ticket for him but Freddie, not having the money to pay, announced that it could be charged to his father's credit card, of which he had the number. Frances said she could not do this without his father's written permission and asked that his father fax this to her, as well as confirming the credit card number. A fax was received the following morning, signed "Earl St Germans". Having a marked paucity of belted earls among our acquaintances, Frances now had to phone the British embassy in Washington to discover how one addressed such a peer of the realm, before she could reply.

Some years later, Frances and I saw a BBC program about the Earl St Germans and his home in Cornwall. In the autumn of 2002, we read in a British Sunday newspaper that Freddie Eliot had decided to change his surname to Freud. Ostensibly the youngest son of the Earl of St Germans, the paper claimed that it had long been an open secret that Freddie was, in fact, the issue of an affair between the artist Lucian Freud and the society beauty Jaquetta Lampson, Lord St Germans' first wife. The artist was alleged to have a large number of illegitimate children and to acknowledge these only after they had grown up. Lucien Freud included a nude portrait of Freddie in an exhibition at London's Tate Gallery. Freddie was now said to have a raffish air, to spend much time dancing and to describe himself as a "mystic dancer standing between the material and cosmic worlds". On reading this, I was immediately reminded of the words of the classical swing ballad "You came a long way from St Louis", the last line of which is "But Baby, you've still got a long way to go!". In late 2004, I read that a nude portrait of the pregnant model Kate Moss by Lucian Freud was to be auctioned by Christie's in London and was expected to realise 3.5 million pounds. Although a great deal of dosh, it would not equal the 5.8 million record for another Freud painting.

Frances, Helen and I had become enthusiastic followers of the Tigers, the name given to all the MU sporting teams. We missed few home football games and also enjoyed the Mizzou basketball games, especially the few that we actually attended, courtesy of a neighbour. Tickets for these were like gold and very difficult to acquire. However, a great number of these games were shown on TV and this rose to almost 100% by the 2004-2005 season. A new basketball coach was installed in 1999. Quin Snyder came from Duke University in North Carolina, a modest-sized college affiliated to the United Methodist Church, established in 1839 and having an excellent academic reputation. It was not noted for football but seemed to have outstanding basketball teams, season after season. Snyder had played there on a very successful team before graduating in Law. He was then an assistant coach in basketball at his Alma Mater before moving on to Columbia.

A press conference was held to introduce him to the media, faculty, students and alumni and there was no doubt, so it seemed, that he could walk across the wide Missouri river. He was given an enormous starting salary, which was increased after a couple of modestly successful seasons to a guaranteed minimum of $815,000. In addition, he was expected to pull in more money if certain academic and sporting goals were attained and he was also paid for a TV show and commercial endorsements. Soon, his annual salary was said to be more than one million dollars! At this time, the President of the four campuses of MU was making an annual salary of $250,000, the Chancellor at Columbia $204,000 and the Dean of the Columbia medical school just $196,000. These obscene athletic salaries were the rule in US collegiate sport and salaries were even higher in professional sport.

Helen was now attending Hickman High School. She was very happy there and went on to the University of Missouri, where she vehemently denied, as I had been informed, that MU students had four main food groups, namely beef, pork, jello salad with marshmallows and beer, and just three spices, salt, pepper and ketchup. Her university charges were largely paid for by a "Bright Flight" scholarship, awarded by the state of Missouri. She spent a good deal of vacation time working in the University Radiology department where she acquired considerable computer skills. She opted to spend her junior (third) year at the University of Manchester, this being one of the many exchange programmes available to MU students. This year proved to be most enjoyable and she later made a return journey to her student haunts there. She graduated in five years with double degrees, a BSc in Education and a BA in English. She then added a Masters Degree in Education before beginning a career in teaching. Mizzou was, about this time, declared to be the "best buy" for university education in the nation.

Frances had by now become a keen quilter. Originally imported from Europe, mainly from Germany and Britain, quilting had largely withered in those countries following the Industrial Revolution. It suffered a similar decline in the USA after World War Two although quilting never died out completely in the Mid West. There was a great revival of interest in 1970, with a landmark exhibition in 1971 and the revival was well underway by the time of the Bicentennial celebrations in 1976. According to Primedia, publishers of the *Quilter's Newsletter Magazine*, there are thought to be more than 5,000 guilds in the country with some 20 million quilters in the USA over the age of 18 years. There are more than 400 quilting guilds in California alone and Missouri has 110.

Meanwhile, I had some problems gaining university tenure, the aquisition of which virtually guarantees life-long employment. The Promotion and Tenure committee looked at three main aspects of the faculty member's time in the institution, namely his performance in carrying out his particular work, his teaching ability and his published work. I thought that I had no worries in regard of the first two of these criteria and, with a book chapter and more than 50 published papers, none also with respect to the last, about which the expression "publish or perish" was frequently quoted. However, the world and his wife seemed to know of my application, confirming the opinion that it was impossible to keep any secrets in a medical school department. Moreover, many seemed to feel a great necessity to write to the Promotion and Tenure committee with their feelings. To my considerable surprise, it turned out that I did have a problem, in regard to a critical letter sent to the Radiology Chairman by some first-year residents, all of whom had entered the residency programme straight from medical school without serving an internship. One of them had been entertained and dined in my home when a medical student, following the original residency interview, but I had developed poor relations with her and other residents. My original application for tenure, much to my chagrin, was refused.

Dr Hugh Stephenson was the Chief-of-Staff at University Hospital at the time, a general surgeon and complete gentleman. He went on to become Dean of the medical school and Chairman of the Board of Curators for MU, as well as winning the prestigious Freeman award from the Freeman hospital in Joplin, in the southwest corner of the state. This was given to him for his work on cardiac resuscitation and presented by no less a personage than Margaret Thatcher. Hugh Stephenson became a true and valued friend and worked hard to obtain tenure for me. His considerable assistance, and a change of Radiology Chairman, worked to my advantage and tenure was later confirmed. In November 2004, Dr Stephenson presented the medical school at Mizzou with a personal gift of two million dollars, the largest donation the school had ever received.

I was now informed that I was listed in the "Who's Who of US Health Care" register but had no idea how significant this was. A few years after this, I was made an honorary member of the department of Orthopaedic Surgery, with whom I worked very closely and whose conferences I regularly attended. I was soon promoted to being a full Professor and this title extended to Orthopaedic Surgery as well as Radiology. This designation seemed to irritate some British acquaintances, especially those having had surgical training. It did not imply, of course, that I would embark now on an orthopaedic surgical career. It was merely an acknowledgement of my close interaction with the Orthopaedic department and this sort of thing is very common in US academic medicine among radiologists and pathologists.

In May 1992, I was invited to visit the University of Tennessee medical school at Memphis as a Visiting Professor. I gave three formal lectures there and spent a good deal of time in the Radiology department with the residents. I was treated with great consideration, given a handsome honorarium and had a most enjoyable time.

In June 1993, we all went to Australia for a holiday. I found the journey very long and tiring. We were picked up at our home by a shuttle, flew out of St Louis to Chicago and then, after a considerable delay, to Los Angeles and finally, after more hanging about, we took off for the very long flight to Sydney. This itinerary was largely of our own making and due to us wishing to fly American Airlines all the way, thereby using and securing frequent flier miles. Peter, my old submariner friend from *Tally Ho*, met us after we had cleared customs and immigration at Sydney airport and drove us some 100 miles to Salamander Bay, just north of Newcastle, where he was now living. We stayed with he and Paddy, his wife, for four days and then flew on to Brisbane, where we were guests of the Higgins family. John had been a resident at University Hospital in Columbia and, after further specialist training in Boston, would return home. We saw the sights of the city, went to fashionable Noosa, north of Brisbane on the Sunshine Coast, and I was pleased to see the Australian RU team play Tonga at Ballymore. I gave an invited lecture to the Queensland branch of the Royal Australasian College of Radiology, where I became reacquainted with an old friend, a former Radiology registrar from Edinburgh.

We then flew to Sydney and stayed with Pedr and Dolores Davis for a few days at Kyle Bay, just south of the city. Pedr had been an apprentice with the Austin motor company after leaving school. He was sent to Australia by them in 1953 and returned Down Under in 1956 to begin what became a most successful career in automotive journalism. He gradually built up his initially small, private company into a nationally recognised entity. His weekly column was syndicated eventually in more than 150 Australian newspapers; he also published in excess of 40 books on motoring and light aviation as well as appearing on television not infrequently. Pedr had more than a few classic cars, which he proudly demonstrated. I gave an invited lecture at Westmead Hospital following which I called on Pat and Richard Guest who were now living in suburban Sydney. Originally from St Helens, Dick had been an outstanding RU wing three-quarter and had also been an England rugby selector. In addition, he was one of only three players to have represented England both before and after World War Two. One of the others was his cousin, Jack Heaton, who had captained Waterloo, Lancashire and England, the same teams for which Dick had played.

Our final visit Down Under was to Melbourne, where I had lived and worked some 34 years earlier. My friend Anne greeted us on arrival and we had a most enjoyable time in that lovely city. This was due in no small measure to the considerable and generous assistance of Anne and her husband Denys, who picked us up in their Roller most evenings and generally squired us about the city. I lectured at the Alfred Hospital, where Frances had worked as a radiographer much earlier. We dined in a restaurant owned by Eric Sandstrom, an outstanding British sprinter of the 1950s and a frequent relay partner of Ken Box. Eric had won a gold medal with the English sprint relay team at Cardiff in the 1958 Commonwealth Games and had become a lecturer in Physical Education at Melbourne University. Changing planes in Auckland on the way home, I met up with Roy Bevan, the well-known Welsh referee who was returning home after refereeing the Australia/New Zealand game of the previous day. We spent three relaxed days in Hawaii, to break up the long haul home, and finally returned to a flooded Missouri.

I was by now an enthusiastic member of the Society of Skeletal Radiology, a national body which met once a year, mainly in Florida. In the late 1980s, I successfully applied for membership in the prestigious International Skeletal Society (ISS) which was largely Anglo-American in formation, had its first meeting in Washington DC in 1974 and whose membership was not granted lightly. The majority of members were radiologists, with a substantial minority of pathologists, some orthopaedic surgeons and the occasional rheumatologist. Annual meetings were held alternatively in the USA and the rest of the world. They were of a uniformly high academic calibre, with superb social events organised by the local host committee, having five years notice. I enjoyed each and every one of these meetings, at venues such as Stockholm, Berlin, Paris, Dublin and many North American cities, such as San Diego, New Orleans, Santa Fe and Toronto, where I had the good fortune to meet many interesting radiologists from all over the world.

At the invitation of my friend Bill, the Chairman of Orthopaedics, I joined the Rocky Mountain Trauma Society. This had an annual meeting in late January at Snowmass, a delightful ski resort near Aspen in Colorado. The vast majority of the members were orthopaedic surgeons and lectures were held before and after sking. New members had to give a lecture immediately after joining the society and I spoke on "Sir Robert Jones. The Founder of Orthopaedic Surgery". I had tailored my talk to my American audience and it was well received.

I still managed to run regularly although lunchtime exercise was now impossible. I took part in many competitive races but was unable to log the substantial weekly mileage necessary for another marathon. In 1994, when Frances was guiding a garden tour around the south of England and our daughter Helen was at home with me, I awoke with mild chest discomfort that I took to be due to reflux oesophagitis. The pain did not subside with antacids, however, but was not severe and my pulse rate never increased above 50 per minute. After several hours, I thought that I'd better get a medical opinion and drove myself to the Emergency Room of my hospital. Initial ECGs were negative but, after spending the night in the hospital, these and blood test became positive on the following morning. There was now no doubt that I had suffered a myocardial occlusion, albeit a clinically mild one. I had none of the "feelings of impending death", said to be classical signs of a heart attack and my only emotion was one of intense indignation! I had a normal blood pressure and optic fundi, a normal cholesterol level and a high level of high-density lipids, the beneficial ones and, of course, a history of sustained aerobic exercise for many years. It was, it seemed to me, all so unfair.

My cardiologist performed a coronary angiogram, identified the area of occlusion and performed an angioplasty, using the technique devised by my former chairman, Charles Dotter; unfortunately for me, this was carried out more than twelve hours after the onset of my symptoms. Some ten years later, I was amused to read in a London paper that a revolutionary proceedure known as "primary angioplasty" was now available for the acute treatment of heart attack victims in the UK and that the Department of Health was investigating its employment! I was discharged home on the third day and began walking immediately. After a couple of weeks off work, during which I gradually increased my exercise, I resumed part-time duties and then began my full schedule. I cycled and swam quite hard after this but felt that my running ability had markedly declined, although I did not push too hard.

Slightly less than a year after my heart attack, I had an isotopic stress test to evaluate my coronary function and this was very abnormal. Another coronary angiogram was performed and this was abnormal also. I knew what this meant and felt very depressed. Coronary Artery Bypass Surgery was indicated, a formidable although commonly performed operation. I hardly considered other centres and was more than happy, if I had to undergo this intervention, to have it in my own hospital; however, I was determined to select the surgeon concerned. Dr Jack Curtis, who lived just down the road from me in a nice house on the lake, was Chairman of the Cardio-Thoracic Surgical Department and a very experienced surgeon who was internationally known. He readily agreed to carry out my surgery. He allowed me to pick my date and I stipulated that I wished to be his first case of the day.

On the day prior to my surgery, I worked from 6.30 am to 5.00 pm with a very short lunch break Frances drove me to the hospital at 6.00 am on the big day, an iv injection putting me to sleep and we were off to the races. The surgery lasted about five hours, so I was told later, with my heart arrested for some 90 minutes during which I was on a heart-lung machine. I awoke in the thoracic intensive care unit, free of any pain but conscious of an endo-tracheal tube in my throat which prevented me from talking. Frances and Helen were at the bedside, looking expectantly and earnestly at me. Frances later said that she was surprised, even somewhat alarmed, at how cold I felt. This was because of the cooling to which I had been subjected, reducing my body temperature to some 80 degrees Fahrenheit to decrease my metabolism. Removal of the tube from my throat completed this phase of my recovery and I was soon moved to a private room on a general surgical floor. I was asked by the nursing staff to walk a little a few hours later and I did so with no problems. I did more walking over the next few days and was discharged home early on the morning of the fourth day.

The total cost of my surgery, including my hospital room and all accessory charges, was $23,500 and my university insurance, in no way dissimilar to that of any other faculty or staff member, took care of all but $60 of this. I walked around the block after arriving home and soon began gradually increasing ambulation. I had some cardiac rehabilitation, which was also included in my insurance, during which I exercised on various machines while wearing an ECG halter and being monitored by the staff. I remained puzzled and a little angry about my infarct and could only suppose that stress, together with a family history of vascular disease, was responsible; but I was thankful that I had been treated so expertly. After a few weeks of increasing ambulation at home, I began part-time work for a short time, then resumed normal duties.

Soon after this, I was delighted to be selected as an examiner for the American Board of Radiology, the orals now being always held in Louisville, Kentucky. Every evening, at the completion of the day's examinations, the examiners would meet together and decide who, among the borderline candidates, had passed and who had not. After this came a drinks party, at which gathering all the great names in American Radiology were present. The examinations began at 7.00 each morning and the examiner's meeting would not be completed until well after 6.00 pm. If one stayed on for the social drinking, as most did, then things were concluded much later. Although aware of the considerable honour in being a Board examiner, I found the whole business extremely tiring and, after a while, somewhat less than exciting. To the amazement of many, I decided that I did not wish to examine in the future.

In the late Spring of 1998, Frances and I went on vacation to Italy. We visited Rome and Florence, which I had already enjoyed many years earlier, and Sienna. In Rome, we stayed at the Casa di Santa Brigida, run by the Bridgidine nuns and just off the Piazza Farnese, near the French embassy. Close to the Casa was the Venerable English College where many English priests, having completed their studies there during penal times, returned to a martyr's death in their home country. This was also the place where Joe Halsall and John Heenan had studied many years earlier. The Casa was favourably critiqued in Frommer's Review and we met people of many nationalities and religions there. We were very comfortable with the food, in particular, being very good.

Of course, we wished to attend the papal open-air audience that was held each Wednesday morning in the Piazza San Pietro. We had writen to the North American College for tickets and we also acquired two more from the English College. Then we were offered two more from the nuns at the Casa. I declined these, already possessing four, but a young nun urged me to accept them, saying that theirs were the best. I was surprised and sceptical at this claim but took the tickets rather than causing any offence.

Arriving rather early for the audience, we walked up the main aisle of the piazza, only to be stopped by a Swiss guard in his magnificent and colourful uniform. After presenting our tickets from the North American College, we were shown into seats that seemed to be a very much at the rear of things. After waiting a few minutes until the guard had moved off, we moved further up the aisle and presented the tickets from the English College to another guard, now obtaining seats that were appreciably better. Finally, at the appropriate moment, we moved off again until being stopped very close to the front of the accomodation by yet another Swiss guard. The nun's tickets from the Casa were now produced and, finally, we ended up in superb seating, level with the canopy under which the Pope would sit but over to one side. After the Pope had arrived by popemobile and taken his place, we found that we were no more than 35 yards away from him. So the young nun had been quite correct in her estimatation of the Casa's tickets.

The hospital scene was changing rapidly. Managed Care had resulted in a whole slew of changes and problems. Our Radiology department had brought in many innovative changes, with some of which I did not agree. We took over most of the radiological work of several small hospitals, with much work being dealt with by Tele-Radiology. Images from these peripheral institutions were sent electronically to University Hospital, Columbia, where they were read and reports sent back to the patient's hospital. This was frequently an arduous job. The images were not as easy to read as films and, if suboptimal, it was a tedious and often frustrating business to obtain repeat studies. Many considered that this sort of work was not in the province of a teaching hospital.

Towards the end of 2004, Apex Radiology of Coral Springs, Florida, announced that they had been searching for a new home in a place with a good quality of life and a relative absence of problematic weather. Apparently, the storms and hurricanes endured by Florida in the past year had knocked out their electrical supply for many days. After such locations as Roanoake Virginia, Hot Springs

Arkansas and Salt Lake City Utah had been considered, they had decided to relocate their main administrative and networking functions to Columbia, Missouri. About 35 people would work here and some 20 radiologists, situated all over the country, would read digital radiographs and scans, this being the principal work of the company. Final reports would, it was claimed, be issued on average in less than two hours from completion of the exmination. Some of these radiologists would work from home and this flexible job, largely free from paper-work, was said to be very attractive to growing numbers of stay-at-home mums and retired doctors and would overcome the recruiting problems posed by a national shortage of radiologists. So Tele-Radiology was becoming very much an accepted form of Radiology, where one person can cover a lot of different places. However, there were said to be medical and legal problems across state and national boundaries.

I carried on working for several more years and we visited Union Hall, County Cork, again. All thoughts of a house purchase there, however, had been long since abandoned because of my cardiac problems. We continued to very much appreciate the area and its people, many of whom we now knew quite well. In 1997, having worked as a physician in many different countries for 43 years and with my working life comprising most of the second half of the twentieth century, I decided to retire. My health was surprisingly good but I had lost some of my earlier zeal and energy. The department hosted a small reception for me, with non-alcoholic drinks and small eats, at which many clinicians with whom I had worked were present. Both the Dean of the medical school and the Radiology Chairman made flattering remarks and I was presented with a nice hardwood chair with the university insignia on its back; also, I was able to keep my hospital computer. I worked part-time, mornings only, for a few months but this did not suit me. I was out of the swim of things and, with the customary lack of clinical histories, was ignorant of many important details of which I would normally be aware. Soon, I quit work completely. Shortly after this, I was given the status of Emeritus Professor at a luncheon attended by senior university figures. After a few weeks of being "out of the saddle", Frances claimed that she saw a huge difference in me. I was said to be much more relaxed and looked as if I was now enjoying life considerably more. I was somewhat worried that, after a busy life, I would find retirement boring but such was not the case.

We never thought of leaving Columbia for my retirement years, being very happy and comfortable here and, of course, my daughter's presence in the town was a major factor. We did, however, think about purchasing a holiday home somewhere but, after prolonged consideration, decided against it. A national shortage of radiologist in the US made the staffing situation in my former department difficult and I was frequently asked if I would return, at least to part-time employment. I had no difficulty in declining these offers. I then did two trips as a Visiting Professor to South America.

FOURTEEN

Ecuador and Brazil

The Radiological Society of North America (RSNA) is a huge organisation with more than 35,000 members. The RSNA monthly journal *Radiology* is read all over the world, a tribute to its excellence. Over 25,000 visitors, many with addresses outside North America, attend the annual meeting in Chicago, said to be the world's largest international medical gathering. As well as a superb series of lectures and exhibits, an enormous floor is used by the leading international commercial firms for displaying the latest radiological equipment. Many radiological departments about to make a big investment in new technology, such as a computerised tomography unit or a resonance imaging magnet, would send their radiologists to this meeting before deciding on the purchase.

The RSNA Visiting Professor programme was instituted in 1986 to assist evolving nations with their radiological education. Individual professors, normally four per year, would travel to a host country, usually for three months, and give didactic lectures to the residents, as well as working with them during the day. Dr Peter Cockshott, a good friend of mine whom I enjoyed seeing annually at ISS meetings, was very active in the preliminary discussions concerning this program and was the first Chairman of the committee overseeing it.

Peter had been born in France and educated there, in Britain and in the USA. He graduated in Medicine from Edinburgh University and had gone on to specialise in Radiology there, several years before I did. He became Chairman of Radiology at University Hospital, Ibadan, Nigeria, where he founded the West African Society of Radiology and began a long association with the World Health Association. He then moved to the new Faculty of Health Sciences at McMaster University, Hamilton, Canada, as Chief of Radiology. He designed the new department there and was much involved in the setting up of the then revolutionary "Problem Based Learning" for medical students. This originated at McMaster before gaining virtual worldwide acceptance, and not only in

Medicine. He was active in many radiological societies and was awarded the Barclay Prize of the British Institute of Radiology and the Gold Medal of the RSNA. I saw Peter for the last time in 1993, at the Toronto meeting of the ISS which he had organised, just prior to his death.

In 1999, I applied to the RSNA for appointment as a Visiting Professor but was not in luck; selection was, I was told, very competitive. I had a great yearning to revisit to Sri Lanka, which had not previously participated in the RSNA program. Hence I thought it might be helpful both to Sri Lanka and myself if a request from the Colombo teaching hospitals for a visit from an RSNA-sponsored professor was made for the year 2000. I had some difficulty in finding the appropriate person to contact in Colombo but eventually was successful in this, after assistance from the Royal College of Radiologists in London. Dr Peiris, a senior and respected physician in Colombo, was most helpful in this regard. The application was duly made from Sri Lanka, the Musculo-Skeletal System was indicated as the preferred sub-specialty and my name was listed as a desired Visiting Professor.

I was reasonably confident of selection for the next year, 2000, and just before Christmas 1999, I had a phone call from the Chairman of the RSNA committee organising these visits informing me that I had been appointed....................to visit Ecuador! I told him that perhaps he was mistaken and that I was really going to Sri Lanka. No, he assured me, someone else was going there and they wished to send me to Ecuador. I felt highly annoyed at this, considering that Sri Lanka would never had made an application to the RSNA without my prodding and that they had specifically asked for me. I was severely tempted to tell my caller what to do with his offer but fortunately resisted this temptation, saying that I would carefully consider it and call him back. On reflection, wiser counsel prevailed and I soon intimated that I would go, after getting confirmation from the academic radiologists in Quito that my ignorance of Spanish would not debar me from teaching there.

Frances and I began an immediate study of the Spanish language by means of books and tapes. We were fortunate to learn of a former high school teacher and she gave us weekly lessons in her home. After nearly three months, I had some appreciation of the language and could slowly annunciate simple sentences; but I was very far from being proficient and was to find the rapid speech of the locals in Quito quite unintelligible. A few weeks before we were due to leave, an armed revolution occurred in Ecuador! Mobs of indigenous Indians, goaded beyond endurance by the endemic corruption in the country, the chronic inflation in the currency and their resultant poverty, occupied the National Assembly and other parts of Quito, the capital, being assisted in this by some units of the Army. The unrest involved other cities, including Guayaquil, the principal port and largest town. The airports were closed and the borders sealed. An intense search was made for the country's President but he was never found. All this made me more than a little apprehensive about visiting Quito but the situation soon became much less threatening and my contacts in the country assured me that all would be well for my visit.

So, in April 2000, we flew to Miami and on from there, arriving at Quito just before midnight after an eight hour flight. The scene at the airport was one of chaos, with the people waiting to greet arrivals apparently being held in a sort of huge cage. After clearing customs and immigration, Dr Guerra, my contact figure there who was the Director of the Radiology residents, managed to find us amid the confusion and drove us to our hotel. He met us next morning and took us to the apartment building that he had selected. We moved in and were reasonably comfortable. I gave an introductory lecture the following day and, as it was Easter week, had the next four days off. One of the residents, a lady from Bogota, Colombia, took us out to dinner with her daughter, who spoke good English, on our second night. At the weekend, we visited the Equator museum and exhibition with them, a few miles north of the city. Frances and I were photographed standing in opposite hemispheres, with the painted line of the Equator running between us. The French had mapped out the Equator in an earlier century and the popular feeling was that it was not quite in the correct position.

From the lounge of our apartment, we could see the slopes of Guagua Pichincha, a 14,000-foot volcano with two peaks, one of which had snow on it despite the underlying cauldron and summer weather. This volcano had erupted just a few months before our arrival, leading to the closure of the Quito international airport for several weeks. We were told that there were another four active volcanoes in the country at this time and, each night from our apartment, we could see the red glow of one of them. This was Cotopaxi, situated about 50 miles to the south, the world's highest active volcano at over 19,000 feet. Some two years after we had departed from Ecuador, El Reventador erupted. This is situated about 60 miles to the north-east of Quito, which it covered in ash to a depth of two inches.

Dr Guerra picked me up each morning soon after 7.00 am and I gave a regular 7.30 am lecture lasting for some 90 minutes. I was flattered by always having at least half-a-dozen outside radiologists in attendance, as well as other physicians ocasionally. At the completion of my lecture, having answered questions, I would then look at films that the residents and physicians from various services had brought along and I would always get a ride back to my apartment from a resident. I was free most afternoons, except when being invited to other hospitals to lecture and discuss films, and everyone was extremely courteous and helpful. I had carefully prepared my lectures using Spanish words for at least the major anatomical parts and the more important pathological processes. With the help of the Dr Guerra and local faculty who spoke some English, we managed fairly well although not without the occasional difficulty. Thus I was never able to translate the word "hatchet", which I required to describe a particular radiographic deformity. My translators had never heard of it and, after quite a long diversion in the middle of a lecture, I had to settle for "machete". I also mispronounced "ano" meaning a year, my effort producing gales of laughter as the sound I produced meant anus!

Quito, a city of 1.5 million, had terrible traffic, with indigenous Indians waiting at every stop sign and traffic light to sell a variety of goods. Their poverty was extreme and obvious. The city is at a height of nearly 10,000 feet but this altitude did not bother us. Although situated virtually on the equator, the altitude gives rise to a very pleasant climate that has been called a "perpetual Spring" as is rarely too hot or too cold. Our apartment was on the tenth floor and was very noisy. Not only was it directly under the airport's main flight path but there was much traffic noise. Most of this came from car alarms that constantly went off at all hours of the day and night. I was told that they were of poor construction, being calibrated at too sensitive a setting, resulting in them being set off by passing traffic, radios and even wind. We soon exchanged our apartment for one at the rear of the building. This brought some improvement in the noise levels but we discovered that a nightclub was immediately adjacent to the apartment building here. Still, for $22 per day, it was good value for a bedroom, lounge, bathroom and small kitchen.

The government had progressively reduced the salary of the residents as the economy worsened and, while I was there, they were paid just $80 dollars a month. Many were married with families and I could only marvel at how they made ends meet. The faculty members were also badly paid and I suspect that few made more than $5,000 per year from their government-run hospitals, although there were a wide variety of differing contracts. Many, therefore, had private practice positions in addition and some did extra work, not always connected with Radiology. At this time, US residents were paid more than $30,000 per annum. The daily allowance given by RSNA proved to be very generous, especially as most things were very cheap. Taxis seemed to hardly ever cost more than one dollar, even for quite long distances, and eating out was a joy. There were many excellent restaurants nearby and rarely did a splendid three course meal for two, with a bottle of good Chilean wine, cost more than $18. There was some violence on the streets at night, thought to be closely related to the terrible economy and the dreadful state of the poor, but only in certain areas. The Old Town, a World Heritage site, was especially dangerous after dark.

The sucre, the Ecuadorian unit of currency, continued depreciating against the dollar. I was informed that it had sunk from 4,000 to no less than 25,000 to the dollar in just three years. Something had to be done, and it was. Soon after we arrived, it was announced that "dolarisation" would occur, with the dollar being substituted for the sucre, although both would be legal tender for a year or more. This was thought to be a good move to stop the headlong inflation of the last few years. However, many were highly suspicious of this change, especially the indigenous Indians, and the banks were unprepared for it. We found it extremely difficult to obtain low denomination dollars and our travellers cheques could not be cashed in many banks, nor would our credit cards work. Much of the population simply did not understand the change and were not conversant with the dollar. When handing one over in a retail situation, it would frequently lead to marked scepticism, with the dollar bill held up to the light and intensely scrutinised. Matters were not improved by reports that drug cartels and rebels in Colombia were sending counterfeit dollars into Ecuador.

We took a day trip to Otavalo, an Indian market about 60 miles to the north and famous for all manner of textiles. Unlike their counterparts in most of the country, the indiginous Indians here were confident and successful. Even those that had moved away, having joined the professions or become successful at business, maintained their ties with the Otavalo area and remain proud of their lineage. The women in the town and market dress in white blouses and elegant long, black skirts. This dress code is said to represent continued mourning for Atahualpa, the last King of the northern Incan empire, who was killed by the conquistadors. A female radiologist from Quito and her lawyer son came with us and their help with translations was invaluable. To my surprise, the Dean of the Postgraduate Medical School provided a car and driver and we had a most enjoyable and profitable day.

I received an invitation to visit and lecture at Loja, a small and pleasant town in the south of the country, not far from the border with Peru. We flew down very early and I went on to give five one-hour lectures. Two of them were in the morning, after which Frances and I were introduced to many new faces and more than a dozen of us sat down to a gargantuan lunch. Loja is famous for its cuy, a small animal that is something like a guinea pig and considered a great delicacy; unfortunately, it is a very fatty dish and so I disappointed my hosts by declining it. I felt very sleepy after this meal but gritted my teeth and ploughed on through three more lectures. My interpreter, a charming female student in her early years at medical school, complicated the afternoon. She did her best but although her English was good, there were many difficulties. This was due to her lack of medical knowledge and she was unable to translate many words.

Meanwhile, Frances was entertained by our host's wife, a former English teacher, and she joined us at the close of the afternoon's activities. The next day our hosts picked us up and drove us to their hacienda, some 60 miles away. This was very nice, had a swimming pool, and was on the fringes of the Podocarpus, a huge national park containing steaming jungle and high Andean peaks. It is home to the puma, armidillo, giant sloth, spectacled bear and the now rare giant condor. We truly enjoyed this very different and exciting experience, which rounded off a most enjoyable visit to Loja and district.

Just before finishing my assignment in Quito, we went on a cruise to the Galapagos Islands, the greatest eco-tourist site on earth, lying some 500 miles to the west of the Ecuadorian coast. We chose a company recommended by Dr Guerra who knew one of the directors, thereby enabling us to receive a substantial discount. Their ships were small, carrying only 22 passengers, enabling the latter to enjoy great attention from the staff. From Quito, we flew to Guayaquil on the coast and then on to Baltra Island, where we boarded our ship. The food was very good and the accommodation comfortable. There were two excellent guides, both speaking good English and possessing a superb knowledge of marine biology, birds, flowers, etc. There were two kinds of landings, dry and wet. In the former, the tourists would disembark onto a dry, firm surface whereas we would have to wade through the sea in the latter type. Although the islands straddle the equator, the water was surprisingly cold because of the Humboldt current running up from Antarctica; this current is said to be also responsible for the Galapagos penguins. Strict ecological rules are maintained at all times. The Ecuadorian government permits only a limited amount of shipping and the tourists are firmly disciplined. An example of this was in the matter of toilet paper. This was not flushed down the toilet after use but collected and eventually burned ashore.

Our cruise began with a visit to San Salvador Island, also known as Santiago, and then we sailed around the north of Isabella Island, the largest of the group, where we made several landings. In all these areas, we saw marine and land iguanas, penguins, sea lions, giant tortoises and a profusion of birds. These included the booby, with blue, red-footed and masked varieties, which is a fish-eating bird closely related to the gannet, sleeps on the water and is especially fascinating. The tameness of all these creatures, because of a complete lack of predators, was astounding. Large sea lions would allow one to approach within a few feet before barking and shuffling off. We landed finally on Santa Cruz, where we visited the Charles Darwin Research Station.

Among many interesting sights here were the giant tortoises (Fig 19). Many measure six feet from nose to tail, weight more than 400 pounds and live to a ripe old age, often more than 100 years.

Fig 19. The author and his wife, with three Galapagos giant tortoises, at the Charles Darwin research station on Santa Cruz Island, Galapagos, Ecuador.

Among them was "Lonesome George". He had been found on the small island of Pinta but had been moved to the research station. There are 11 different varieties of Galapagos giant tortoise but, most unfortunately, George appears to be the last of his kind. No similar species can be found and attempts to mate him with a variety of females have been unsuccessful. Because tortoises are easily killed and provide excellent eating, their numbers had been greatly reduced over many years by pirates and whalers. We were driven across this island to view lava fields, have lunch and head back to the airport. It had been a fascinating five days and quite unlike anything we had previously encountered anywhere.

My time in Quito was now nearly over. Dr Guerra hosted a farewell party for us and, to our dismay, the residents presented us with a lovely hand-painted tea service. It must have cost more than $100, even in this country where goods were very cheap, and I wondered how they could afford it. More to the point, Frances wondered how she was going to pack it and get it home! However, we managed it somehow and, with several new friends seeing us off at the airport with entreaties to return soon, we left beautiful Ecuador for home. The country has oil fields, is one of the leading world suppliers of shrimp and has a booming tourist industry, yet is very poor. A major reason for this is corruption, of which many varieties were present. Some relate to bribes being taken for various licences, others involved dodging many taxes and still others involve officials simply stealing money, bonds, etc. Soon after arriving back home, I read that the former President of Ecuador had surfaced in Boston and was lecturing at Harvard! In November 2002, Colonel Gutierrez, who had led army units involved in the uprising of 2000, was elected President of Ecuador, the sixth to hold this office in just six years. Despite support from a small marxist party, radical Indian groups and leftist unions, he asserted that he was not a communist but a sincere Christian who respected private property and he travelled to New York to reassure Wall Street investors.

I applied again for another Visiting Professor slot for the following year although, having secured one in the year 2000, was not optimistic about getting a consecutive assignment. To my surprise and delight, I was successful once more and went to Curitiba, in the south of Brazil, in January 2001. I had established that all the residents and faculty spoke English and this was welcome news. I simply could not face trying to handle Portuguese! I wished to go in January, to escape the mid-western winter and enjoy the Brazilian summer. This took a good deal of arranging, and some residents there had to reschedule their vacations, but it all worked out satisfactorily. Unlike Quito, which was more-or-less on the same longitude as Columbia, Curitiba was considerably to the east and the overnight flight from Dallas took all of 11 hours.

After changing planes at Sao Paulo, we flew south for another hour to Curitiba's modern, pleasant airport. There we were met by Dr Arnolfo Carvalho Neto and his wife Denise. Arnolfo was the Director of the residents and Denise was also a physician. They took us into town and established us in what was called an apart-hotel. We had a combined living room and bedroom plus a bathroom. However, breakfast was included in the $35 per day charge and this meal was, in my opinion, one of the highlights of our trip. All manner of fresh juices were on offer as well as fruits such as melon, pineapple, papaya, mango, oranges, bananas, apples, etc. There were eggs and bacon, a huge range of cold meats, a wide selection of cheeses, all manner of confectionery, pies and custards, and delicious coffee. Apparently, this sort of thing represented the typical Brazilian breakfast and few of my new friends could appreciate why I so rhapsodised about it.

Curitiba is a city of 1.5 million, said to be the ecological capital of Brazil, with garbage collected six times a week. It is the capital of the state of Parana, so-called because of the former profusion of the parana tree, a form of pine whose wood was highly prized. The tree branches curve upwards in graceful arcs giving an appearance something similar to a menorah. Unfortunately, huge forests of these trees were cut down without any significant reforestation and parana trees are now few in number and highly protected. Parana and the two provinces to its south are atypical of Brazil. As well as having a more temperate climate, large-scale immigration of Europeans occurred towards the end of the nineteenth century, especially of Poles, Germans and Italians; there was even some entry of Americans from the defeated Confederacy at the end of the American Civil War. There is a relative absence of former African slaves, who were mainly employed further north in mining and on sugar cane plantations, and all this has given the south of Brazil a European-like population.

The lectures to the residents were similar to those in Ecuador. I also gave a series of lectures to the department of Orthopaedic Surgery and, as in Quito, many physicians from other departments attended my lectures. I set the residents a multiple-choice examination virtually every week, just as I had done in Quito. In both locations, my announcement of this test gave rise to equal measures of terror and anger, despite my assurances that all questions would be based only on my lectures and that no-one, not even the Director of the Residency Program, would see the results. In the event, it all went off smoothly and formed, in my view, an important aid to teaching and revision. I spoke at a couple of dinner meetings, including the Parana Rheumatological Society and the Curitiba Radiological Society. As in Ecuador, everyone was most courteous and helpful although there was again the occasional radiologist who tried to score brownie points. This was usually done by showing me, quite out of the blue, very difficult cases with no prior warning. Collected over a professional lifetime, these would invariably consist of a few tacky plain films with no additional views and certainly no computed tomography. I did my best in these circumstances to reach at least a differential diagnosis and made sure that I did not overreact or appear annoyed. However, those in the local community of radiologists who knew me were both embarrassed and angry by this sort of thing and made their views clearly known to the guilty party.

There was a small and interesting old part of town but most of Curitiba was of modern construction, with skyscrapers prominent. Shops were not very different from the USA and few retail items were missing. Many of the broad thoroughfares had been pedestrianised and cafes and restaurants with outside tables for eating and drinking were common, lending an almost Parisian air to the city. Although goods, food and drink were not as cheap as in Ecuador, they certainly were by US standards. There were a few beggars on the streets but nothing like the profusion seen in Ecuador; this represented, of course, the much superior Brazilian economy, the strongest in South America at the time. However, just as in Ecuador, we were advised not to drink the water and to use the bottled variety, even when cleaning our teeth. I consider the provision of a safe water supply to be the number one requirement of virtually all Central and South American countries and cannot understand why this has not been expedited, instead of other expensive and far more dubious projects.

Dining and wining was a joy. Brazilians are carnivorous and consume great quantities of meat. Many restaurants are specifically known as "churrascarias" where the service is "rodizio" in style. This is somewhat unusual, with waiters coming to the diner with long skewers loaded with cuts of all sorts of meat and poultry. These offerings continue interminably, with no effort made to limit any customer. After this, there is often a self-service buffet, with fish, seafoods, fruits, deserts and cheeses on offer. Brazilian ice-cream is often made using coconut, not cow's, milk and this variety is truly delicious. We entertained a resident to dinner at one of these churrascarias one evening. We simply gorged ourselves, had fresh raspberries and cream for desert, enjoyed two bottles of excellent French wine and the bill for all three of us was just $31!

There seemed to be a great antipathy to Canada and things Canadian in Brazil and, perhaps because I did not sound like an American, I was often regarded with some suspicion and asked if I was a Canadian. It took me some time to understand this attitude but I gradually learned that it was due to two main factors. The first involved rivalry between Brazil's very successful Embraer aircraft company and the Canadian Bombardier group. The two were apparently involved in the rather specialised and highly competitive small-to-medium aircraft construction field and their rivalry was becoming increasingly fierce and nasty. The second problem involved trade between the two countries, where Canada had a very considerable export-import edge. The World Trade Organisation had already intervened on Brazil's behalf in response to changes in Brazilian interest rates to counteract this imbalance. Canada then blocked the import of Brazilian beef, alleging there was a possibility it had been contaminated with mad cow disease. I tried to keep out of all this controversy and would sometimes preface invited lectures with a declaration that I was not Canadian.

Arnolfo and Denise proved to be extremely hospitable. They took us out for many dinners and Denise would escort us about the city and its many parks most afternoons. One weekend, we went to the coast by train. This single-track line represents just about the only export route for Paraguay and its products. It had been constructed by the French towards the end of the nineteenth century and thousands had died during this work, almost like a mini-Panama Canal disaster; the principal cause of death here was malaria, now long since eradicated. The trip was spectacular, through the coastal range of mountains, with acute bends where the train and carriages seemed suspended over precipitous gorges. We alighted at the small town of Morentes with the train proceeding to Paranagua, a large and busy port. Denise and Arnolfo met us after we alighted and we had a typical Brazilian meal in a nice restaurant overlooking a lazy river. Only an Englishman slurping his soup and wearing a Manchester United football shirt spoiled the scene! We went then to Arnolfo's seaside apartment near Matinhos for two very pleasant days.

After a few enjoyable weeks, I was invited to Blumenau, a small but pleasant city in Santa Catarina, the next state to the south of Parana. Blumenau has a large population of German origin and that language was extensively spoken here until quite recently. In many places, the city looks as if it should be in southern Germany, with attractive houses having triangular pointed roofs, carved bal-

Fig 20. The houses of Blumenau, Santa Catarina state, Brazil. The pointed roofs, balconies and overall appearance are typically Bavarian.

conies, timber exterior framing and other Bavarian characteristics (Fig 20). Dr Fernando, one of the residents at University Hospital, Curitiba, had driven us down and we dined with him and his family at their home. His father was Chairman of Radiology in the local medical school at Blumenau and his brother was also a radiologist there. I gave three lectures on the following morning, a Friday, and then looked at films with the residents. We then had a very pleasant surprise, learning that we were to stay the weekend with the family. After lunch, Dr Fernando drove us to the coast, where the family's new beach-front house had just been completed. His father and brother joined us after work and we had a pleasant evening, sitting on the veranda with drinks and then enjoying a nice meal. On the following day, we swam and sunbathed in the morning and then, after a light lunch, Dr Fernando took us into nearby Camboriu. This was the local equivalent of Brighton or Blackpool but with high apartment blocks rather than bed and breakfast establishments and small hotels. It was quite new, with a population said to be less than 200,000 during a non-summer week but more than a million during the holiday season. It has been built, unfortunately, with little regard for planning considerations and this is expected to give rise to serious problems in the near future. There was a long cable car just to the south of this town, which we rode. From the top of a small hill, a splendid bird's eye view of the town and surrounding country can be obtained and hence the ride is very popular. We returned to the house for a brief rest and shower, then went back into Camboriu with the whole family for dinner, eaten alfresco on a sidewalk. A lazy day on Sunday followed, after which Fernando drove us back to Curitiba. I was again most impressed by the generous hospitality showered upon us.

Our next trip was a three-day visit to the world-famous falls at Iguacu, that were extensively featured in the movie *The Mission*, starring Robert de Niro and Jeremy Irons. A one-hour flight took us to the town of Foz de Iguacu, some 400 miles west of Curitiba but still in Parana state, where Argentina, Paraguay and Brazil come together. The falls themselves are caused by the Rio Iguacu plunging down in a large number of separate cataracts, never less than 275 and, in the rainy season, sometimes as many as 350. They occur in several huge arcs, being nearly four kilometres in length (Fig 21), and are taller than Niagara Falls in their highest parts. They produce a deafening roar and a cloud of water vapour that can be

Fig 21. The huge multi-arc system of waterfalls, set among forest and lush vegetation at Iguacu on the Brazil-Argentina border. The multitude of falls can be seen, extending over a consider able distance, with mist and water vapour in the air.

seen from miles away. On our first day, we walked along the Brazilian side where the panoramic view is best. At the end of this stroll is a catwalk which extends into the river right across from the "Devil's Throat", a terrifying mass of water. Frances was quite uncomfortable here and wanted to get back to terra firma as soon as possible.

On the following day, we crossed to the Argentinean side, drove a couple of miles in an open-topped bus through a temperate jungle and entered a launch. After donning life jackets and oilskins, we headed downstream and came right under one of the larger falls. We were, of course, soaked to the skin and some of the ladies became very nervous. The helmsman played games with us, bringing the boat nearer and nearer the waterfall. He finally sailed away, only to return a few minutes later and repeat the process. The falls in both countries are surrounded by national parks, containing paved roads, museums and hotels. The vegetation is lush and many wild animals, including jaguar and puma, make their homes here. On the days that we visited, there were many brilliantly coloured butterflies and several coati, an animal resembling a raccoon with a pointed head and striped tail. These had become tamed by visitors and were searching for handouts. Brilliant rainbows are very common and we enjoyed these also.

The Rio Iguacu arises to the west of Curitiba and flows in a westerly direction to the falls. The Rio Parana flows south and joins the Rio Iguacu just below the falls. The combined river is called the Parana and flows on south across Argentina, finally becoming the River Plate and emptying into the South Atlantic at Montevideo. Some 13 miles upstream from its junction with the Iguacu is the Itaipu dam. This is the pride of Brazilian civil engineering and represents the world's largest and most productive hydroelectric power plant. The main structure is five miles long and its powerhouse alone is over a mile in length. The Guri power plant in Venezuela is its nearest competitor but turns out much less power than does Itaipu; however, the new Three Gorges Dam in China may produce eventually even more power than Itaipu. This Itaipu dam and plant supplies 25% of Brazil's total electrical power. Brazil and Paraguay theoretically share the electrical power but, in practice, Brazil purchases nearly 80% of Paraguay's share.

The Brazilian town of Foz de Iguacu is quite close to the

Paraguayan border. Ciudad del Este is a nondescript town in Paraguay immediately across the border that has become something of a low-priced shopping mecca. All manner of electrical, photographic and other goods can be bought there quite cheaply. Many of these items are of Chinese manufacture and their sale gives some help to the very poor, beleaguered Paraguayan economy. We did not visit it.

Another trip took us at Carnival time to the beautiful island city of Florianopolis in Santa Catarina state, some 60 miles beyond Camboriu and 230 miles south of Curitiba. This state is renowned for its gorgeous beaches which not only surpass those of Parana and Rio Grande do Sul, its neighbour to the south and Brazil's most southerly state adjoining Uruguay, but especially those of Argentina. It is estimated that more than 300,000 Argentineans come north each year to the warmth and splendour of this state's coastline. Florianopolis once represented the most southern extent of Portuguese conquest and rule and was the site of several battles with the Spanish before settled borders were established. The city itself lies on the island of Santa Catarina, and two bridges connect it to the mainland. There are many well-known beaches around the island, which measures some 16 miles in length and seven in width.

In the more northern cities of Brazil, Carnival sees thousands of people taking to the streets in costume, singing and dancing for days. Rio, Salvador, Recife, Forteleza, Belem and many other cities do this, with several having their own style of celebrations. In the southern three states, Carnival is less exuberant. People simply regard it as a vacation and many go to the beach. We had some problems in making our reservations as we had left things rather late; and we were unable to get any flight reservations. However, Dr Fernando kindly said that he would run us down, although this would add some 150 miles to his journey to his family's beach home. We had a lovely, relaxing four days on the island, walking on the beach, swimming, sunbathing, eating and drinking. We intended to explore at least some of the island, and a nearby beach called Ingleses was intriguing, but never got around to it. There were many visitors from Porto Alegre and other towns of Rio Grande do Sul as well as thousands from Argentina.

We became quite friendly with an Argentinean married couple, both physicians who spoke good English. They spent a good part of each morning telling us how hard life was in Buenos Aires, with sky-rocketing prices and taxes and a depreciating peso. In the best tradition of *Fawlty Towers*, we never mentioned the Falklands war. We were returned to Curitiba by Dr Rodrigo, another resident. I had imagined that he was staying near us for Carnival but this was not the case. In fact, he had come miles out of his way to pick us up and probably driven an additional 200 miles! This was yet another example of the superb consideration that we were constantly shown.

Only too soon after getting back to Curitiba, it was time to leave. The residents and faculty dined us out in great style and we were presented with a most attractive clock in the geographical shape of Brazil. It was certainly much easier to pack than was the tea service in Quito! Despite it being a working day, both Denise and Arnolfo drove us to the airport for our one-hour flight to Rio, where we had planned a final four days before finally heading home. On the first afternoon, we took a bus tour and, soon after leaving our hotel, saw the bar where two men would sit and lust after *The girl from Ipanema*, as they described in their popular song of the early 1960s. The girl in question is now in her late 50s and is a grand-mother. Antonio Jobim, the writer of the music for this song, later played piano each night at the hotel at which we stayed and during this time wrote *Blame it on the Bosanova*, another big hit.

After this, we went to the Sugar Loaf mountain and ascended to its summit via two cable cars. There we had a great panoramic view of Rio and its environs (Fig 22) and I was able to appreciate what I thought was a very characteristic feature here; namely, that many high hills and peaks are situated about the city and close to the sea. I remembered that this sort of thing was not seen in other lovely cities by the sea, such as Sydney, Durban, San Francisco, etc. On the following day, we visited Corcavado, the name meaning "hunchback". This is 2,300 feet in height and can be climbed by foot or ascended by a cogwheel train, after which a climb up a steep staircase gives access to the summit. There on a pedestal stands the figure of Christ the Redeemer, with extended arms as if embracing the city, over 100 feet tall. The statue weighs more than 700 tons and was sculpted by a French team in 1921 to commemorate the centenary of Brazil's independence from Portugal.

The wide Avenida Atlantica runs along the beaches and has

Fig 22. The Sugar Loaf mountain and wonderful coast line of Rio de Janeiro, seen from Corcavado and the statue of Christ the Redeemer.

heavy traffic with considerable noise. There are cafes, bars, prized apartments and hotels, including the elegant *Copacabana Palace*. This was built for the visit of the King of Belgium in 1923 and was the first luxury hotel in South America. Thousands of celebrities have stayed there, including Princess Diana. The beaches are extensively used by the Cariocas, the citizens of Rio, for recreation. Here, people skate, cycle and promenade constantly with stalls every few yards, selling ice cream, cocoanut milk and soft drinks. Games of handball, volleyball and especially soccer are played on the sands. Copacabana and Ipanema are the most popular and best known of the beaches, both being crescent shaped and almost adjacent to each other, although separated by a rock formation. They are very similar although Ipanema is somewhat smaller and quieter.

I was fortunate in having two friends in Rio, both resulting from my ISS connections. One was Dr Julius Smith, a South African who had trained in Radiology ahead of me at Bristol and, at his request, I gave a lecture to his residents at the Brazilian National Cancer Institute. The other was Dr Philipe Matoso, probably the best known radiologist in Brazil. Both friends entertained us to dinner, showing us the sights en route and answering our many queries, with Dr Matoso and his wife taking us to the *English Country Club* in Ipanema, said to be the most exclusive establishment in the city. Rio was undoubtedly an exciting and vibrant city but I doubt if I would wish to live there permanently. We flew out of Rio to Sao Paulo, a city of 17 million souls that is noisy and polluted and yet loved by the Paulistas, its inhabitants. We did not venture outside the airport. The flight home was again a long 11 hours, with a change in Dallas followed by a direct flight to Columbia. This service was a godsend and avoided travelling through St Louis but was, most unfortunately, discontinued a little later.

FIFTEEN

Continuing Retirement

Arriving back in Columbia, I soon picked up the routine of my retired life. In this year of 2001, the stock market began to decline, led by a spectacular collapse of technology shares. The "dot com" companies soon became "dot bombs" and gloom then spread to the manufacturing sector. America's problems caused even more serious troubles throughout the world and Britain was officially in a recession in July of that year. However, unemployment figures grew only slowly in the USA and not at all in Columbia, where they were virtually absent. House construction here proceeded apace and one wondered who would occupy all the new homes. It was far from easy to get a contractor to do any job and long delays were encountered before plumbers, painters, joiners, electricians, etc could be engaged. Supermarkets could not get enough staff and there was a real job-seekers market.

My daughter Helen was working happily as a teacher of English in the Columbia Public Schools system, being the only educator in the state who, in my view, spoke English correctly. She also coached the flag corps of *Marching Mizzou*, part of the university marching band which performed during half time at every home football game. This was a very onerous and demanding position, requiring two hours of work daily as well as three or four hours before every home football game. After 14-15 weeks of this, she accrued 2,000 dollars in salary, a not over-generous wage rate. She felt unable to continue with this taxing work after one season but still helped out in an unpaid, voluntary manner, by assisting the photographers and press corps. She was then promoted to being Head of English in her Junior High School, where more than 700 children between the ages of 13 and 15 were taught by over 70 teachers, of whom ten plus a university fellow were involved with English. She was now able to buy a house, arguing that paying off a mortgage with associated tax relief made more sense than paying rent for an apartment. Her house was just nine months old, had three bedrooms, two complete bathrooms, a spacious fully-fitted kitchen, a nice living room/lounge and a two-car garage. The garden front and back was large and all this cost just $92,000, or about 65,000 pounds sterling. Her relatives and friends in England were green with envy and some could not believe this figure! However, in southern California, where housing prices are absurdly high, such a house would have cost something like $250,000, or even more! Helen had secured a special mortgage for teachers and had inherited some money, which she used towards the purchase. George Bush helped later with the financing, giving her a tax rebate. This was the second such windfall Americans had enjoyed, Ronald Reagan having given us a similar rebate many years earlier. In her second year as titular Head of English, she was flattered by being appointed to lecture and supervise the university fellows, those graduate students working towards a master's degree in Education who taught under supervision in the public schools; in addition, she did a good deal of administration for the school district. She now did little actual teaching of the school children but continued as Departmental head.

September 11th 2001 shook America to the core although Missouri was isolated from any direct impact. Initially, the principal effect of the disaster was the appearance of thousands of US flags outside residences and on cars. Many Americans put out their flag in front of the house on Sundays and this gesture was repeated daily for many weeks. KOMU, an affiliate of the National Broadcasting Corporation (NBC), now came in for a great deal of flack. This local TV channel was also an "auxiliary enterprise" of the University of Missouri, where journalism students received some training. The News Director of KOMU banned all staff from wearing ribbons or other patriotic symbols while on the air. Despite the University Board of Curators asking for wide latitude in this area, and angry protests from many Missouri state legislators, the Director held firm to his position. He claimed that his ban "helped to avoid the appearance of outside influences" and was about "teaching journalism and journalism ethics the right way". This explanation was as incomprehensible to me as it was to many others.

Shortly after this terrible day, the Last Night of the Proms was shown on BBC America and we were able to enjoy it thoroughly. The program was relayed to outdoor crowds in Hyde Park, Gateshead, Cornwall and Liverpool, where a large audience watched in William Brown Street, between the main entrance of the Mersey Tunnel and the Walker Art Gallery. Leonard Slatkin was conductor of the BBC Symphony Orchestra, having earlier been conductor of the St Louis Symphony, which plays regularly on the campus of the University of Missouri at Columbia; in fact, I had enjoyed a conversation with him after one of these performances. This particular *Last Night of the Proms* must have been difficult for him. He was relatively new in his position and the almost jingoistic nature of the occasion, as well as its occurrence so soon after September 11th, posed several problems. The programme included *Tromba Lonata* by American John Adams, Michael Tippett's *Spirituals* and Barber's *Adagio for Strings*, which Slatkin explained had become almost America's "music of grief". In fact, the conductor handled things extremely well. To the waving of many American flags, as well as ubiquitous Union Jacks, he made appropriate comments in what was a more than usually memorable evening.

The Dow-Jones financial index is an important and closely watched number, being obtained from a weighted average of certain key stock prices on the New York Stock Exchange. Often referred to simply as "the Dow", this and the stock market fell even more steeply after the horrendous events of what came to be widely known simply as 9/11. Most investors lost money, as I did. However, my portfolio was largely composed of blue chip, non-speculative investments and my losses were much less than were those of many friends. The US economy and stock market were recovering nicely in 2002 when a series of corporate scandals hit the headlines, one after another. Martha Stewart's commercial empire was in serious trouble, with the widely-known home and garden guru accused of insider trading. She was convicted in March 2004 of charges of obstruction of justice, making false statements to federal investigators and conspiracy in relation to covering up a $45,000 stock market profit. In July 2004, the domestic icon was sentenced to five months in a minimum security prison and also to five months of home confinement. Share prices in her company shot up, however, after the sentence was announced and many supporters greeted her as she emerged from the courthouse. However, most legal experts considered that she had got off very lightly.

Much bigger scandals hit giant corporations such as Enron, World Corp, Tyco, Global Crossings, Im Clone, Adelphia and Quest.

Enron had indulged in highly questionable accounting practises and it was alleged that Ken Lay, the Chairman and Chief Executive Officer of the energy giant, which had been the seventh largest company in the USA, had disposed of company stock after the economic plight of the company had become clear, while employees were still encouraged to continue investment. It was claimed also that Lay invested 4 million dollars, more than his total annual salary, in variable annuities in his home state of Texas, where they were protected from creditors.

Ken Lay was a graduate of Hickman High School in Columbia, where Sam Walton, the founder of the retail chains Wal-Mart, Sams and Asda had been a pupil, as had my daughter Helen. Lay went on to be awarded BA and MA degrees in Economics at the University of Missouri in the mid-1960s. In 1999, he had donated Enron stock to finance an endowed chair in his name in the Mizzou Economics Department. The endowment stood at more than one million dollars in the summer of 2004, when heated discussion broke out between the MU Chancellor, the Economics Chairman and his faculty as to the morality and advisability of retaining Lay's donation.

As if the association of the Enron Chairman was not bad enough, the news now broke that Mrs Huda Ammash, allegedly in charge of Iraq's biological weapons program and certainly a member of Saddam's inner circle, had enjoyed close ties with the University of Missouri. In fact, the lady known as "Chemical Sally" had worked in the Department of Microbiology here and been awarded a PhD by MU in the early 1950s.

In January 2002, Frances and I enjoyed a most pleasant vacation on the Yucatan peninsula in a superb hotel. A charming old friend in Oregon used to claim that he experienced diarrhoea if he even flew over Mexico! Perhaps the Mexican hotel standards left something to be desired in the 1950s but those days are long gone and hotels there are, in general, are now the equal of those in Europe and North America. Nevertheless, the tap water in most of the best hotels is still not recommended for drinking. I was shocked at first to find that the language of many road signs and other letterings was quite incomprehensible. I felt better when someone explained that this was Mayan, not Spanish. There were problems in travelling to Mexico and other warm spots in winter. Early morning flights out of St Louis frequently required an overnight stay in that city, when snow on the ground and cold weather would make warm clothing obligatory. Of course, on arriving at our vacation destination, the much warmer tempratures would cause discomfort.

I had resolved to make a more serious attempt to learn Spanish. This was largely for the enjoyment of mastering the language but partly in case that I was asked to visit Central or South America again as a Visiting Professor. However, changes in that program made it less likely that I would be invited again, or indeed should wish to go. The advent of Managed Care had virtually made sabbaticals a thing of the past for university based physicians. Being retired, this had worked in my favour at first but RSNA had now decided to send many more radiologists abroad each year, with all going to one regional location but only for a couple of weeks. This much shorter time requirement meant that the assignment, although less attractive, would be open to many more applicants and that someone like myself, who had already enjoyed two long such appointments, would be much less likely to be selected again

I joined a Spanish Two class at MU on returning home from Mexico, having missed the first week because of my vacation. I soon realised that I should have been less ambitious and that a Spanish One class, begun on time, would have been a better choice. The 18 youthful students with me had all taken Spanish One and most of them had also enjoyed three years of High School Spanish. I was in deep trouble at once although I found that the little Latin that I remembered from my distant school days was very useful with Spanish verbs. However, several embarrassing weeks ensued before gradual improvement occurred. In this I was greatly helped by Ebion DeLima, a Brazilian friend who was fluent in some half a dozen languages and was a retired professor from the MU department of Romance Languages. He helped me greatly with general grammar and I was able to gradually catch up with the bulk of the class and pass the written and oral exam at the end of the semester.

It both irritated and amused me that even the most intelligent and anglicised Hispanics, like Ebion, appeared to find considerable difficulty in spelling out Spanish words. They would, instead, make the Spanish sound for each letter, instead of naming the individual letters, a process that I found very confusing. I imagine that this was due to the great emphasis placed on pronunciation by these always helpful people, an emphasis that unfortunately I did not share. I became convinced that many of the problems that my fellow students encountered were due to their deficiencies in the English language. There were all manner of examples of this, with the failure to discriminate between the different parts of speech being especially pronounced.

There were many memorable incidents during this semester, some hilarious and at least one that was a considerable shock to me. This involved an oral exam in conversation which had to be taken in pairs, just before the final written exam, and would count towards the final grade. We were informed of four general areas about which the exam would be conducted and my female partner and I did some preliminary work together on these in the time allocated for it during classes. In addition, I memorised great chunks of language for each subject, even covering situations where my partner might stray from the agreed path. Thus I had committed to memory phrases like "returning to what we were discussing previously", etc. On the morning of the exam, I was horrified to discover that my partner had failed to turn up at the specified time and so the lecturer told me that she would act as my partner. She was a most pleasant lady from the Republic of Panama and I was sure that she would be as helpful as she could; but my carefully laid plans were now in disarray. She handed me an envelope, told me to read the contents and be ready to enter the exam room and begin conversing in three minutes.

On opening it, I discovered that the topic appeared to be nothing like any of the four previously advised. The instructions read "You are well-known to be an expert in heart problems. A young lady has such a concern and wishes to consult you. She will tell you about herself and you must advise her accordingly". I thought that this topic must have been specially made for me, a physician, and considered this rather strange. However, having little time for idle thought, I at once began to assemble the vital words that I must use, like family history, chest pain, palpitations, shortness of breath, drugs, etc. I entered the room and my new partner immediately began talking to me. I couldn't believe my ears and had to ask her, several times, to repeat phrases. Apparently, the young lady in question was suffering from a "broken heart" following an unhappy love affair and wished to consult me about this! My astonishment was profound and I had difficulty in getting my wits together, especially as I had given no thought to this particular scenario or vocabulary. Eventually, I managed to get out a few bland sentences and then, feeling less flummoxed, the conversation continued rather better. I passed this oral with quite a good mark and, off the record, the lecturer told me that I had done very well after a poor start during which she was very concerned for me.

In common with most US Universities, MU had two semesters each year, from January to May and from August to December, there being a week of vacation in each semester. After the spring semester of 2002, Frances and I went to Cuernavaca in June for three weeks. This city of about one million people is some 75 miles southwest of Mexico City and is said to be one of the most attractive towns in Mexico. The multi-coloured houses, red-tiled roofs and beautiful gardens confirm this view. Various celebrities such as Cortes, Archduke Maximilian, a variety of film stars and many foreign diplomats have had homes here. Frances did not take the highly intensive course of study at the private language school, which was very respected and much used by MU. In fact, 23 Mizzou students were there simultaneously with me, where their six weeks course of study would give them the equivalent of one entire semester. We stayed with a local family, in a house with lovely gardens and an open-air swimming pool, this being one of the key features of the program to assist in the learning of Spanish conversation. I worked from 8.00 am to 2.00 pm each day and had homework nightly. There was also an exam each Friday. The standard of tuition was excellent but it was all much more serious, heavy-going and demanding than I had expected.

Several side trips were organised by the school each week, the two most popular undoubtedly being to Teotihuacan, the major archeological site in Mexico, and to Acapulco. We went to neither as the first involved a round trip of more than seven hours in a bus and the latter an entire weekend, leaving on Friday morning. We did go to Taxco, a beautiful hilly town which has been declared a national monument, its lovely cobblestone streets and colonial style buildings having been preserved by local legislation. The surrounding mines bring forth 65% of the country's silver and help to make Mexico the world's biggest producer of this precious metal. The city also has hundreds of silver stores, all selling absolutely genuine 100% silver objects but at varying prices. Taxco is the site of the annual World Silversmiths Conference and Exhibition. A wonderful baroque cathedral, full of pictures by Miguel Cabrera, the Mexican Michelangelo, is another great attraction.

We also went on a half-day excursion to Xochicalco, a relatively nearby site of Indian temples, pyramids and other interesting archeological remains where several different indigenous cultures had been fused when it became necessary to adjust the mesoamerican calendar. Because of this, a fascinating astronomical observatory built in the sixth century AD becomes illuminated by the sun every year at the summer solstice. This strongly reminded me of the prehistoric ruins at Slane, Count Meath, Ireland where astronomical calculations, including the summer solstice, were observed in a similar manner. Returning from this trip, we called at the hacienda of Cortes, now a hotel, on the outskirts of Cuernavaca.

At the conclusion of many of my lectures, I would chat over a coffee with a genial and informed American who taught at the language school at Cuernavaca, also had an appointment at the University of Mexico City and had lived in the country for many years. We would discuss many aspects of Mexican history and culture and one day we got on to the subject of politics. He amazed me by saying that no-one could get elected to public office in the country, or have any sort of political life, without being a member of a masonic lodge. I questioned him about this but he added little more information, being entirely emphatic in this opinion. I longed to ask him if he himself was a mason but thought it better not to do so. I was aware that many of those who had liberated Central and South America from Spanish rule, such as Simon Bolivar, were masons. However, my friend's disclosure amazed me. It seemed as if not all lodges had the largely benign characteristics of those in the United Kingdom and the USA.

After church one day, when an entire mariachi band had played during the service, I was introduced to John Spencer, an elderly Englishman. He was courteous and softly spoken and told us that he had lived in Cuernavaca for some 30 years. It emerged that he was a well known local artist who was currently engaged in restoring an old convent, which he eventually intended to present to the city as an Art museum. He invited us to see what he was doing and we arrived at his large but considerably run-down building the next day. It was clear that he had already accomplished much restoration but a great deal more lay ahead of him and he appeared to have only two local workmen to help him. As we got to know each other, he opened up a good deal and we learned of his busy and artistic life. I formed the distinct impression, however, that he was more than a little lonely. Later, it emerged that he was quite a close relative of the late Princess Diana and, of course, he shared her family name.

In late August, 2002, I began the Spanish Three course, which comprised 31 different classes. There were just 21 students in my particular class and I thoroughly enjoyed my time in it. The teaching was excellent and at last I began to feel I was making real progress. The course book was heavily weighed with subjects such as Illiteracy, Pollution, Malnutrition, Poverty, AIDS, etc. I had no problem with these except for the fact that they were all dealt with in a most liberal and even left-wing fashion. Pop stars, movies, the soaps, etc were also much bandied about, presumably in an effort to keep the attention of young students, no doubt many of whom hoped to follow in the show biz traditions of Cheryl Crowe, Brad Pitt and Tom Berenger, all former MU students. Individuals such as Gloria Estefan, Jennifer Lopez, Ricky Martin, Enriqe Iglesias, etc were discussed in class, several of these being completely unknown to me, and I was forced to enlist the assistance of my daughter Helen in identifying and categorising them before I could tackle some course projects which involved the so-called popular culture. Having made a variety of silly mistakes in the final exam, I was more than pleased with my final grade of 83%.

Towards the end of 2002, I was asked by my friend Dr Smith in Rio if I would revisit the National Cancer Institute in Rio for several weeks in the coming year for further lectures and teaching. This was an exciting offer but, after prolonged consideration, I declined with reluctance. The funding for my visit would have been poor, with expenses being much less generous than those given by the RSNA. In addition, I was now really enjoying my Spanish studies and was loathe to abandon them.

At the suggestion of Helen, I now made enquiries as to whether or not I would be required to take some extra courses in addition to Spanish, should I decide to advance to the degree. I expressed surprise at this possibility, never having been an undergraduate in the USA, but Helen thought it best to get this sorted out at an early stage. US university education is very broadly based in the early years and science students frequently are required to study various arts subjects at this time, with arts students having to study scientific subjects. These enquiries were addressed to the Associate Dean of Arts and Science, a conjugation of disciplines that I thought extraordinary but which was found in most US Universities.

To my horror and disbelief, I was immediately told that I could never be awarded any degree in the Arts and Science faculty of the University of Missouri! This was because the possession of a degree higher than a masters, i.e. a doctorate, debarred me. I was told that this ruling might have been aimed at preventing Arts and Science graduates, for whatever reason, staying on at MU and beginning another degree in a different subject. For the life of me, I couldn't see any harm in any student wishing to obtain more than one degree and thought that the ruling was highly anti-academic and silly. Having been told that I could, of course, appeal against this ruling, I asked where I might read the relevant details and was told that there was nothing in writing. The edict involved had apparently been passed "by acclamation" of the Arts and Science faculty. So an ordinance, limited just to Arts and Science and having no written basis, was in place. I marvelled at what an aggressive lawyer might make of this!

However, I didn't wish to start appeals and legal proceedings, at least not at this stage, and suddenly realised that I was not a doctor, at least not an academic one. In Britain and much of the Commonwealth, the MD is a prestigious post-graduate degree. However, the US medical student, having an undergraduate degree in the vast majority of cases before beginning his medical studies, becomes an MD on graduation. Although I, and many like me, had been strongly advised to write MD after our names having passed the Flex examination and obtained a state licence, I would never dream of using MD in Britain or in any publication. In fact, my qualifying academic degrees were simply MB ChB, two Bachelor degrees. My elation was soon quenched when I was told that although it was clear that I could now proceed to the baccalaureate degree in Spanish, I would have to take various additional course subjects. These might include such subjects as Psychology,

Anthropology, Geology and even Writing! Protestations that I had many published scientific papers, an invited chapter in a medical textbook and a published work of non-fiction were simply waved aside. Eventually, after my transcript had arrived from the University of Liverpool, I asked for a meeting with the Dean of Arts and Science. He proved to be a much more helpful and relaxed individual than his associate with whom I had been dealing. It was established that I would have to do a short course in Modern American History, this being mandated by the state of Missouri, but no other additional courses would be required.

In January 2003, Frances and I spent two weeks in Costa Rica. This stable, small country, which disbanded its army more than 50 years ago, has lovely beaches, tropical forests and volcanoes, together with a huge and varied bird population. The trees surrounding our hotel were full of monkeys and there were many sloths dangling from branches nearer the beach, all apparently asleep. Unfortunately, Costa Rica has now been discovered by American tourists and is very popular during the high season. Following this vacation, I embarked on an "Intermediate Spanish" course which I thought was very difficult, and much more so than the two earlier courses that I had taken. I found the Lecturer's Mexican accent hard to understand but I stuck at it, worked hard and managed to get a decent pass.

The onset of the war against Iraq saw a rash of signs on the lawns of Columbia homes. "We Support Our Troops" competed with "Peace Is Patriotic. No War". The latter slogan was later replaced with "Bring Our Troops Home" and "End The Occupation". Both the pro and contra war signs often appeared together in groups, with large numbers of similar signs, and seemed to say more for the industry of some local zealot than any indication of popular feeling. Many local reservists went off to the war and the B2 "stealth" bombers at the Wightman Air Force base, some 50 miles to the west of Columbia, soon joined them. These planes, costing some $2 billion each and built by Northrop Grumman, had amazing capabilities and it was claimed that just a couple of them could do the work of 75 conventional aircraft. They were well known to inhabitants of Columbia as one would frequently fly over the university football field, at great speed and with enormous noise, just before football games.

At the war's end, the US Navy's huge *Abraham Lincoln* atomic-powered carrier arrived back at her home port, having been away for a little over ten months. This was said to be the longest deployment of any US Navy ship for years. I thought back to *Barossa*, and many other RN ships that were on regular commissions of two years and more in the late 1950s, although admittedly they were of a different era and not on a war footing.

Meanwhile, much of the political argument and rhetoric of the presidential campaign seemed to centre on the Vietnam War and few seemed to find anything strange in this. Shortly after this, during the later stages of that campaign, some British presenters of world news on BBC America from Washington exhibited considerable hostility towards President Bush and the Republican Party on a regular basis. I am uncertain as to how much individual freedom the various announcers are allowed and if these views expressed personal opinion or represented BBC bias. Most Americans had good feelings about Britain and a majority were grateful for British assistance in the Iraqi war and its aftermath. However, I had to defend my adopted country not infrequently when on holiday in the UK.

In early May 2003, ten days of terrifying weather hit the Mid West, with more than 300 tornados being reported there and no less than 562 twisters in the country as a whole. This was, by far, the largest number experienced since accurate records were begun to be kept in the early 1950s. The experts were of the opinion that large, stationary anticyclones, technically known as "blocking events", had become established over the north-eastern Pacific and the west-central Atlantic. This situation had forced the jet stream south over the Mid West and southern plains, and with cool Canadian high pressure to the north, a large mass of moist, warm air was embedded thus setting up the "clashing conditions" needed for tornado formation. Despite fantastic claims in some well known newspapers, these phenomena had absolutely nothing to do with global warming.

A huge area extending from Georgia to South Dakota, and from Mississippi to Wisconsin, was involved, with Missouri, Kansas and Oklahoma being the states most affected. A total of nearly 50 people were killed, with Missouri having 18 fatalities, the greatest number of deaths in any state. Damage in Missouri ran into millions of dollars but Columbia was, as usual, unscathed. The twisters had

Fig 23. The characterisic "funnel cloud" appearance of a tornado, seen just to the east of Kansas City, Missouri, in May 2003 (Reprinted by permission of the Department of Atmospheric Sciences, University of Missouri, Columbia).

a typical funnel appearance (Fig 23), seemed to ocur regularly at night and would frequently contain debris such as metal sheeting, large pieces of wood, etc within their vortices, thus increasing their potential for damage. Sirens would go off, indicating that residents should take shelter in a basement area, this being strongly reminiscent of the sirens and the World War Two blitzes that I still vividly remembered from my boyhood. These warnings created a problem for Frances and I as our house, which we loved, did not possess any basement. In fact, this had been one of the reasons that we had purchased it, as many basements in the area tended to be damp, with flooding problems frequent. So we would sit on the floor, between the kitchen and family room, for as short a time as we thought fit. Mobile homes were said to be particularly at risk and their inhabitants were urged to leave the home and seek shelter in a ditch. This draconian advice also applied to any motorists in the area at the time of a tornado warning.

In June 2003, we went to Spain for four weeks. The US dollar had now depreciated more than 20% with respect to the euro.

This, of course, was good for US exporters and many felt that the Bush government was cooperating in keeping the dollar weak; but it made for an expensive visit to Europe for most Americans. However, I still had accounts and monies in England and the use of these enabled me to avoid the expenses experienced with a weak dollar. Initially, we stayed in Minorca at the villa of Frances' sister. As in Mexico, I was disturbed to find that I could not read any road signs nor begin to understand the locals. The problem now was that a regional form of Catalan, not Spanish, was in use. We then enjoyed 12 days in Madrid which was hectic but most enjoyable. In addition to all of the city's delights, such as The Prado, the Palacio Real, the Rastro, etc, we also made visits to Toledo, Segovia, El Escorial and Alacala de Henares. Although experiencing some problems with rapid Spanish speech, I was quite pleased with my understanding of the spoken language and managed quite well. I had been deeply interested in the Spanish Civil War for many years and was disappointed, as I had been on many earlier occasions, by a complete refusal of all the Spaniards with whom I became friendly to discuss the war in any terms.

Immediately on returning home, I began the summer school course in Modern American History that I had agreed on with the Arts and Science Dean. In fact, this turned out to be a typical 14 week semester course squeezed into just four weeks; and I began it three days late because of my vacation! To my amazement, no less than six books were required for this four week course, which was well taught and very interesting. However, I noted once more a definite liberal bias both in the teaching and in the text books. The work load was immense and 140 pages of required reading for one night was not uncommon, with many mini-quizzes and long essays to be written. I found it all very interesting although heavy going but "hung in there" and managed to achieve an "A" grade.

The Dow had reached an all time high of 11,7223 on January 14th, 2000 but had fallen to just 7181 by October 10th, 2002. US unemployment had by then risen steeply and many were complaining bitterly of their financial losses. In fact, this nadir of the Dow was no lower than its status had been on October 28th, 1997. The Dow closed at 8341 on Dec 31st, 2002 but Wall St began the 2003 financial year in great style with the Dow up a whopping 260 points, representing a full 3.2% of the market.

In the late summer of 2003, I was delighted to hear my financial advisor tell me that he was feeling very bullish and able to confirm that I had now not only recovered all my earlier losses but was "ahead of the game". The Dow closed on December 31st, 2003, at 10,454. This was an increase of nearly 25% on the year, the jobless total was at its lowest level for three years and only the feeble dollar, now at just $1.25 to the euro, spoiled the picture. I had first entered the market, in a very small and conservative manner, towards the close of 1980, when the Dow was standing at only 964!

The Dow continued to climb until the Iraqui war, rising oil prices and a disappointing US economy led to a continuous, gradual fall to below 10,000 with the dollar reaching a new four year low against the euro. The approaching US election halted this decline, for reasons for that were not clear, and the Dow reached 10,387 on November 5th. There was an announcement of 337,000 new jobs in October and the Dow closed for 2004 at 10,783, with plenty of momentum. However, the greenback began to depreciate again and soon reached new record lows. Quoted at 83 cents to the euro when the latter became legal tender on January 1st 2002, it now sank to just $1.33 per euro.

American TV continued to bore me, as it had for many years, ever since arriving in the country, in fact. The national news on the three major channels was just about bearable, although much less overseas news was given compared to the BBC. The big weekly evening shows left me cold. The Public Broadcasting System, whose TV arm was being increasingly criticised as unnecessary and expensive, had the occasional good program. All in all however, the entire TV scene was quite bleak and seemed to be designed for morons; of course, there was no license fee. Because of the poor program choices, we paid for Cable TV, costing some $54 per month. It gave us Sky Sports, with a nightly one-hour news, mainly about soccer and with many English games shown but also some live international rugby. The Cable packet also included BBC America, a product of BBC Television.

Some BBC programs were shown repeatedly on the BBC America channel, including very old repeats of shows such as *The Avengers* and *The Saint*, and, of course, not all BBC programming was available. So it was better than nothing but far from perfect. The daily news, from London or Washington, seemed to differ somewhat in presentation from the BBC news shown in the UK and had its own British news readers. This was, in my opinion, the best feature but, inexplicably, it was available at weekends only at 5.00 am. A source of chronic annoyance for me was the insertion of advertising material into the news, often with a reader being interrupted in mid-sentence. Personally, I never tired of *Dad's Army, One Foot in the Grave, People like Us* and similar shows. However, one got fed up with endless repeats of *Blackadder* and even *Poirot* could be indigestible if repeated too often. As for *Changing Rooms, House Invaders, Ground Force, Can't Cook, Won't Cook, My Hero, Coupling, My family* and *Faking It*, which were constantly repeated, the less said the better.

I thought that the BBC's standards had considerably declined over the last 15 years, with little evidence now of anything even vaguely Reithian but with much evidence of considerable "dumbing down"; but they were were, on the whole, still better than US TV. Of course, this perception of mine might be flawed because of the incomplete selection of the Beeb's output that viewers in the USA see on their screens. However, reading the British press and talking with British friends, I doubt if this is the case. I was not surprised to learn that the Burns report, published in July 2004, announced that more than half of the British public thought that the BBC was "getting worse" and did not give value for money. Even strong supporters of the Beeb said that its TV programmes had lost ground where it had previously been prominent. Max Hastings made an important exception to this damning perception in the *Speccie*. While pointing out that vulgarity had overtaken parts of the Beeb, its presentation of what might be called "Events" was still exemplary. In this category would be included royal weddings, funerals, similar occasions and historical celebrations, with the coverage of the 60th anniversary of the D-Day landings being a case in point. I would agree with this opinion and imagine that the production excellence in this area is probably due to a long, successful tradition, going back to Richard Dimbleby and before.

Parkinson annoyed me occasionally on his show, on which Pop stars are eager to appear and whose careers, I had read, are then hugely boosted in many cases. Although invariably avuncular and easy going, he would in many cases fawn obsequiously over meretricious guests, pouring excessive and mellifluous praise on them. Parky had upset me years earlier when, in my view, he had been dismissive of Colin Cowdrey's claims to the England cricket captaincy, favouring those of a fellow Tyke. However, I was very much in his corner during the infamous Meg Ryan interview in late 2003 and also recognised his input concerning the problems of the state of British cricket in 2003, together with Michael Atherton, Bob Willis and others via the Cricket Reform Group.

In March, 2004, I read that Alistair Cooke had, at the age of 95 years, decided to retire. As a great admirer of his, I thought it would be impossible to replace him with anyone vaguely similar. Born in Salford and educated at a Blackpool grammar school and then at Cambridge, this legendary Anglo-American journalist had delighted millions for nearly 60 years, mainly with his *Letter from America*. Many attempts to persuade him into an earlier retirement had failed, sometimes after Cooke had invoked the assistance of his many friends in high places. I was saddened to learn of his death a few weeks later.

The horrific Tsuami disaster shocked the world in late December, 2004. I felt particularly saddened by the damage and loss of life in Sri Lanka and became alarmed when unable to con-tact my friend Dr Peiris in Colombo. I heard from him at a later date and was relieved to learn that he was quite safe. I was puzzled as to how Galle, situated on the west coast of Sri Lanka and about which I retained happy memories, was so devastated and was frustrated by a great lack of news from towns on the east coast. After a week or so, the small eastern towns of Mullaittivu and Kalmunai received some mention but there was nothing about major Tamil towns such as Trincomalee, even after many weeks. I imagined that this was due, at least in part, to the Tamil Tigers being in control in the north and east of the country but, nevertheless, found it very strange.

A small team from the International Centre for Psycho-Social Trauma at MU, members of which had previously been in such areas as Bosnia, Kosovo, Palestine, etc, visited Sri Lanka in early 2005. They trained mental health professionals, social workers and teachers in counselling and related matters. "Doctors Worldwide" assisted with the travel and housing arrangements and the sessions were held in Colombo. I spoke with two of the MU team, who had not traveled to the east coast. They agreed with me about the influence of the Tamil Tigers in the east and could not add a great deal although they had heard that Trincomalee had been severely damaged. In addition, they confirmed reports that the Sri Lankan government was distributing international aid very slowly, and also very unevenly, with little getting through to the north and east.

Then in late February 2005, Prince Charles visited Batticaloa, which was said to have been ravaged by the Boxing Day disaster. As President of the British Red Cross, he met with Tamils, but not Tamil Tigers, and was said to have been careful in skirting around the political situation. Reports of his visit added little to my appreciation of the situation in eastern Sri Lanka and made no mention of the casualties on the east coast.

Many volunteer physicians from the USA had arrived in Aceh, and some 20 or so US Navy ships carried out relief operations, immediately after the disaster. The *Abraham Lincoln* had been commissioned again and was in the vanguard of this work in Sumatra. Its large array of choppers, hovercraft and landing craft was ideally suited for the important role that they were playing. Many thousands of US soldiers and marines were also soon working there, ably assisted by units of the Australian Army. To my knowledge, this invaluable work was never reported by BBC America except for a cursory mention after the date of their withdrawal had been announced. These omissions were highlighted by, among others, Christopher Booker in the *Sunday Telegraph*. However, other networks did comment on the work of these US forces, including the Chinese News Agency. A BBC America presenter agressivly questioned Bill Frist, the Senate majority leader, just before he left for a fact-finding tour of the affected countries. Doubts were cast on the intention of the US to provide long term relief efforts and on the ability of US forces and agencies to work with countries who had opposed the Iraqi war. Booker felt that BBC employees are so enthralled by their collective mindset that they are unable to see how unprofessional they had become. In late January 2005, it was announced that the BBC will be made to sign up to a specific commitment to broadcast news that is "balanced and fair" as part of its new royal charter. While this was not aimed principally at its coverage of US affairs, I could only hope that the latter would be included in the new brief.

British friends often argued with me on the subject of urban violence in the USA, when we met on vacation or, less commonly, by letter and e-mail. There is no doubt that this is a serious problem in many cities and multiple shootings like those in an Atlanta courthouse and at a religious service in suburban Milwaukee, both occurring in March 2005, were particularly worrying. The situation in general, however, has improved over the last few years with New York city, for instance, reducing its figures for violence very dramatically. This problem, of course, is linked to gun ownership and the right to carry such weapons. Personally, I am very much opposed to the gun culture but many law abiding, intelligent and educated friends are strongly in favour and claim that it reduces crime. I find it of interest that many in the UK now feel that householders, at least, should be able to possess and use weapons to defend themselves against intruders.

However, I have never remotely come close to violence of any kind when living in the USA. Cleveland is regarded as being a dangerous city with considerable violence but I never felt threatened while living there, or in Portland. Of course, my family and I would rarely, if ever, visit those areas associated with high risk. In Columbia, we leave our garage open for much of the day, displaying tools, garden implements, bikes, a snow blower, athletic clothing etc and have never suffered any loss. The only disturbance from which we suffer is the very occasional noise in summer from high spirited youths on their way to and from our neighbourhood lake. By contrast, I have felt threatened on many occasions when visiting the UK, especially when travelling by train or walking at night. The constant reporting of drunken, yobbish and violent behaviour in many British towns, especially at the week-end, and the attacks on many elderly in their homes, would seem to confirm my impressions, as well as the extraordinary admission of the Chief Constable of Nottinghamshire. In March 2005, the latter stated that his force was being overwhelmed by violent crimes and could no longer cope. Many feel that the recent increase in the licensing hours, leading to a potential for round-the-clock drinking, will only exacerbate this situation.

There had been a severe shortage of influenza vaccine in the USA in the autumn of 2004, leading to a rationing of available supplies' with only those at greatest risk having the vaccine injected. There were no domestic US manufacturers of vaccine, largely because it was not a very profitable business, and all US supplies are imported from the UK. In early 2005, the US press announced that the British plant responsible for this shortage had delivered vaccine in 1999 and 2003 that had been improperly made. The entire subject was complicated and reports were not entirely clear but it seems unlikely that anyone had suffered any ill-effect from this. However, as a result of these problems, the UK authorities closed down this plant in October 2004, resulting in no vaccine from the UK being available for the US market in 2004. The latter then had only 50% of its expected vaccine. The plant re-opened in March 2005.

The earlier vaccine had been made by Powderject Pharmaceuticals of Liverpool before Chiron bought the plant in 2003. It was widely known in Columbia that I was not only British but hailed from Liverpool. Following these media allegations, I came in for a great deal of flak from friends and especially from acquaintances at my health club! The day after these revelations, news broke of the impending marriage of Prince Charles to Camilla. The matter of the flu vaccine was all but forgotten by my friends and, instead, I was questioned closely on a variety of aspects of the forthcoming nuptials. Being largely disinterested in this wedding, I could answer few of their queries and thought that, in general, my questioners were much better informed on the subject than was I. As I had noticed on many former occasions, events involving the British royal family seemed to attracted far more interest in the USA than in the UK.

Frances and I continued to enjoy drinking wine in summer and early Fall, sitting on the deck at the rear of the house before dinner (Fig 24), where we would peruse the British *Spectator* and *Sunday Telegraph*, received weekly by airmail. We greatly enjoyed them both, in spite of the poor quality of the printing ink used in the latter, which came off on hands and clothing in a most annoying manner. The local evening paper, full of very local and even parochial issues, was disposed of in a maximum of 15 minutes and was also read at this time. Despite volcanic eruptions, tornados, ice storms, temprature extremes and cultural differences, I had absolutely no regrets about coming to the USA 28 years earlier, except for wishing I had come earlier. I certainly missed many things British and these publications would sometimes strike a nostalgic spark in me. Most of these feelings related to Sport, usually with some bibulous association, such as drinking with friends in a pub, in

Fig 24. The author reading the Spectator, with wife Frances (to the author's left) and daughter Helen, all enjoying a drink before dinner on the back garden's deck.

a rugby pavilion after a game or sitting in a deck chair watching cricket. I enjoyed American football, especially the college variety, and basketball to a lesser extent, but could never warm to baseball.

I would occasionally tease Frances by asking if she thought we should return to Albion for the rest of our lives. This invariably produced a spirited response, with her asking me if I wished to leave my daughter and a robust declaration that I could jolly well go alone if I was set on such a crass action. Being highly perceptive, I took all this to indicate some reluctance on her part to leave the USA in general and Columbia, Missouri, in particular and in this I was, in fact, in total agreement with her.

However, I still tended to support Britain and England in sporting competitions, although some of this represented my perennial backing of the underdog. In rugby, for instance, I would back the USA against any of the Home Unions although my support would rarely if ever result in the *Eagles* winning such encounters. I enjoyed my not infrequent visits to England. These never took place in the high summer, as we felt it preferable to holiday there in the Fall. Not only was it then less crowded but the rugby and soccer season would be in full swing I noted that many Brits seemed to be setting new standards now for casual dressing, especially at dinner, even surpassing those established for many years by younger Americans. Simon Heffer, who deplores "dressing down", would not have been amused.

I recalled the maxim of Aristotle that education was the best provision for old age and wondered if I had enough of it to be contented and happy. On balance, I thought so and my retired life was certainly satisfying, with Spanish studies, time on the computer, reading, writing, exercise, travel and wine studies, both theoretical and practical, keeping me busy. All the vacations and trips we had made had proved to be highly entertaining and most enjoyable and I felt certain that this would continue. However, I thought that walking and jogging on the Katy trail and sitting on our deck drinking wine before dinner were, in all honesty, probably even better and my favourite pastimes by far! My wife asserted that most of the things I missed about England were no longer present and, to a large extent, I agreed with her. I had come to relish funerals and I did miss old friends when their deaths were reported to me, feeling sorry that I could not pay my final respects, but there was nothing I could do about this specific regret. I still had difficulty in coming to terms with my heart attack, now some ten years away, but I told myself that I should be grateful for my current good health, as well as my busy and enjoyable existence. And so life goes on, considerably more leisurely and relaxed than when working and a good deal more contented. I can think of no better explanation for this state of affairs than the ally that has fortuitously served me for so long and so well - Serendipity!

GLOSSARY

Amah. Word used extensively throughout the Indian sub-contient and the Far East to mean a baby's or child's nurse.

Anaphylaxis. A reaction to the introduction of foreign protein into the body, especially after injection. Symptoms can vary from being mild to severe and can be fatal. Penicillin and multivalent anti-snake venom are two examples of drugs leading to anaphylaxis.

Ayurvedic. A system of Medicine in Sri Lanka and India, based on traditional, herbal and naturopathic principles. In the 1950s, the practitioners of this did a two year course of study.

Beat Retreat. The re-enactment of the ancient practice carried out at dusk by a detachment of soldiers or marines, who marched around the walls of a fortification, making sure that all doors were secured and that all was well. Now only performed ceremonially, famously by Royal Marine bands

Beecham, Sir Thomas. English conductor and impressario who founded the London Philharmonic Orchestra. He championed the music of Delius and brought much operatic and ballet music into England.

Bibulous. Meaning addicted to alcohol.

Black Rod. The Gentleman Usher of the Black Rod is an official of the House of Lords. The position was created in 1350 and is today largely ceremonial. Black Rod is usually a former senior member of the Armed Forces, who acts as Personal Attendant of the Sovereign in the Lords, Serjeant-at-Arms and Keeper of the Doors of the House. The position exists in several Commonwealth countries, such as Canada.

Blighty. Originally the corruption of a Hindi word, it long signified England or Home, especially for servicemen overseas. Its usage was maximal during World War One and has declined since.

Bradman, Sir Donald. Legendary Australian cricketer and captain, one of the greatest batsmen of all time.

Brig. A ship's prison.

Brow. The Navy's term for the landlubber's gangway for boarding a ship.

Burgess, Anthony. Born and educated in Manchester, he worked in the colonial service in Malaya and Borneo where his first three novels were written. He went on to become a very well known writer with *A Clockwork Orange*, which was filmed, probably his best known work.

Cardus, Sir Neville. Outstanding writer for the old Manchester Guardian, who was both cricket and music critic of that newspaper.

Dench, Dame Judy. Well known actress, who has appeared in a large variety of roles in films, TV comedies and many plays. One of the most versatile, accomplished and respected British performers.

Dhobi. Word widely used in the Indian sub-continent and the Far East, indicating laundry.

Digs. English slang word for rented accomodation, as used by students or itinerant workers.

Dog Watch. The 24 hours of the day are divided into six watches in most navies. The four hour period between 4 pm and 8 pm has, for many years, been split into two "dog watches" by the Royal Navy. This period is traditionally used for sport and other leisure activities. Hence "half a dog watch" literally means one hour and colloquially indicates a very short period of time.

Enosis. The union of Cyprus with Greece.

EOKA. An acronym for the Greek words meaning "National Organisation for the Cypriot Struggle". It related to the Cypriot Greek activists, led by Colonel Grivas, who favoured Enosis. They were active in guerrilla activities in the island, aimed at the Cypriot Turks and British, mainly between 1955 and 1959.

Extant. Still existing.

Feral. Meaning brutal, wild or untamed.

Flyco. Abbreviation commonly used for Flying Control, the place from where all flying operations on a carrier are controlled. Invariably, this is situated high in the carrier's island, close to the funnel, with excellent views of the sky and deck. Commander (Air) runs all aeronautical things from here, with assistants.

Flag Officer Aircraft Carriers. The Admiral responsible at sea for the carriers of the Royal Navy.

Heffer, Simon. Columnist for the *Daily Mail*, who deplores "dressing down", especially the lack of ties.

Jackstay. A line or cable, passed between two ships at sea, often being fired across from one to the other. A jackstay transfer is the pulling of a man, suspended from a jackstay, from one ship to another. This is frequently a wet and even hazardous experience

Johnston, Brian. Often known as Johnners, was an Old Etonian and former Guards Officer. He was said to be the greatest natural broadcaster of them all. His career spanned nearly 50 years and, after being removed from regular TV, he re-emerged as a much loved figure on Test Match Cricket TV. He not only got away with much schoolboy humour, such as describing the cakes and other goodies sent to him by admirers, but made a highly successful forte of it.

Johnson, Paul. Well known writer and historian, the son of an artist who was Head of an Art school, Johnson was educated at Stonyhurst College and at Oxford. Politically to the left of centre in his early career and editor of the *New Statesman*, he became much more right wing. Currently, he writes regularly for *The Spectator*. A prolific author, he has more than 40 books in print. *His History of the Jews* and *A History of The American People* are particularly well known.

Lower deck. The collective term for all non-commissioned naval ranks who, unlike officers, historically did not live and sleep on the upper deck.

Managed Care. A complex system of medical care, where the financial costs mainly involve insurance companies. The latter had become much more restrictive in paying for various examinations, drugs and treatments to patients since the early 1990s.

Menorah. The Jewish seven-armed candelabra, symbolic of the creation and used in Jewish religious ceremonies.

Meretricious. Showly attractive.

Meridional. Meaning an inhabitant of Southern Europe.

Methaemoglobin. A denatured form of haemoglobin, the oxygen-carrying component in red blood cells, which does not transport oxygen.

Mickey Finn. Usually taken to mean an adulterated alcoholic drink, due to the addition of some "knock out" ingredient. There appears to be no general agreement on its derivation. The most popular alleges that it was used in the late nineteenth century by a notorious Chicago saloon proprietor of the same name, who also acted as a fence for stolen property and ran pick-pockets and prostitutes on the side. Chloral formed the earliest additive but now all manner of drugs are used including barbiturates, opiates, tranquilisers and many other substances.

M.R.C.P. Member of the Royal College of Physicians. An important medical qualification, taken by a difficult and prolonged examination having a high failure rate.

NAAFI. The Navy, Army and Air Force Institute, which provides creature comforts for the British Armed Forces by means of canteens, bars, restaurants, etc.

National Service. Also known as "Conscription", it involved all males who had been declared medically fit in two years of service. It was abolished in the late 1950s. Corresponds to "the Draft" in the USA.

Pettah. The word used in Sri Lanka for a native shopping area or bazaar.

Pratique. Universally used to indicate a "clean bill of health" and freedom from any communicable disease, for ships about to enter a port. It is usually only given after a Port Medical Officer has visitsed the ship. The flag representing the letter "Q" means "Ship is healthy and I desire free pratique". A square, yellow flag, known as the "yellow jack" or quarantine flag, means "I have infectious disease on board".

Recusant. One who refused to worship in the Church of England. Historically applied to Catholics and Dissenters.

Reith, Lord John. The first Director General of the BBC, who made Information, Education and Entertainment, independent of government, the basis of his Public Service Broadcasting.

Roller. Slang word for a Rolls Royce car.

Round-down. The most aft part of the flight deck, which curves smoothly backwards and immediately in front of which are arrester wires. It is well displayed in Fig 12.

Royal Navy (RN). The regular navy of Great Britain, active in peace and war.

Royal Naval Volunteer Reserve (RNVR). Unique to Great Britian and the Commonwealth, it consisted of men who joined up during wars, when RNVR officers and men would serve side by side with the Royal Navy, and those who served when conscripted in times of peace. The RNVR was formed in 1903 and was merged with the RNR about 1960.

Royal Naval Reserve (RNR). Originally comprised professional seamen and officers of the Mercantile Marine who served with the RN in times of war. Amalgamated with the RNVR in 1960.

Scouse, Scouser. Scouse or lobscouse was originally a dish, consisting of potatoes and Sunday left-overs. The terms now refer to citizens of Merseyside and can be used humorously or pejoratively.

Scrimshank. Somewhat dated British slang for one who shirks duty or work.

Sillitoe, Alan. Son of an illiterate and often unemployed Nottingham labourer, he was a writer and one of the post-World War Two "Angry Young Men". Probably his best known works are *Saturday Night* and *Sunday Morning* and *The Loneliness of the Long Distance Runner.*

Sods Opera. A skit or comedy in which the roles of females are played by males.

Taoiseach. Prime Minister and Head of Government in Ireland.

Thoracotomy. The surgical opening of the chest, usually followed by another procedure, e.g. the arrest of haemorrage or coronary artery by-pass surgery.

Tinnitus. A sensation of "ringing in the ears", often very unpleasant.

Tyke. A Yorkshireman.

Tyler's toast. The tyler is the outer guard of the lodge who prevents non-masons from entering during lodge meetings. He traditionally has a dagger and his toast completes the cabalistic, or secret, part of the proceedings.

Volunteer Aid Detachment. Assistant nurses of World War Two, who continued into the late 1950s.

Vin d'Honneur. Literally "wine of honour", given in the Royal Navy when an officer is leaving the ship and has not been dined out.

Wisden. More properly Wisden Cricketer's Almanack, this fat, yellow book has been published annually since 1864. It now appears in the Spring and contains all important cricketing scores, news and information from the previous year. Generally considered to be the best source of cricketing information in the world.

The Women's Royal Naval Service (WRNS). Formed in 1916 and of whom there were 75,000, known as wrens, in 1944. As well as cooks, clerks, telegraphists, etc, wrens served in other positions such as radar operatives and air mechanics. The WRNS was amalgamated into the Royal Navy in 1993. The WRNS was very similar to the US Waves.